A WOMAN'S GUIDE TO PERSONAL FINANCE

VIRGINIA B. MORRIS

LIGHTBULB PRESS ®

LIGHTBULB PRESS

Project Team
Design Director Dave Wilder
Editorial Staff Janet Hollander, Joe Hollander, Bess Newman, Tania Sanchez
Design Karen Robbins
Design Assistant Mercedes Feliciano
Production and Illustration Justin V. Bender, Antonina Colbert, Holly Duthie, Christopher Engel, Gary Lingard, Terry Marks, Thomas F. Trojan
Photography Mercedes Feliciano, Katharina Menner

SPECIAL THANKS

Christine Oldham Butterworth, Linda J. Denny, Darcy H. Johnson, Siobhan D. Onthank at ING Aetna Financial Services

American Express, Experian, MasterCard International Incorporated, Sears, Roebuck and Co., The Wall Street Journal is a registered trademark of Dow Jones L.P, Visa U.S.A.

Carl Arnold, Nathalie Casthely, Joanne Charles, Charlotte Hamilton, Ken Hamilton, Nadine Hamilton, Kara W. Hatch, Isabelle Hunter, Kim C. King, Diedre C. Meyerson, Fanny Neira, Carla Noriega, Anna Reggio, Thia Reggio, Dr. Philip Robbins, Tina Sbrigato, Sarah Sweeney, Jeanette Vasquez, Laura Yoshida, Lily Yuen

Lightbulb Press, Inc., 112 Madison Avenue, New York, NY 10016
Tel. 212-485-8800, www.lightbulbpress.com
ISBN: 0-9740386-3-6

LIGHTBULB PRESS

Each year more women are earning, managing, and investing money. Whether you're creating an investment plan, buying a home, or growing your own small business, you need to be armed with the knowledge to help you make educated choices. We've written this guide to provide you with the information you need to make these financial decisions with confidence and ease.

This guide can help you in many facets of your financial life. If you're just starting out, you can learn about establishing good credit, avoiding or reducing debt, and choosing investments to help you meet your goals. Since everyone runs into unexpected hurdles, the guide provides information to help you protect your money in the event of an illness, divorce, widowhood, or other unexpected circumstance. And if you're nearing retirement, the guide can help you learn more about estate planning, retirement investing, and how to create wills, gifts, and trusts. Finally, there is extensive information for women who own small businesses, including funding your business, choosing benefits packages for your employees, and networking effectively with other business owners.

Feeling confident about money matters, and understanding essential financial topics, can help you plan effectively for your present and future financial security. We hope that you find this guide a helpful resource in making decisions, both big and small.

Virginia B. Morris

A WOMAN'S GUIDE TO PERSONAL FINANCE

Life Stages

Setting and Meeting Goals

Building a Financial Base

Potential Hurdles

Protecting Your Resources

Enjoying Financial Security

Managing Your Business

Getting Started

Looking ahead is crucial to your financial success.

What's the biggest difference between being dependent on someone else and being on your own? For many women, it's taking financial responsibility for themselves and perhaps for dependents as well.

Being financially responsible usually means earning enough money to support yourself. That may be something you experience for the first time as a young woman ready to move into a home of your own. But financial independence isn't as much an age issue as you may think. If you're widowed in your 40s or 60s, divorced or separated in your 30s or 50s, you may also be just starting out on your journey to personal financial security.

Whether you're living on your own for the first time, have just gotten married, or made some other change, you may be facing the challenge of making your money stretch far enough to cover your needs.

In addition to a savings account, you might want to start investing some of your money. So learning about stocks, bonds, and mutual funds can help boost your financial position. Because investments are risks, your earnings may build higher and faster through them. Unfortunately, there is no guarantee that this will be the case.

As a general rule, separating your needs and wants is one of the best ways to create a workable budget. But don't think of a budget as a rigid spending plan. Its real value is serving as a guideline for managing your money

A WORLD OF QUESTIONS

As you take responsibility for managing your own finances, you're likely to have a number of questions about the decisions you have to make:

- How do I pick a bank?
- Are all credit cards the same?
- Why is it important to have a good credit history?
- Should I pay off my education loans now?
- Do I need health or life insurance?
- Should I be saving for retirement?

MANAGING YOUR MONEY

Two basic resources for successful money management are choosing the right financial institution to handle your money, and establishing a good credit rating through the careful use of credit cards.

Finding the bank that's right for you means comparing the fees and rates that various banks charge for different accounts. You may want to open just a checking account, but maintaining a savings account as well can be a good way to establish an emergency fund to fall back on.

Getting a credit card can be a good way to build your credit record. You'll have many choices when you decide to get your first card, but the main things to think about when choosing a card are your buying habits, your tendency to keep a balance, and your desired credit limit.

KNOWLEDGE IS POWER

Going back to school, either to college or graduate school, is a common goal. You may realize once you start working that more training or another degree could lead to better job opportunities.

More education can be beneficial in many ways, but it can take a toll on your wallet. Many scholarships, financial aid programs, and student loan options exist for people who want to further their education, but need some financial help.

If your classes pertain directly to your job, you might also check to see if your employer will reimburse you for your tuition. Sometimes an employer will include this opportunity in an employee benefits package.

THE VALUE OF EDUCATION

While women with at least a bachelor's degree make more than those with only a high school degree, both groups make less than men.

	WOMEN	MEN
Median weekly income with a bachelor's degree	$713	$957
Median weekly income with a high school diploma	$429	$595

Source: Bureau of Labor Statistics—Third Quarter 2000 Usual Weekly Earnings

Building Your Career

Steady employment creates a path to valuable benefits.

Building your career can mean getting a new job, moving up in the company where you are currently employed, or even starting a business of your own. Setting goals for yourself in the workplace, and taking steps to meet those goals, can increase the amount of satisfaction you get from your job. As you take on more responsibility, you also become more valuable to your employer.

Although the most concrete way your employer can reward you for your work is to give you promotions and salary increases, you stand to gain in other ways if you're dedicated to your job. Here are just a few of the possible advantages available to you:

- Expertise in your field
- Upward mobility in the workplace
- Job security
- An extensive benefits package, including insurance and retirement plans

SEEK OUT YOUR DREAM JOB

You might have an idea of what your ideal job is. Do you know what it would take to find and get hired for that job? Researching the qualifications of your dream job can put you one step closer to reaching that goal. Does the position require specific skills or a particular educational background? You might try taking courses, reading books, and talking to people already in the field to broaden your knowledge.

Also, be sure to establish yourself in your current position. The best basis for moving ahead is having a solid history of hard work and dedication behind you. Keep in mind that new employers often look for recommendations from previous employers, so think about how you would want to be described—and try to live up to that description.

USE FLEXTIME

The nine to five work schedule is no longer a rigid standard for many companies. Employers are aware of the growing desire for **flextime**—which can include creating your own hours, working part-time, or compressing a

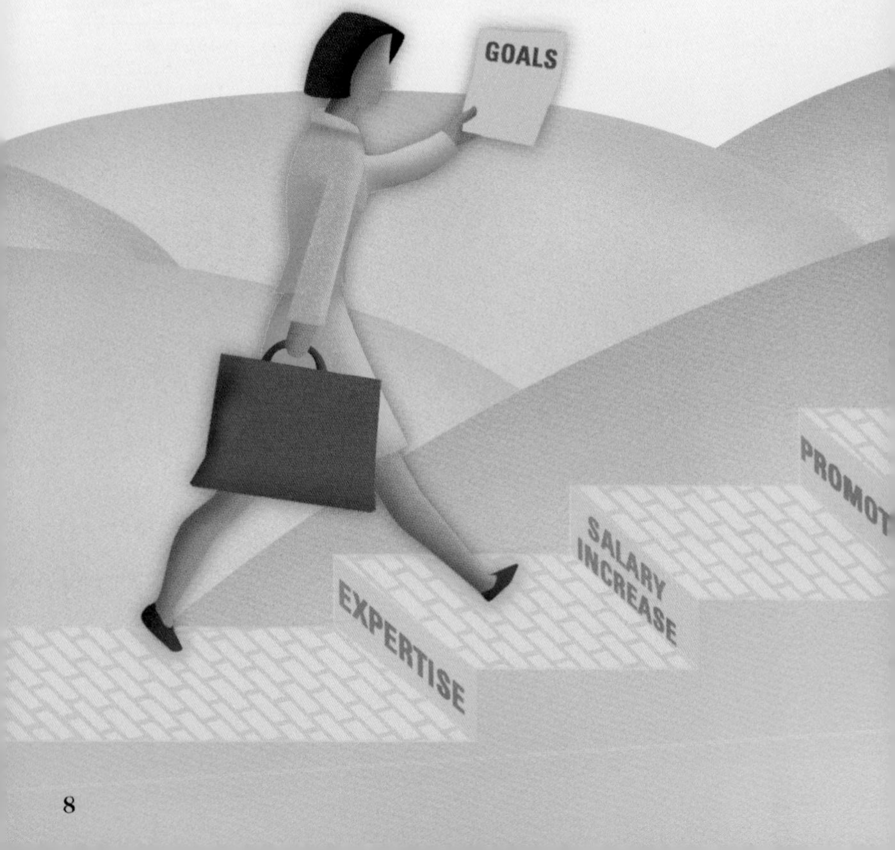

FIND A MENTOR
As a woman, finding a female mentor—someone who has an established career in your field who can give you sound advice—may be a challenge. It might be particularly hard if you are trying to work in a traditionally male-dominated field, such as investing, engineering, or construction. Having a mentor, however, can show you that it's possible for you to move ahead in your industry, and can inspire you to expand your career goals.

Of course, there's nothing wrong with a male mentor either. If he has confidence in you and your ability to succeed, he can give your career a boost.

work week into three or four days—and have started offering these options to their staff.

If you are the primary caretaker in your family, having a job that will allow you to pick your child up from school or take a family member to a doctor's appointment can be an invaluable benefit.

If your idea of flextime includes being able to work at home rather than at the office, you can ask your employer if the company allows **telecommuting**. If you have access to a phone, computer, or fax machine, it's easy to work outside the office.

Telecommuting also means you can work and correspond with your office from planes and trains, or from different cities, as well as from your home.

REJOIN THE WORKFORCE
Many women choose to take time off from work—rather than negotiate a flextime schedule—to have children and raise a family. On average, women spend 11.5 years out of the workforce at some point in their lives, as opposed to 1.3 years for men.

With technology advancing so quickly, you might find that spending several years away from the office could leave you without the necessary skills to perform your job. For example, think about the challenge of reentering the workforce now, if you had little experience with computers or the Internet before you left.

If you decide to take time off, stay current with what is happening in your field. Try to stay in touch with people from your previous job to keep up to date on what's happening. And stay abreast of new technologies. For instance, you don't have to be an expert at using the Internet, but it will help to be familiar with what it is and what its capabilities are.

AT THE INTERVIEW
When you're looking for a new job, be sure to ask about employee benefits. Will you have health insurance? Can you cover your dependents? Is there a retirement savings plan? You're not being greedy or pushy. You'll need that information to weigh one offer against another.

Settling Down

Cultivating your finances now can improve your future peace of mind.

There's not a fixed timetable to help you decide when it's time to buy a home, commit yourself to a long-term personal relationship, get married, have children, or any of the other landmark events that are bound to change your life. But by anticipating the financial responsibilities that settling down is likely to bring, you can eliminate some potential problems right from the start.

IN THE HERE AND NOW

What can you do to be in a secure financial position in the present?

Control debt. You can maintain your financial footing by watching your short-term debt. If you owe money on your credit cards, it's smart to limit the number of cards you use and lower the balance you keep on them.

Calculate your net worth. Subtract your **liabilities**, or the total amount of debt you owe, from the total value of what you own. The result is where you stand financially.

Build a good credit history. Pay your bills on time, and stay up to date on the status of your credit cards and bank accounts.

BUILDING A CREDIT HISTORY

For most people, the word credit immediately brings credit cards to mind. Although the two are related, building a credit history is a bit different from merely using a credit card.

Your credit behavior is tracked by three major credit reporting agencies, which gather data from all your lenders and create a profile that shows your payment history, collections that lenders have had to make from you, and bankruptcy filings, if you've had any. If you've had a history of these events, your credit rating will suffer and you may find it difficult to

A recent Roper study found that two-thirds of women believe it's very important for them to save for retirement, but less than half regularly put money into a 401(k) or IRA account.

According to *Money* magazine, a typical US family has 14 credit cards and carries an average balance of $5,800.

borrow money. But paying your bills regularly and on time can help you maintain a solid credit rating and keep you in good standing for loans when you need them.

BUYING A HOUSE

When you're ready to buy a home, you generally start by looking for a mortgage, a very specific type of loan. Without a mortgage, you'd have to save the full purchase price—not something that most people can do. As an added bonus, mortgage interest is tax deductible, so you can reduce what you owe Uncle Sam as you put a roof over your head.

Qualifying for a mortgage requires good credit. Because a mortgage is a long-term loan, you'll need to show your lender that you have a solid history of repayment, as well as a steady source of income and a strong job history.

GETTING MARRIED

If you and your partner are thinking of making a lifelong commitment, you can decide together how you want to handle your finances. Will you file your taxes together or separately? If you buy a home, will you have joint ownership?

Every couple handles their money differently. Some combine their funds in joint accounts, while others keep their savings separate—and some choose to have both joint and separate accounts. No matter which approach you choose, it's crucial that you both agree to it, since unsettled money matters can lead to arguments, financial problems, and even divorce.

RETIREMENT PLANNING

Have you been putting money in an IRA? Do you contribute to a 401(k) plan? Your retirement planning can forge ahead at this time. Companies often wait until you've worked at least a year before offering you the opportunity to participate in a salary reduction plan. If you've reached your eligibility date, now is the time to start contributing to your retirement account or accounts.

Having Children

Becoming a parent is a full-time financial commitment.

Starting a family means a big change in your lifestyle—and your finances. Some of the changes are simple, such as adding another exemption on your tax form or changing your will to include your child. Others involve a deeper commitment. Being ready to pay for your children's college expenses, for example, requires careful, long-term planning.

It's hard to anticipate all the possible costs of raising a child. Today, many women continue to work or start a career while their children are young. Although maintaining a job while your child needs constant care will give you an income, working can also increase your expenses. If your job requires you to put your child in daycare, for instance, you could end up paying out a large part of what you are earning.

As you learn more about money management through the process of raising your child, you can pass on your financial knowledge to him or her. Having your child understand and respect your efforts to prepare for the future will increase your motivation to do so.

SHARING YOUR KNOWLEDGE

Being open about money at home can introduce your child to the financial world. If you devote careful attention to your finances, your child will be more likely to adopt a similar approach.

Teaching him or her about money doesn't have to mean explaining the details of your investing plan or your tax reduction strategy. To start out, you can simply include your child in discussions about the family's saving and spending plans. For example, you might teach your child how to prepare a vacation budget and live by it. Or you can even get your child a toy bank with two slots—one for saving and one for spending—to explain the importance of money.

PLANNING FOR COLLEGE

With the cost of college escalating each year, it's never too early to start planning for your child's education. It's smart to set up a separate college savings account and contribute some money each month, even when your child is very young. The sooner you begin, the less pressure you're likely to feel later. There are a number of ways to get started, including putting money into Education IRAs, state-sponsored savings plans, tuition pre-payment plans, or US savings bonds.

As your child gets older, you might adjust your saving plan and investments. A financial planner could help you find the best way to handle your accounts during each stage of your child's life.

SUPPORTING A CHILD ALONE

While the cost of raising a child may seem overwhelming, having to pay the bills on your own may seem truly monumental. If you are single, divorced, separated, or widowed, you need to develop a specific strategy.

In cases of divorce, child support will most likely be a primary consideration. Each state uses its own guidelines in setting the amount of child support to be paid. If you are already receiving child support, you should do your best to put some of that money away for college. During your divorce agreement negotiations, it's also important to decide who will pay for college, especially if your former husband is in a position to do so. It's dangerous to simply assume he will pay.

Also remember that financial aid programs consider both parents' circumstances when distributing loans and awards. You can't assume that just because you are a single parent, your child will be eligible for financial aid.

ADOPTION

Research has shown that 2% to 4% of US families have adopted children. While that may seem like a small percentage of the total population, it's estimated that these adoptions have created homes for two and a half to five million children.

Although adopting can include a long waiting period and significant expenses, there are benefits available to make the process easier. A federal tax credit was created in 1997, and some companies offer adoption benefits for employees to cover legal fees and birth mother medical costs.

Being Prepared for Change

Financial stability can be rocked by an unexpected storm.

It's rewarding to enjoy financial security. You have probably worked hard to establish your career and earn a comfortable income. You may have already survived the pressure of buying a home and paying college tuitions, and are looking forward to predictable monthly expenses. While breathing a sigh of relief is tempting, it can be dangerous to relax so much that a drastic change can blindside you and your finances.

How would you manage economically, for example, if you couldn't work because of illness, disability, or job loss? Although thinking about these issues is never fun, you'll want to prepare for the unexpected to protect your financial security.

A major change in your relationships can also surprise you. If you're married, you might lose your husband through divorce or death. The financial factors might be especially hard to face because of the emotional impact of this type of event.

FOOD FOR THOUGHT
20% of all women never marry. 47% of first marriages and 49% of second marriages end in divorce. And 75% of married women are eventually widowed.
A Woman's Guide to Investing, 1998

For example, you'll probably have to open new bank accounts or take your husband's name off existing ones. You may need new credit cards if you don't have one in your own name. And you'll have to prepare a will and change the designations on retirement savings plans and insurance policies.

RIDING OUT THE STORMS

While facing disability, illness, or job loss is never pleasant, making certain preparations can help you survive these financial strains.

If you do become ill or disabled, the greatest costs are those that medical providers charge, including hospital,

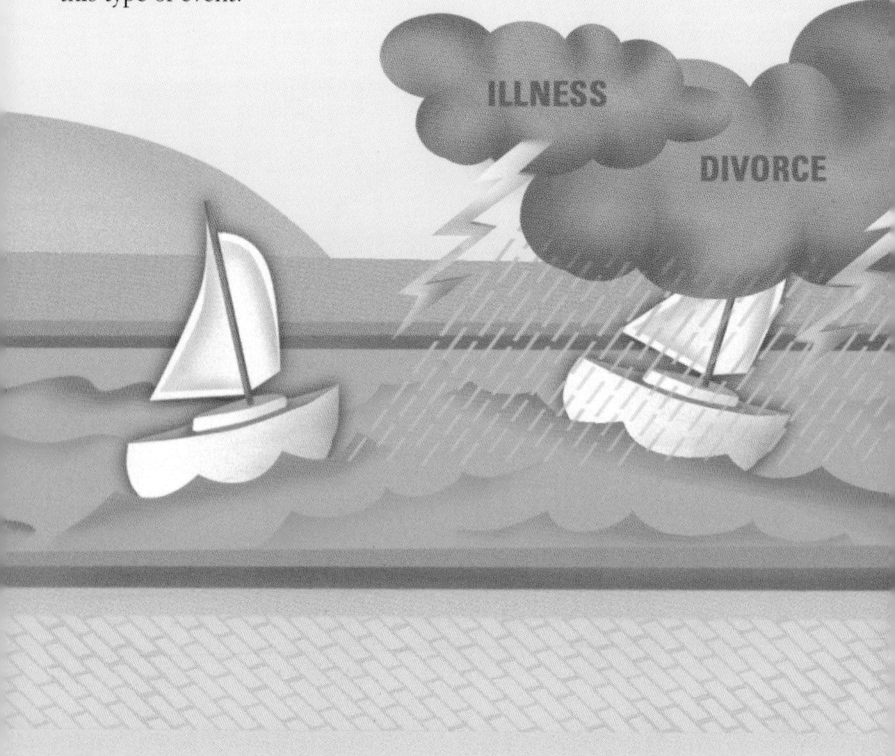

loctor, and medication bills. That's vhy it always pays to have health nsurance, especially if you can get a educed rate through your employer's group plan. You may also want to con- ider disability insurance. If you care- ully research different policy options, ou can get the right kind of coverage o protect yourself.

Losing a job can also be alarming. That's why you need to have an emer- gency fund to cover your expenses if ou're between jobs. And look at the right side: Job loss can lead you to new career, or a better position in our current field. And since most eople hold an average of eight jobs n their lifetime, you're not alone if ou decide to shift career paths at ome point. You may decide to take ome time off to travel, spend time vith your family, or pursue a hobby.

FLASH OF SUDDEN INDEPENDENCE

f you've been married for much of our adult life, the financial inde- endence that comes with divorce or vidowhood can seem overwhelming. ou'll need to be prepared for some hanges, depending on your situation nd the circumstances around the oss of your partner.

You're in an especially strong position if you're comfortable with all of the aspects of your family's finances because you played an active role in financial decisionmaking. In that case, you are prepared to make choices that will protect your future and provide for your dependents. The advice of a professional can be helpful as well.

AGING PARENTS

As you age, your parents age as well, of course. You may find them struggling with illness during their advancing years.

As their daughter, you may be responsible for their care, since 82% of women in your position wind up with this responsibility. The emotional impact and financial strain together can be exhausting. It's quite possible that your commitment may compromise your career or your family.

Grappling with illness can naturally spark concerns about your parents' deaths. Do you know how carefully your parents have planned their estate? It can be quite difficult to ask the questions that you need answered, but it might be worse to wonder about their wishes when it's too late to find out.

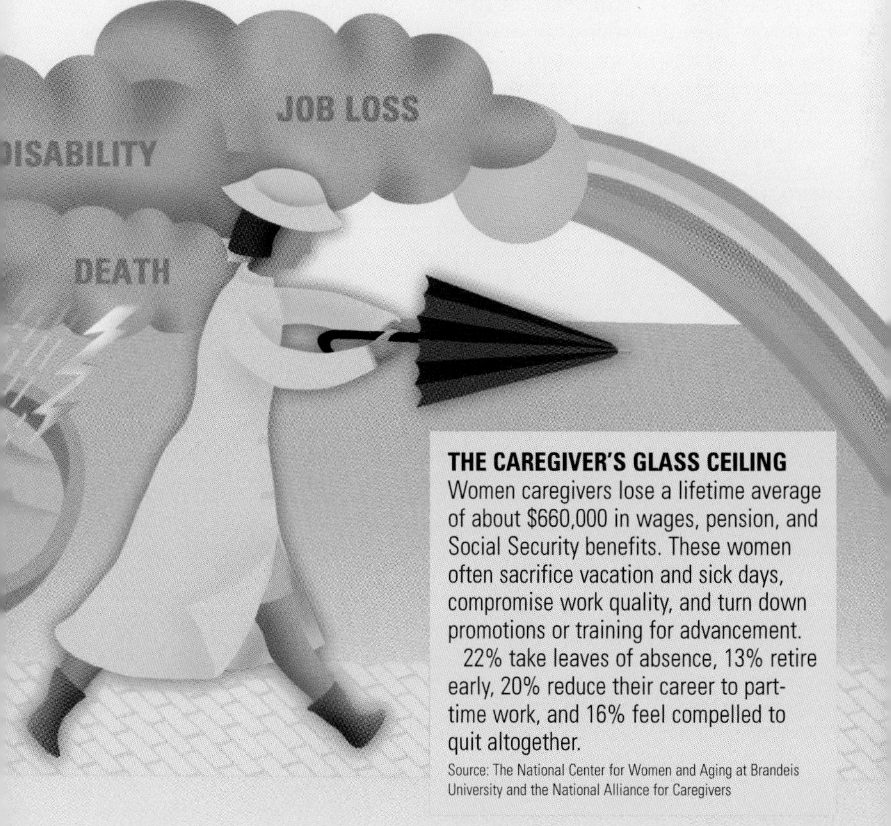

THE CAREGIVER'S GLASS CEILING

Women caregivers lose a lifetime average of about $660,000 in wages, pension, and Social Security benefits. These women often sacrifice vacation and sick days, compromise work quality, and turn down promotions or training for advancement.

22% take leaves of absence, 13% retire early, 20% reduce their career to part-time work, and 16% feel compelled to quit altogether.

Source: The National Center for Women and Aging at Brandeis University and the National Alliance for Caregivers

Retiring Right

Your retirement challenge is knowing where your money will come from and where it will go.

Retirement can be all you've hoped for: a new home, new interests, or new involvement in familiar activities. But if you're worrying about money, it can be hard to live as you'd like to, or really enjoy retirement. A realistic view of the financial changes to expect—both in your income and in your expenses—can help. Once you identify your financial questions and know where to find the answers, you can really begin to enjoy retirement.

THE INCOME JIGSAW

If you're used to living on a regular paycheck, getting income from a variety of sources during retirement can be a bit unnerving initially. But you'll eventually be comfortable when more than one check arrives each month.

In the meantime, having a clear picture of your anticipated income can reassure you that you can be financially secure without your former salary. How can you sort out all these options? You may want to focus on three main kinds of benefits: Social Security, retirement plans, and personal investments.

You're probably counting on **Social Security** income, based on the contributions you've made during your working years. But you'll need to decide when to start receiving these benefits, and anticipate what you may receive.

If you have participated in a **pension** plan at work, now is the first time you can touch the funds that have been set aside for your retirement. With a **defined contribution plan**, the amount you'll receive depends on how well the investments in the plan have done over time. However, a payout from a **defined benefit plan** will be based on how long you worked at your company, and how much you earned.

You may also be looking forward to withdrawing money from a salary reduction plan, Individual Retirement Account (IRA), or some other type of retirement plan. To make the most of what these plans offer, you'll want to review the rules for naming beneficiaries and making required withdrawals with an experienced adviser.

Investments are a key part of the financial picture for many retirees. They require decisions that carry real economic consequences. For example, you might wonder if you should change your investment strategy or even take all your money out of the market.

'he choices you make can be crucial o ensuring your financial stability luring retirement. For example, you nay need to adjust your portfolio to reate income, as well as tap into our existing investments to cover our needs.

:HANGING EXPENSES

'o construct a financial plan that vorks well with your retirement eeds, you might also want to rethink our expenses. A retirement budget nay be a bit different from the budg-t you had during your working years.

Specifically, you may want to set nore aside for leisure during retire-nent. Since you will no longer have ypical work costs, you can devote nore money to travel, hobbies, or ven a new vacation home.

You may also face increased ealthcare expenses. The government oes insure you through Medicare, ut that may bring up more questions nd uncertainties. You may also won-er about extra treatment that extends eyond your regular insurance, ike medication, hospital visits, nd long-term care.

While retirement economics are certainly an adjustment from your former financial situation, a clearly outlined budget can be the key to soothing your anxiety. It's quite possi-ble to enjoy retirement without serious financial woes. If you maximize your sources of income and spend within reason, you can look forward to a financially secure retirement.

WORKING DURING RETIREMENT

Although most people view retirement as freedom from the demands of their career, second jobs are popular as well. A second career can be an opportunity to pursue a passion, and a part-time job can nicely supplement your income.

But there are financial and lifestyle implications. If you earn too much, you can jeopardize your Social Security bene-fits. And the demands of employment can interfere with your priorities during retire-ment. So volunteering might be a better choice for you.

Planning Your Legacy

The best estate plans have detailed blueprints.

When you die, what you've accumulated is given away—both your valuable possessions and your money. Do you want to provide lifelong support for your children, or give to a favorite charity or your alma mater? Or can you afford to do both? You might also consider the extended future. For example, you might want to make sure that a cherished heirloom stays in your family even after the death of your initial heir. Decisions such as these are outlined in your **estate plan**.

You may be deciding now—or are already certain—how your legacy will be distributed. But you may be wondering for the first time if estate planning is something you need, and if so, where to begin.

WITHOUT A SKETCH

Dying without a will, or **intestate**, creates a world of confusion for those trying to settle your estate. If you die intestate, the courts follow state laws for distributing your wealth, which means your possessions may not go to the loved ones you would have chosen yourself. And without an estate plan, part of your estate could be subject to federal estate taxes, plus 8% in fees.

The thought of estate planning may seem morbid, but it's worth the effort to protect your loved ones—especially your children, if you have any—from letting the courts guess what you would have wanted. It's crucial to have a plan in place, even if you're young and healthy, since there's no way to tell when it might have to be used.

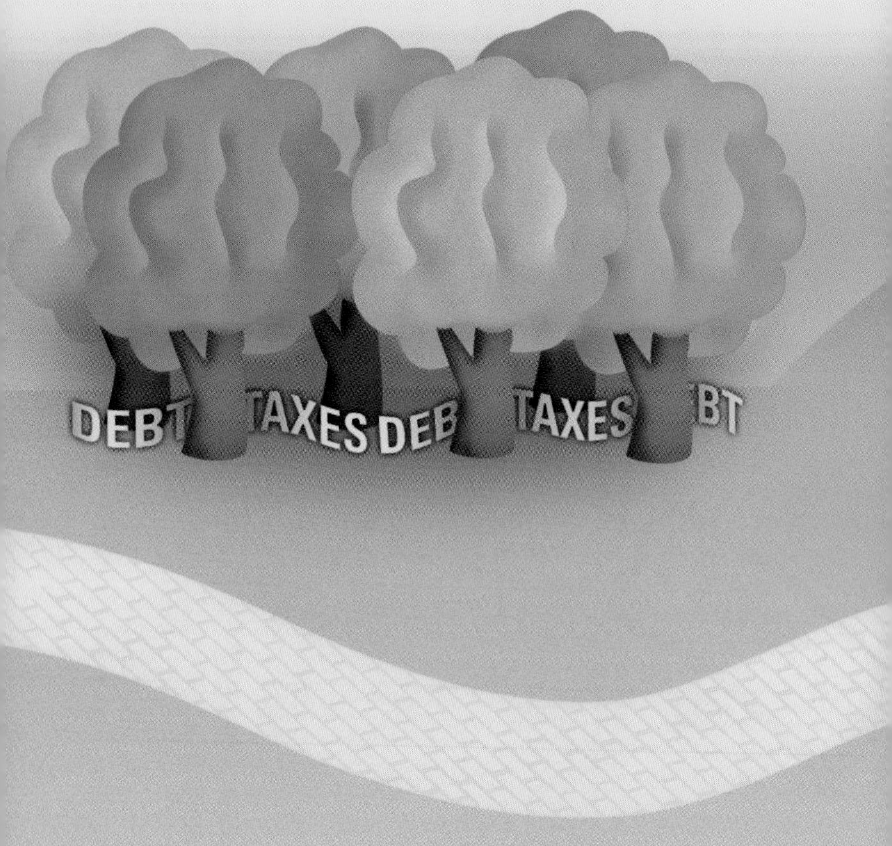

SSESSING THE SITE

o construct an estate plan, you must illy consider your possessions and our goals. The size and scope of your state will determine what you can nd should do with it. When you're guring out what is included in your state, remember to include real state, bank accounts, investments, nd life insurance. Your personal roperty—jewelry, furniture, art, ntiques, and other valuables—is lso part of your estate.

An estate attorney, along with your nancial adviser, can help you esti- nate the value of your estate. They an also give you advice on estate lanning strategies, as well as help ou create a plan to maximize what ou can pass on.

SCALE MATTERS

Estate plans may seem like a concern for the very rich. But that assumption is often the reason that mid-sized estates are hit with unexpected taxes. If you own a home and an insurance policy on your life and have personal investments and money in retirement savings plans, it's possible that the value of your estate may exceed the dollar amount that's exempt from federal estate taxes. That's $1.5 million for 2004 and 2005.

Even if your estate will not face taxes, having a plan is usually in the best financial and emotional interests of your loved ones. Your written instructions should prevent, or at least lessen, arguments among your heirs about the possessions they're entitled to inherit.

DRAFTING THE SKETCHES

The most obvious place to name your heirs is in your will. But complete estate plans also use a variety of tools to distribute wealth.

If you need to limit the estate taxes you face, you can give away a good por- tion of your money while you're still alive. If you intend to give away your valuables to someone you trust, you can transfer or share ownership with them before your death. To secure income for dependents, you may set up trusts to pay a regular stipend after your death—or you may name the next person to receive income from your retirement plan.

Defining Your Financial Goals

To get where you want to go, you need clearly defined goals.

Do you remember the first time you set a financial goal and had the satisfaction of reaching it?

Maybe it was buying your first bicycle, saving money to go on a vacation, or using your own money to buy your mother a special gift. The process you followed to achieve the goals that were important to you during your childhood is the same process you follow to reach major financial milestones as an adult.

- **Decide when you hope to meet your goal**
- **Figure out how much money you need to meet that goal**
- **Determine how you'll manage your current income as you try to meet your goal**
- **Be sure you're protected against unexpected financial events that could stand in the way of meeting your goal**

HELPFUL HINTS
Studies show that adults are more likely to meet their financial goals if they write the goals down on paper. So you can start out by writing (or typing) your goal, including specific details to define it. Then write down the timeframe and steps that you predict you'll take as you try to achieve your goal. Finally, post that document in a place where you're likely to see it daily.

Start by asking yourself the following:

- What goal do you want to achieve?
- When do you want to reach that goal?
- What obstacles might arise?
- How much money will it take?
- Have you protected yourself from obstacles that may sidetrack you?

OALS AND VALUES

Iost goals are linked to the things ›u value. If, for instance, you have family to support, then your goals ay be to provide a house for them to 'e in, food to eat, a solid education, ıd a nurturing environment for your ıildren. If you're building a career, ›ur goals may include more educa- ›n. Or you may want to travel ound the world.

NE TUNING

very day brings changes in the orld around you and in the financial imate. You need to take all of those ıings into account as you manage ›ur short- and long-term plans, view where you stand, and make ljustments in what you want or ›lieve is attainable. Experts suggest ıat you conduct a review of your ng-term goals once a year and more equently of your short-term goals.

BE SMART

By setting SMART goals, you can clarify not only your targets but the directions to follow to reach them.

Specific. If owning a home and enjoying a secure retirement are important to you, set specific goals. Determine the kind of house you'd like and where you'd like to live. Figure out when you want to retire, how much income you're likely to need, and where it will come from.

Measurable. Every financial goal has a price tag, so you have to ask yourself how much it will cost. If you don't know specific prices, your immediate task is to do some research.

Achievable. It's very tough to assess how achievable a goal is, since some people like challenges, while others feel safer with more easily attainable targets. You should spend some time doing an honest assessment of your own attitudes. For example, are you really willing to sacrifice things you enjoy now to put money toward your future goals?

Realistic. Be careful about putting aside too much money toward your goals, which could leave you without money for everyday expenses or small luxuries. Realistically budget money toward your goals so you can allow for small frills.

Timely. Each of your specific goals should be part of a master timetable. You need to set dates, since a goal's timing affects your strategy for meeting it.

If you can't figure out the cost and can't set a date, you probably need to do some research to find the missing numbers. Similarly, if you are uncertain about how achievable or realistic your goals are, you might want to discuss them with a family member, your husband or partner, or a knowledgeable friend. Then consult with a professional financial adviser.

Financial Plans

It's worth the effort to put your plans in writing.

One way to figure out how you'll pay for the things that are important to you is to create a **financial plan**. A financial plan is a written document that spells out where you are in your financial life, where you want to be, and the investment strategies you'll follow to meet your goals.

It can be a detailed description of different investments, and a discussion of the strategy that's been prepared by a professional planner. It can be a letter or memo from your adviser, summarizing what you hope to achieve and how to approach those goals. Or it might simply be a list of objectives and actions you've drawn up yourself.

While experts have different opinions on how detailed a plan should be, they all agree that getting your ideas on paper is essential to getting started and can be used as a valuable benchmark to measure the progress of your financial goals.

GETTING STARTED

One way to begin your financial planning is to create a record of all your savings and investment accounts, along with their current balances. Then consider linking each of your existing accounts to a particular goal, such as buying a home or paying for college. As you set aside money for your goals, you put it into the designated account.

The most obvious examples of goal-specific accounts are tax-deferred retirement savings plans, including a 401(k), 403(b), or 457 plan that your employer may offer, and individual retirement accounts (IRAs) that you set up on your own. When the relationship between the goal and the account name isn't as obvious, you may want to give your accounts descriptive names.

You can link almost any account to any goal, though you'll discover that certain ways of putting your mon- to work are better suited to meeting certain types of goals. That's because some accounts are designed to preser- your **principal**, or initial investment amount, for short-term use while others are better suited for growing your assets over the long term.

WOMAN-CENTERED PLANS

As a woman, your financial plan should reflect several realities:

- You're likely to live an average of seven years longer than a man, so

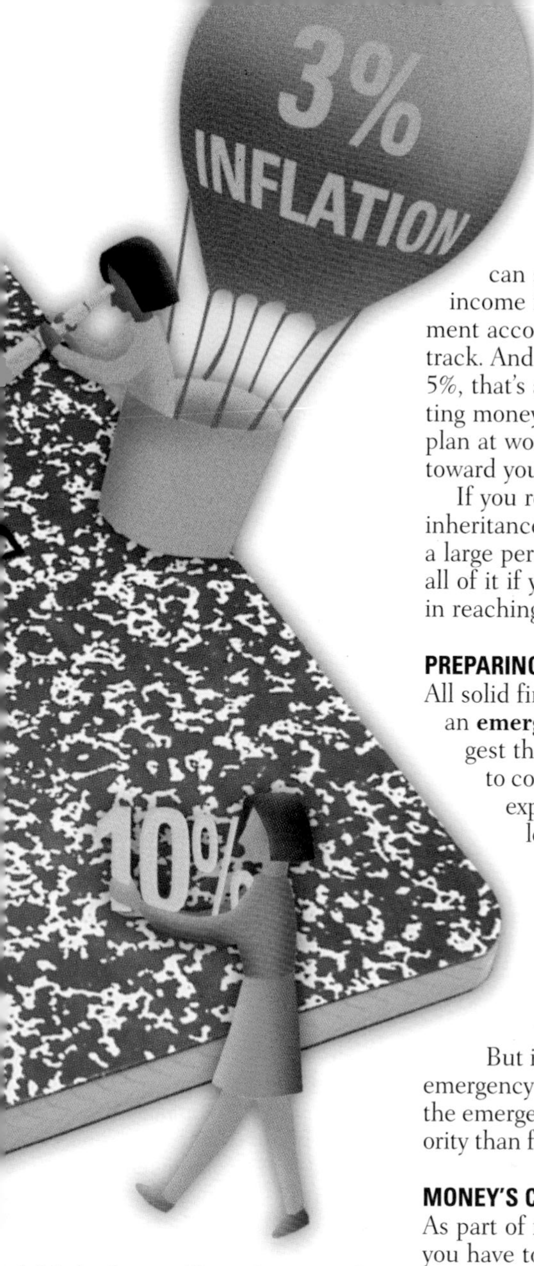

it's likely that you'll need income for an extended period after retirement
You may dedicate years to caregiver responsibilities, both for your children and your aging parents, and not invest in an employer sponsored retirement plan during your nonworking years
You may spend fewer years in the workforce, resulting in smaller retirement income
You may face gender discrimination when you apply for mortgage and business loans

AY YOURSELF FIRST

lentifying the savings and investing :counts you'll use to meet particular oals lets you establish the routine of lding to those accounts regularly. hat's sometimes described as paying ourself—and ideally you'll do it as your first priority when you deal with your bills each month.

Generally speaking, if you can set aside 10% of your gross income for your savings or investment accounts, you're on the right track. And if you can manage only 5%, that's a good start. If you're putting money into a retirement savings plan at work, that percentage counts toward your total gross income.

If you receive a large bonus or an inheritance, you might want to invest a large percentage of that money—or all of it if you have a long way to go in reaching your goals.

PREPARING FOR THE UNKNOWN

All solid financial plans incorporate an **emergency fund**. Experts suggest that you keep enough money to cover three to six months of expenses—or perhaps even longer, if you're single and supporting yourself—in a liquid account. That way, if you face an unforeseen event, you won't have to stop contributing a portion of your savings toward your previous goals.

But if you haven't established an emergency fund, paying off the bills for the emergency should be a higher priority than funding your investments.

MONEY'S CHANGING VALUE

As part of making a financial plan, you have to take the effect of inflation into account. The reality is that the cost of meeting your goals increases each year, typically due to inflation, which has averaged 3% a year on and off for almost a century.

At that rate, prices double about every 24 years. That means if you're living on $45,000 now, you'll need $90,000 in about 20 years to maintain your lifestyle. Complicating the picture is the cost of goals, such as buying a home, starting your own business, or paying for college, which tend to increase at a higher rate.

On the bright side, any money you invest today has the potential to grow faster than money you invest in the future. For instance, if you've invested $10,000 by the time you're 35, and it averages 8% growth for 30 years, you will have an account that's worth $109,357 when you're ready to retire.

Financial Planners

It can help to have someone to talk to about your financial plans.

Financial planners specialize in helping you reach your personal finance goals, from identifying what you want to accomplish, to writing a financial plan and putting that plan into practice. They can't make decisions for you, but they can help enormously by laying out the choices you face and the consequences of the decisions you make. They can also help you assess your current financial situation. Most importantly, they should be able to answer your financial questions clearly or help you find the answers you need.

WHO NEEDS ADVICE?

Most people can benefit from financial advice. It's particularly important to get help if your self-assessment shows that you're uncertain about making financial decisions. You may want a planner's unbiased look at your current financial plan.

And if you've been handling money for some time, you may want advice about expanding your horizons to more sophisticated investing or estate building.

Many financial plans falter because people procrastinate. A planner may provide the encouragement you need to start putting your plan into action.

HOW ARE ADVISERS PAID?

Advisers are paid in different ways. Some earn **commissions**, which means they get a percentage of the cost of stocks, bonds, mutual funds, insurance policies, or other financial

CHOOSING THE RIGHT ADVISER

Finding the financial adviser who's right for you is like choosing any other professional. Start by talking to friends and family who've worked with advisers themselves. Ask your lawyer, accountant, or tax adviser for a reference. Investigate the services your banks or other financial service companies you already do business with provide. Many of them have planners on staff.

Schedule appointments to meet with several advisers. Because you're looking for help in managing an extremely important part of your life, you'll want to choose someone you're comfortable working with.

Here are some questions you'll want to consider as you make a decision:

Is the adviser interested in who you are and what you want to accomplish?

One clue is to monitor how many questions the adviser asks about your goals and your financial experience.

Has the adviser worked with people who have goals and financial situations similiar to yours?

Ask the planner to describe his or her typical client.

RESOURCES

If you want more information about financial planning and professional planners, check these resources:

The Financial Planning Association
800-647-6340
www.fpanet.org

The National Association of Personal Financial Advisors
888-366-2732
www.napfa.org

The American Institute of Certified Public Accountants
800-862-4272
www.aicpa.org

roducts you buy on their recomıendation. These commissions, or ales charges, vary based on the roduct. Sometimes they're added) the cost of the investment so that ou know what you're paying. But ometimes they aren't broken out s a separate expense. You should lways ask about the method of payıent, and get an estimate of the cost.

There are also advisers who ıanage your investment portfolio s well as provide advice. This type f adviser may charge an **annual fee**, /hich is a percentage based on the alue of your account, or a flat month- or annual fee for their work.

Fee-only advisers charge an hourly ate for the advice they give, but no ıanagement fee or commission on /hat you buy. Other advisers receive combination of fee and commission, nd still others earn a salary plus ommission or just a flat salary.

You can find good advisers paid ı any of these ways. Or you can use ne type of adviser for planning and another for investing. Most important, you want to be sure that the advice you're getting is right for you and not just profitable for the financial adviser that you hire.

Vhat investments does the adviser ecommend most often?

There's reason for concern if the adviser tresses one type of investment rather han a range of investments to meet lifferent goals.

:an the adviser explain planning :hoices and investment alternatives :learly?

If you can't understand what the adviser ells you, you probably won't willingly ollow the advice you get. The adviser nay have some different points of view han you do and may want to open your eyes to new approaches or ideas. So being able to explain them is critical.

Is the adviser certified or accredited?

You'll want to work with someone who has met professional standards as a financial planner (CFP), retirement consultant (CRPC), insurance agent (ChFC, CLU), or a CPA accredited as a planner (PFS).

Does the adviser have several years of experience?

Someone who has been in the field five years or more has probably worked with a number of clients and in a variety of market conditions.

Balancing Your Financial Goals

Effective financial planning means keeping many balls in the air.

Timing plays an important role in your investment plans and goals. Chances are that you want to meet some of your goals in the immediate future. You look forward to achieving others in a few years. And you keep those that won't become reality for a long time in the back of your mind.

Timing also influences the specific investments you make to achieve particular goals. And the emphasis you put on one of your goals during a certain period of your life has a direct impact on your progress toward meeting the others.

For instance, you may be trying to save 10% of your income to divide among your various goals. But if you're making the down payment on a new home in the next few months, you'll need your cash to cover all the expenses of moving. Can you do both? Perhaps you can't. But if you have to skip meeting your savings goal for a few months, your overall plan doesn't have to suffer.

Put another way, taking timing into account means looking at what you can afford to spend today and still meet your long-term commitments. Similarly, it means asking what investment risks you should be taking for the long term without putting your short-term security in jeopardy. All this balancing is aimed at finding the place where you are both comfortable and reasonably confident of meeting your goals.

HELPFUL HINTS

What's short term for some may be long term for others. For instance, if your twin daughters are sixteen, funding their college tuition is a short-term responsibility for you. But if your sister's daughter is five, she has a much longer span to work with.

SHORT TERM (UNDER TWO YEARS)

Your challenge in the short term is to be sure that you're meeting all your day-to-day obligations while also accumulating money for immediate goals, such as buying a car, getting married, or taking a big trip.

Planning for short-term goals isn't as difficult as for those that are farther in the future. Their immediacy makes it easier to get motivated to save the money you need. Because the effects of inflation are minor on

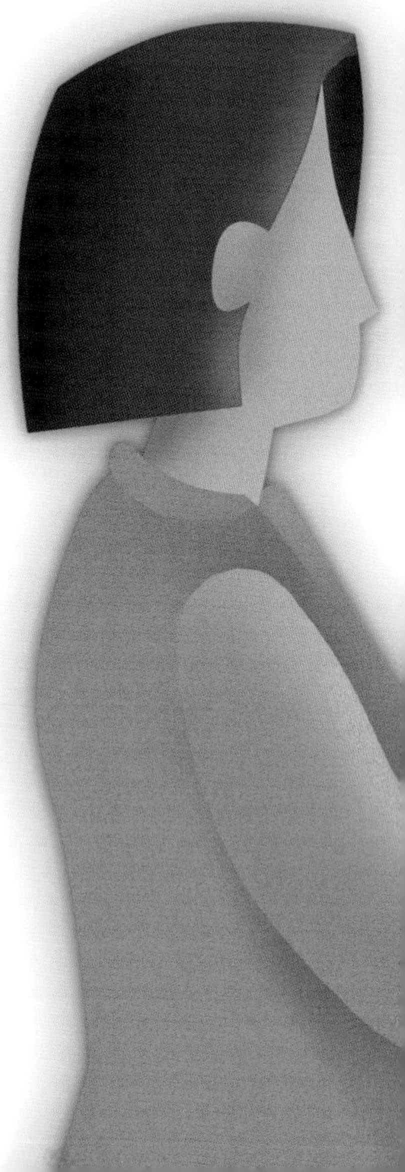

noney you're spending fairly soon, :'s relatively easy to estimate the ctual cost.

The complicating factor is that hort-term expenses affect what you an invest for longer-term goals. You nay picture yourself sitting behind he wheel of a brand-new convertible r moving from your apartment into house. You've calculated that you an afford the payments. But you lso have to ask yourself how spending the extra money now might affect our plan to expand your business or ttend graduate school.

1EDIUM TERM (TWO TO TEN YEARS)

ou may need more time to ccomplish some of your ther goals.

If, for example, you ave a passion for making product or providing a ervice that you believe you can do better than anyone else, you may want to turn it into a full-scale business. Before you actually open the door, you'll need to learn about potential customers, competitors, and the requirements of the market. And you need to be building as much of a financial cushion as you can to keep the business growing until it begins to make a profit.

As energizing as a medium-term goal may be, you have to deal with demands on the money you had planned to invest—perhaps to replace a car unexpectedly. But there may also be times when you choose to put all your financial energy into meeting a specific goal, resolving to catch up on the others later. It's not ideal, but it's realistic.

LONG TERM (TEN YEARS OR BEYOND)

Retirement is the most common long-term goal. But caring for an older family member or sending your grandchildren to college are also examples of things you may need or want to pay for in the more distant future.

There's a paradox in financial planning for the long term. On the one hand, goals that are 20 or 30 years in the future seem remote and even unreal. It can be hard to motivate yourself to give up some income now to provide income later, or to sacrifice things you want to do because you've been warned you have to save more.

On the other hand, it may be easier to achieve long-term financial goals than short-term ones because certain investment categories, such as stocks and stock mutual funds, can lose as well as gain value quickly in the short term. But these investments tend to increase in value over longer periods of time.

Buying a Home

Buying a home may be one of the biggest financial decisions you'll ever make.

The same process that helped you make an overall financial plan can help you decide whether and when to buy a home. Start by defining your goals. Consider where you want to live, the features you're looking for, what you can afford, and a realistic date for having the money you'll need. Then apply your knowledge to making this key decision.

RENTING VERSUS BUYING

Because purchasing a home is a huge investment, you need to take the time to weigh the benefits of renting versus buying a residence.

Renting may be a smart financial move for these reasons:

- The initial cost of renting is usually lower than making a down payment on a house, though the security payment, advance, last month's rent, and so on, can mount up
- You probably won't pay property taxes and upkeep directly though your rent may reflect these expenses
- With no money tied up in real estate, you should have more cash or savings to invest, producing more growth in value than owning real estate
- You run no risk that the value of your property will decline
- Renting gives you more mobility to take advantage of a job opportunity in a different area

Buying a home has its advantages as well:

- You can deduct the interest on your mortgage and your local property taxes on your tax return, which can reduce your taxes and free up cash for investing
- You build equity as you pay off your mortgage, increasing your share of the property's value
- You may be able to borrow against your equity and deduct the interest payments on the loan
- If your house increases in value over time, you may make a profit when you decide to sell
- While the effects are harder to measure, owning a home has enormous emotional and psychological advantages

THE COST OF BUYING

The actual amount you'll spend to buy a home depends on the part of the country you live in and the type of home you want. While the dollar amount will vary, certain guidelines apply wherever you buy.

It's likely that you will need cash for a down payment and will get a **mortgage**—a long-term loan you use to buy a home. Traditionally the down payment has been between 10% and 20% of the sale price, though there are some government sponsored programs that let you put a smaller amount down. But the less you put down, the larger your mortgage payments will be and the greater the risk

ıat you will default, or not be able
› make your payments.

What a mortgage costs depends on ıree factors: the **principal**, or amount ou borrow, the **finance charge** you ay for using the money, and the **term**, r length of time the mortgage lasts. ou should also expect to pay an up-ront interest charge to your lender, of ne or more **points**. A point is usually % of the mortgage amount.

ıORTGAGE REQUIREMENTS

Vhen you apply for a mortgage, you ill have to qualify to be able to bor-ow. Typically, lenders require you › spend no more than 28% of your ıonthly income to repay the com-ined total of your mortgage loan, roperty taxes, and homeowners' ısurance. For example, if your gross ay is $54,000 a year, or $4,500 a ıonth, your housing expenses could e up to $1,260.

Most lenders also consider your ther financial responsibilities, ıcluding car payments, personal ›ans, college loans, and other debts. 'hey don't want these expenses—plus our housing costs—to be more than bout 36% of your monthly income. ı short, they want to be sure you'll e able to pay your mortgage before ıey let you borrow.

USING A REAL ESTATE AGENT

A real estate agent can provide valuable assistance in buying a home. An agent knows what's available in a particular neighborhood, what the price trends are, and how current asking prices relate to actual sales prices.

You can look for an agent the same way you look for a financial planner or other professional. Ask your friends and family for recommendations, check out your local resources and various real estate websites, and interview several people before you decide on the person to work with. It could turn out to be an extended relationship, and you want it to be a productive one.

Traditional real estate agents and the real estate firms that list homes for sale are paid by the seller and represent the seller's interest. That doesn't mean that, as a buyer, you can't establish a good relationship with sellers' agents or use them to find a home at a price you can afford. Some buyers, though, prefer to hire buyers' agents to represent their interests and negotiate the sale price and contract terms.

Planning for College

Paying for college can be a drain on your resources.

A college education has enormous value for its own sake, and can have monetary value as well. On average, women with college degrees make about a million dollars more over their lifetimes than high school graduates. But education can be expensive. The cost of an undergraduate degree has increased approximately 6% to 8% a year for several decades, while overall cost of living has increased about 3% a year. Graduate programs can be costly as well.

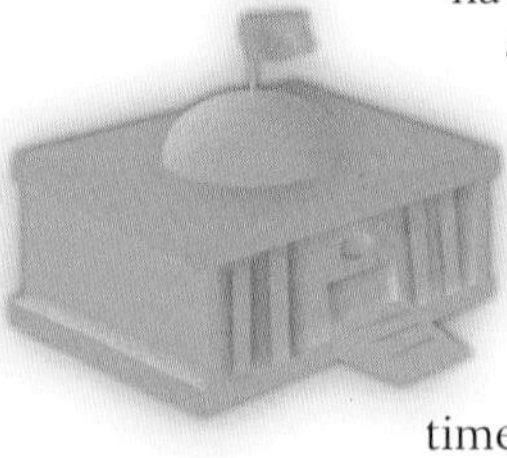

If one of your goals is paying for a child's education, it's important to start building your investment early. If you put away education dollars steadily—every week or every month—and invest for growth while your child is young, you've got a stronger chance of reaching your goal. You can move the money into less risky instruments as the date for that first tuition payment gets closer.

LONG-TERM COLLEGE PLANNING

It pays to check out some of the ways to make the cost of higher education more affordable. Be sure to check for any income restrictions that may make you ineligible for certain plans.

Join a savings plan. All 50 states offer qualified college savings plans authorized by Section 529 of the IRS Tax Code. You contribute money for a specific beneficiary, either as a lump sum or over time. Any earnings are tax exempt when you withdraw them if the money is used to pay tuition and other qualified expenses at any eligible institution.

Prepay tuition. Some states let you pay future tuition charges at today's rates, either as a lump sum or in monthly payments. An association of private colleges and universities offers its own plan for prepaying tuition at any of the participating schools. You can find more information at www.independent529plan.org.

Open an education savings account (ESA). You can contribute up to $2,000 a year for a child under 18. Earnings aren't taxed if the money in the ESA is used for education expenses before the beneficiary turns 30.

Consider a custodial savings account. You can put money into an account in a child's name and act as custodian or trustee. After the child reaches 14, earnings are taxed at his or her rate, which will probably be lower than yours. However, at 18 (or 21 in some cases), the child has the right to total control of the money.

Buy US savings bonds. Based on he amount of income you have, you nay be able to avoid income taxes on avings bond interest if you use the noney to pay college expenses.

DUCATION FOR YOU

f you're planning to further your wn education, you may have less ime to accumulate the money you eed. But there are some cost-saving lternatives to explore.

Your employer may be willing to oot some or all of the bill if your

degree will make you a more valuable employee—or there may be a tuition plan in place for which all employees are eligible. If you're planning to work in certain occupations, such as education or medicine, and are willing to work in certain needy areas, you may qualify for reduced rate loans or have your loans entirely forgiven.

You may qualify for government programs like a Hope Scholarship tax credit or Lifetime Learning Credit. These plans mean you can subtract college expenses to reduce the income tax you owe. And if you've lost your job or are getting divorced, you may be eligible for special government assistance.

A number of colleges and universities offer flexible programs for adult students to combine work and study. Others may give credit for life experience or let you take exams to qualify for a certain number of credits rather than having to pay the full cost of the course.

THE TIME IS NOW

If you haven't done the kind of planning ahead you wish you had, or if some unexpected financial setbacks have drained the savings you put aside for education, there are still ways to pay for school. No one solution will work for everyone, but there are many options that you can investigate.

Probably the most common way to pay for education is by taking student or other types of loans. You have the option of borrowing against the value of your home. Interest on home equity loans is tax deductible, which can be a significant saving. However, you must begin repayment right away, and if you should default on the loan, your home would be at risk. Your financial planner can help you decide what option could work well for you.

Choosing a college that's part of your state university system can mean significant financial savings, since tuition is usually significantly lower for in-state students. Spending the first two years at a local community college and then transferring to finish a bachelor's degree may also save you money. And military programs, such as ROTC, will pay your tuition and book costs in exchange for a commitment to serve in the armed forces.

Creating a Secure Retirement

Whatever your age, planning for retirement should be a priority.

One of your most challenging financial goals is creating a steady stream of income after you retire. Nobody wants to be a burden on her family, and nobody wants to struggle to make ends meet. But being sure you'll have enough money for the 30 or more years you could live in retirement requires both planning and action. If you haven't begun working toward this goal yet, it's smart to start saving immediately.

DETERMINE YOUR NEEDS

It's hard to know for certain what your long-term needs will be. Most financial planners suggest that you'll need between 70% and 80% of your preretirement income to live comfortably during retirement. Some experts who specialize in financial security for women believe that if you've been supporting yourself, you may need 100% of your preretirement income. That's because women, on average, earn less than men, collect less Social Security, and are eligible for smaller pensions—if they get pensions at all.

Some costs are likely to go down. Your mortgage may be paid off, and you may not be paying as much in income tax—though withdrawals from individual retirement accounts (IRAs) and employer sponsored retirement savings plans, as well as pension payments, are taxed.

But certain costs—such as medical expenses or the cost of household help—may increase throughout retirement. While fewer than 10% of Americans between the ages of 65 and 69 need help with tasks like bathing or getting around, almost 50% of people over 85 do.

You may also hope to move when you retire. Among the financial issues to consider are whether the cost of living in your new home will be lower or higher than your current expenses.

TAKING A HARD LOOK

Whether you do your long-term planning on your own, use one of the electronic worksheets available on the Internet, or enlist the services of a financial planner, you'll need to provide the same type of information. Some you'll know, but some you might have to collect. You may want to create a retirement file that you can access easily.

As you analyze your personal situa-
ion, ask yourself these questions:

- What year do you hope to retire?
- What's your current income?
- How much do you already have in accounts you're designating as retirement accounts?
- What real rate of return are you earning on those accounts?
- How much are you adding to your retirement accounts each year?
- What income can you realistically expect from other sources?

VHO IS THE MONEY FOR?

\t the same time you're trying to ›rovide adequate retirement income or yourself, you may also be thinking ıbout leaving money to the people ›r institutions that are important o you. Those goals tend to require lifferent approaches.

Retirement savings plans can be ›ne source of regular income. But the ;overnment requires you to withdraw ı minimum amount from your IRA or etirement savings plan—such as a 401(k), 403(b), or 457—each year.

Similarly, annuities and pensions ıre paid only as long as you or you ınd your beneficiary live or until a ›ayout period you have chosen ends.

A WORKING LIFE

If you're doing a job you love, or you're ready to start a new career, you may plan to work past customary retirement age. This age will gradually increase from 65 to 66 in 2009 and to 67 in 2027. New Social Security rules mean you won't lose any part of your benefit for earning money after you reach 65.

In contrast, you can purchase other types of investments to build the value of your estate and increase what you can leave to your heirs. You can leave these investments untouched for as long as you choose, and often save capital gains taxes by passing them along to your heirs. Or you can choose to sell the investments at any point during your lifetime and use the gain for yourself. Be careful to consider all tax implications when you make those investment decisions.

GETTING THE TIMING RIGHT

Your goal may be to retire as soon as you qualify—a date that varies based on who your employer is and how much money you've saved during your working years. You can retire from some jobs after 20 years, and from others when you turn 55. Some require you to work until 65 to get full retirement benefits, including retiree healthcare.

You can apply for Social Security benefits at 62 if you choose, either based on your own earnings or on your husband's, if you're married. But keep one caution in mind: The people who face the risk of running out of money in old age are widows whose husbands retired early and began taking Social Security before they reached 65. That doesn't mean retiring early is bad, but it does mean you should create financial projections to figure out if the money you have will sustain you for the rest of your life.

Banking Basics

When you shop for a bank, consider convenience and cost.

With over 9,000 banks, at least 11,000 credit unions, and a growing number of other banking options to choose from, how do you decide which one is best for you?

Since most of these institutions offer the same basic services, the key things to consider when you make your choice are the costs of banking, hours and locations that work for you, and customer service.

CONVENIENCE

When shopping for the best deal on basic banking services, look for features that help make managing your money easier.

With **direct deposit**, you can have your paycheck or Social Security check automatically transferred into your checking or savings account—or sometimes split between them.

Many banks offer **bank cards** that you can use as a debit card when you shop. The money is deducted directly from your account. Sometimes these debit cards are also ATM cards.

You can get **credit cards** linked to your bank account, sometimes with lower interest rates or a lower fee than what's available on comparable cards. You may also have a line of credit in case of an emergency.

If you get **overdraft privileges**, checks you write will be paid, even if there's not enough money in your account. While you'll have to repay the amount the bank advances to your account with interest, your check won't bounce and you won't owe a bad check fee.

Automatic transfers let you make monthly investments or schedule payment of your regular bills, often without a charge.

HELPFUL HINTS

You may qualify for reduced banking rates if you're old or young enough. Ask your prospective bank about special programs they offer to seniors, college students, or other groups.

COST

As you compare costs, you'll want to pay particular attention to the charges for services you're most likely to use.

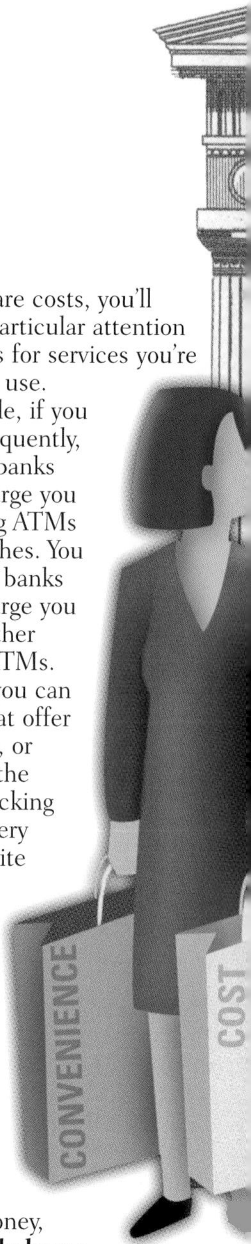

For example, if you use ATMs frequently, you can find banks that don't charge you a fee for using ATMs at their branches. You may also find banks that don't charge you for using another institution's ATMs.

Similarly, you can find banks that offer free checking, or banks where the fees for a checking account are very low. If you write a number of checks each month, it could mean big savings.

You may find that the banks tie free checking and ATM use to keeping a certain amount of money, or **minimum balance**, in your combined accounts at all times. That includes money in savings and checking accounts, as well as money in certificates of deposit (CDs), and sometimes even the balance on your mortgage. If you have that amount—which may be as little as $25 in some credit unions and as much as several thousand dollars in some commercial banks—it can help to reduce banking costs.

If being able to handle your banking online is a priority, be sure to compare the cost of that service at various banks as well. One alternative may be to use a virtual bank for most of your money and a convenient local bank for day-to-day cash withdrawals.

BANKING CHOICES

TYPE OF BANK	BENEFITS	DRAWBACKS
Commercial Bank	Full range of services, often including online services Many branches with ATMs	Relatively high fees Bigger banks may offer less personal service
Credit Union	Low fees As a credit union member, you have a say in setting policy	Need to meet membership requirements Limited ATM access
Savings and Loan	Lower fees than some commercial banks Personal service and some evening/weekend hours	Fewer branches than commercial banks Limited ATM access
Virtual Bank	Higher interest on deposits, since there's little overhead No need to visit a branch Banking at your convenience	No personal contact Have to mail in non-electronic deposits Fee for ATM access
Brokerage Firm, Mutual Fund, or Insurance Company	Low-cost or free checking, often linked to interest-paying money market funds May provide loans against investment balances	May require high minimum balances Potentially high fees

BACK-UP SERVICES

Banks provide additional services you may not need to use often. But they can come in handy when you do.

If you lose a check you've written, or write a check and then decide that you don't want it to be honored, you can place a **stop payment order** to halt payment. As long as you make the request before the check is paid, your bank must honor your order. If the bank pays the check, you can still get your money back, but you have to offer written proof that you ordered the payment stopped.

You can usually get **bank checks**, sometimes called cashier's checks, and money orders from your bank if the person or company you're paying demands a guaranteed check.

OTHER FEES

While you may not be faced with paying them very often, you should also compare bank charges for certain other services. Some fees you might incur include:

Debit card fees. Some banks charge you for a debit card or impose a fee when you use it.

Check-printing fees. Most banks charge you more to print checks than you'd pay if you ordered them from a check-printing service.

Balance inquiry fees. Some banks charge a fee if you request information about your account by phone or ATM. Others charge a fee for talking to a teller.

Online Banking

With online banks, your financial transactions are just a mouse click away.

As long as you have access to a computer, you can now do almost anything—make travel reservations, find movie reviews, or even shop for a new car—without having to leave the comfort of your home.

Online banking is yet another way the Internet can help simplify your life. Not only do many banks and brokerage houses offer online services to their customers, but a growing number of **virtual banks**, which exist exclusively on the Internet and have no physical branches, are up and running as well.

THE ONLINE BASICS

If you bank online, you can expect to get the same basic services traditional banks offer. That includes electronic bill payment, transferring money between accounts, and checking your balances whenever you want. You can also find out when your checks have cleared, trade stocks and mutual funds, or even apply for loans.

Before you start banking online, you should investigate what the fees and costs may be, since you may be charged for using non-bank software, or for the number of transactions you do online.

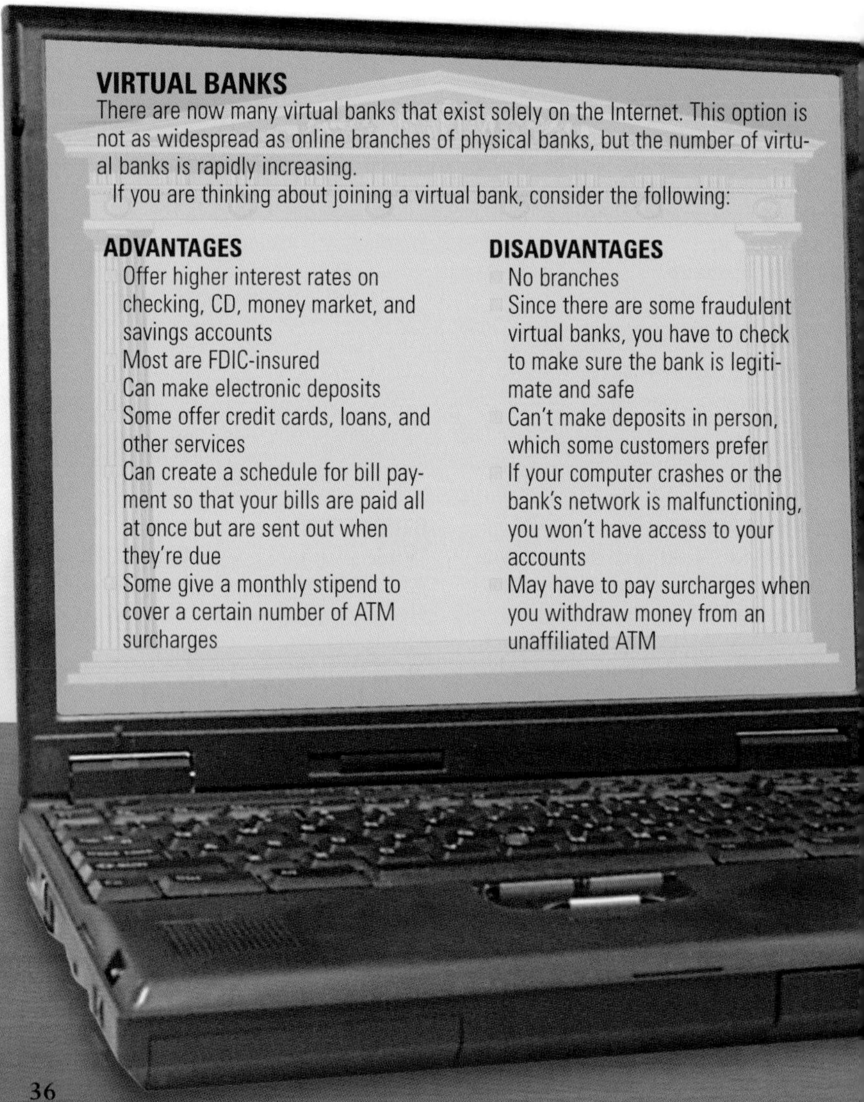

VIRTUAL BANKS

There are now many virtual banks that exist solely on the Internet. This option is not as widespread as online branches of physical banks, but the number of virtual banks is rapidly increasing.

If you are thinking about joining a virtual bank, consider the following:

ADVANTAGES

- Offer higher interest rates on checking, CD, money market, and savings accounts
- Most are FDIC-insured
- Can make electronic deposits
- Some offer credit cards, loans, and other services
- Can create a schedule for bill payment so that your bills are paid all at once but are sent out when they're due
- Some give a monthly stipend to cover a certain number of ATM surcharges

DISADVANTAGES

- No branches
- Since there are some fraudulent virtual banks, you have to check to make sure the bank is legitimate and safe
- Can't make deposits in person, which some customers prefer
- If your computer crashes or the bank's network is malfunctioning, you won't have access to your accounts
- May have to pay surcharges when you withdraw money from an unaffiliated ATM

THE SOFTWARE

If you want to use your computer to do your banking, but don't want to spend a lot of time online, you can purchase personal finance software, such as Quicken or Microsoft Money. These programs let you do most of your banking offline, and when you're ready to complete a transaction, you connect to your bank's online branch.

You can handle most of your basic banking needs with this software. Some added features include bill payment reminders, analysis of your investments according to market indicators, and yearly tax planning advice.

Some banks offer their own software to use on your home computer. The main difference between using a bank's software and other types of programs is that you can access your bank through a secure network, rather than publicly through the Internet. In addition, using the bank's program lets you access your account from any computer, not just the one on which you've installed the personal finance software. That can make it easier to manage your money when you're away from home.

WHY TO BANK ONLINE

If you're used to bricks-and-mortar banking, switching to the electronic option may not appeal to you immediately. There are many advantages to online banking, though. If you're hesitant, consider the following benefits:

- No lines or red tape
- Open 24 hours a day, 7 days a week
- Access to real-time account information, including your monthly statements
- Ability to invest, pay bills, and check deposits you've made

> **DID YOU KNOW?**
> According to Dataquest, an information technology research firm, 24.2 million people will be banking online by 2004. That's up from 7 million people banking online in 1998.

- Increasing availability of investment research, loan and credit card applications, and many other online bank services

SAFETY

You may worry that banking online is not as secure as banking in person. However, your fears may be put to rest once you understand the three-layer system most online banks use to ensure safety and privacy.

First, online banking sites have a **firewall**, which is a computer used to connect the bank's internal network to the outside world. A firewall's purpose is to make sure that the bank's computers (and your personal data stored on those computers) can't be accessed by any outside parties.

The second layer is **data encryption**. Once you enter your personal data and passwords, they're scrambled so outsiders can't detect what they are. Encryption guarantees that your data can't be intercepted and stolen by a third party as you're sending it over the Internet.

Finally, online banks offer **personal identification numbers (PINs)**, which you're probably familiar with from your traditional bank. The PIN you choose (or are given by the bank) is your way of identifying who you are whenever you log on to your bank's site.

Good Credit

Get on the road to good credit.

Having good credit is like getting good grades in school. With a solid transcript, you can choose from a wide array of colleges or jobs. And with a good credit rating, you have access to the money you may need to pay for things that are important to you.

That can mean having a large enough spending limit on your credit card to be able to buy what you need. Or it may mean being able to get a loan to buy a house or a car, pay for higher education, or start and build your own business.

THE ROAD TO GOOD CREDIT

You can build a strong credit history if you plan ahead. It's important not to wait until you need to borrow to think about whether you'll qualify.

Get a credit card. You need to show that you have an established credit history (to help you get loans and mortgages, for instance), and the best way to do that is to get a credit card. If you're turned down for a Visa or MasterCard, start with a gasoline or retail store card.

Show stability. It's important to be able to show that you have a regular source of income. The longer the amount of time you've spent at one job can also be a plus in the eyes of lenders.

Make payments on time. Although your credit history won't be affected by one late payment, three payments (more than 60 days late each) can damage your ability to borrow. And paying late is expensive because you owe a penalty.

Build your assets. Although it's not as important as a steady source of income, lenders like to see that you have assets, such as savings and investment accounts.

Obtain credit references. One of the best ways to qualify for credit is to establish a relationship with a bank or credit union.

Limit your credit applications. Your credit report shows every loan and credit card you have applied for. If you apply often, lenders may see it as a sign that you're in (or have the potential to be in) financial trouble.

IMPROVING BAD CREDIT

If you've run into credit problems, it's a smart idea to stop using credit cards. You might want to keep one for an emergency, but don't carry any cards with you. Make paying off what you owe your priority.

When you're debt-free, you might reintroduce one credit card at a time, as long as you keep your spending under control.

You can also seek professional advice from a credit counselor, who can provide educational materials and guidance on how to get out of debt and control your spending.

UNFAIR CREDIT PRACTICES

If you apply for credit and are turned down, you have the right to know the specific reason why your application was rejected. Under the Equal Credit Opportunity Act, it's illegal for a lender to give vague or indefinite explanations. So if you are denied credit but aren't given a specific reason, you should request an explanation immediately, in writing. The lender must respond within 60 days under the Equal Credit Opportunity Act.

Among other things, you can't be denied credit for your sex, race, marital status, religion, ethnicity, or age.

But not having a regular source of income or a strong credit history are legitimate reasons for rejection.

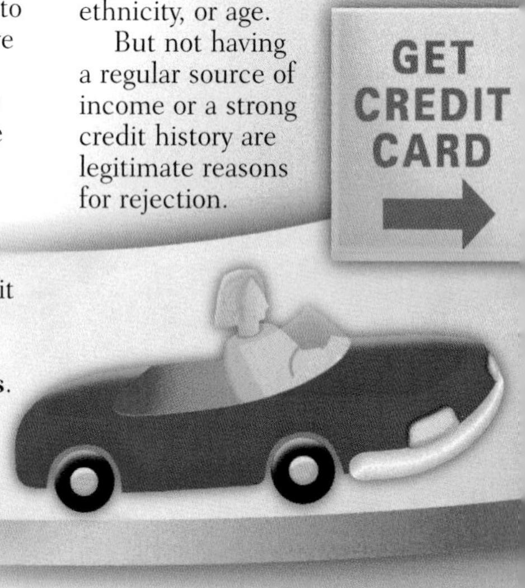

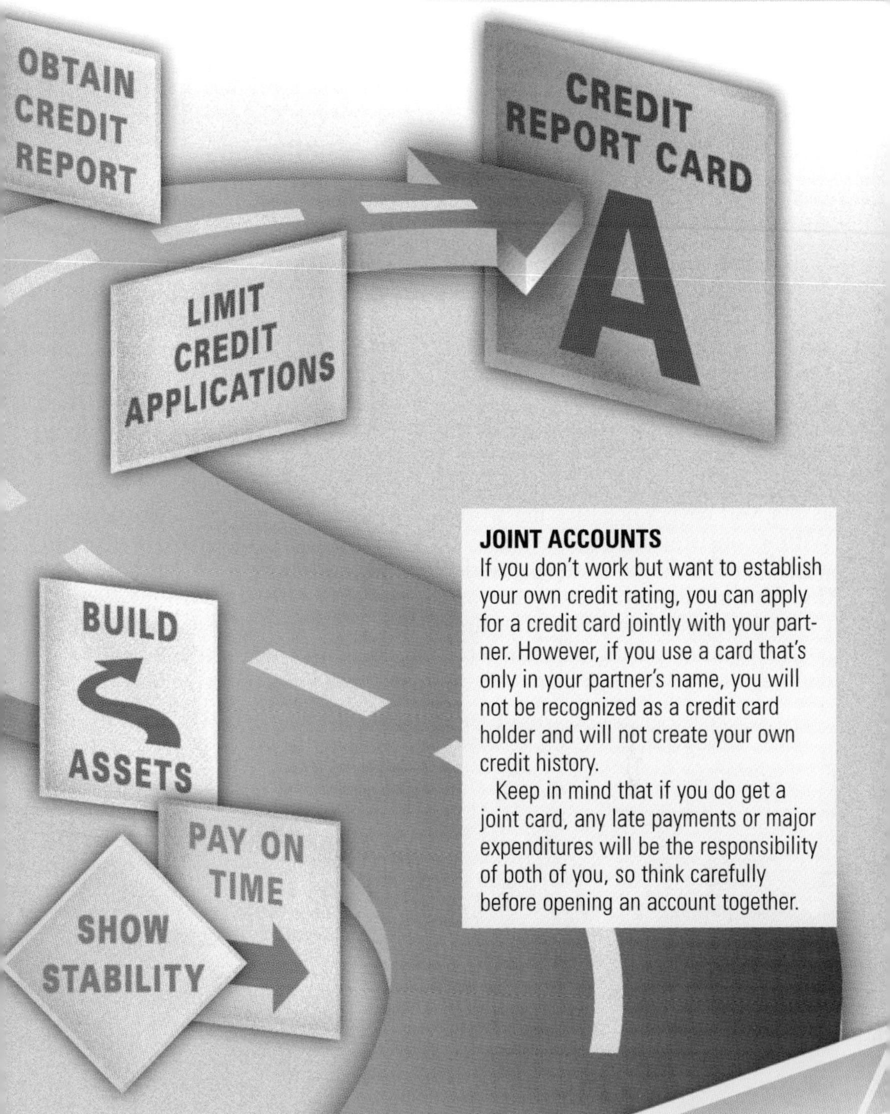

JOINT ACCOUNTS

If you don't work but want to establish your own credit rating, you can apply for a credit card jointly with your partner. However, if you use a card that's only in your partner's name, you will not be recognized as a credit card holder and will not create your own credit history.

Keep in mind that if you do get a joint card, any late payments or major expenditures will be the responsibility of both of you, so think carefully before opening an account together.

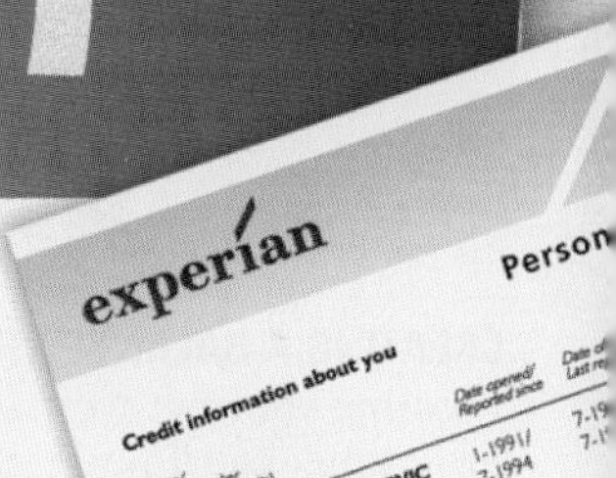

NATIONAL CREDIT SYSTEMS

How do companies find out about your credit history? It's from a national credit system, which collects and reports credit history information. There are three major national credit systems—Equifax, Experian, and Trans Union—that provide credit information about you (for a fee) to institutions, such as banks and employers, that have been approved as recipients.

According to the Fair and Accurate Credit Transaction Act, you have the right to dispute any information on your credit report that you believe is inaccurate. You can also write a 100-word explanation, which will be sent out whenever your credit report is requested.

To get a copy of your credit report, you can contact the following organizations directly. If you've been turned down for credit, you can get a copy for free. If you just want to see where you stand, there may be a small fee.

Equifax
800-685-1111
Equifax Credit Information Services
PO Box 740241
Atlanta, GA 30374
www.equifax.com

Experian
888-397-3742
Experian National Consumer Assistance Center
PO Box 2104
Allen, TX 75013-2104
www.experian.com

TransUnion
800-888-4213
Trans Union Corporation
PO Box 2000
Chester, PA 19022
www.transunion.com

Your Net Worth

Your net worth statement is a simple equation of your financial situation.

To figure your **net worth**, or where you stand financially at a given time, you use a simple equation: Your **assets**, or what you own, minus your **liabilities**, or what you owe, equals your net worth.

If your assets outweigh your liabilities, you have a positive net worth. But if you have more liabilities than assets, you have a negative net worth. With a consistently negative net worth, you could get so deeply in debt that it would be difficult to pay what you owe. Most advisers say your first goals should be paying off your debt and beginning a savings plan.

are owned jointly, but you want a sense of your individual net worth, divide the value of those items in half. The same is true of assets you hold in common, such as property you own with brothers or sisters. And it's also important to include your share of the liabilities.

When you've finished your calculation, keep your net worth statement on file. That will make it easier to update—something you'll probably want to do once a year as part of evaluating where you stand financially and the progress you're making toward your goals.

CREATING A BALANCE SHEET
Figuring your net worth takes a little time. You'll need to gather your financial records—recent bank statements, credit card bills, and other documents—to have the numbers you'll need to create your personal balance sheet. If a lot of your assets

FAIR MARKET VALUE
One tip for calculating your assets is to use the **fair market value**, which is the price a buyer would pay on the open market for something you are willing to sell. Fair market value assumes that the buyer and seller are both well-informed consumers and that neither is under any pressure to buy or sell.

WHAT YOU OWN

Cash and Cash Equivalents. Figure out what you have in your checking, savings, or money market accounts, as well as CDs, US Treasury bills, and the cash value of your life insurance policies.

Personal Property. Add up the value of your cars, boats, electronic equipment, fine art, jewelry, and antiques. Remember that some assets, like antiques, may increase in value (or **appreciate**) over time, while others, like stereo equipment, may decrease in value (or **depreciate**). You may want to have some of the more valuable things you own professionally appraised.

HELPFUL HINTS
One thing a net worth statement doesn't include is your income. One way to tip the balance in your favor is to make investments that you can expect to increase in value over time.

Investments. When you calculate our investments, include the market alue of your bonds, stocks, mutual unds, and other investments. Long-erm investments, such as money in etirement savings plans or annuities, re also considered assets.

Real Estate. If you own your ome, it's an asset. So is any other eal property you own on your own or vith other people. Estimate the mar-et value and include the full amount vith your assets. You'll subtract any nortgage due under liabilities.

If your mortgage payments include real estate taxes and homeowner's insurance, don't count them again as separate items.

THE POWER OF YOUR WORTH
When potential lenders review your loan application, they examine your net worth. In fact, one reason to have a fairly up-to-date net worth statement on hand is that you'll have an easier time completing a loan application. Lenders look very closely at your current assets and liabilities, as well as what you could owe if you charged up to the credit limit on your credit cards. In general, lenders like to see that you have considerable investments, as well as a retirement plan, since these are assets you could tap if you found yourself in financial difficulty.

Financial aid is based on your net worth, so if you have children applying for college loans, you have to give a full report of your assets and liabilities as part of your child's application.

Finally, if you want to make certain types of investments, including putting money into start-up companies, you may be required to have a minimum net worth, $1 million or more.

VHAT YOU OWE

Short-Term Debts. Your current ills, credit card charges, insurance osts, personal loans (such as car or ducation loans), and real estate taxes re all short-term debts. Include the mount you owe on your credit cards, ven if you always pay the outstand-ng balance in full.

Long-Term Debts. Enter the alance on any mortgages or home quity loans, car loan or lease pay-nents, or any liabilities you pay in nstallments over a period of years.

Other Liabilities. This category nay include alimony payments, nnual real estate taxes, personal ebts, and liens against your property.

Household Budget

Making a budget can help you organize your household finances.

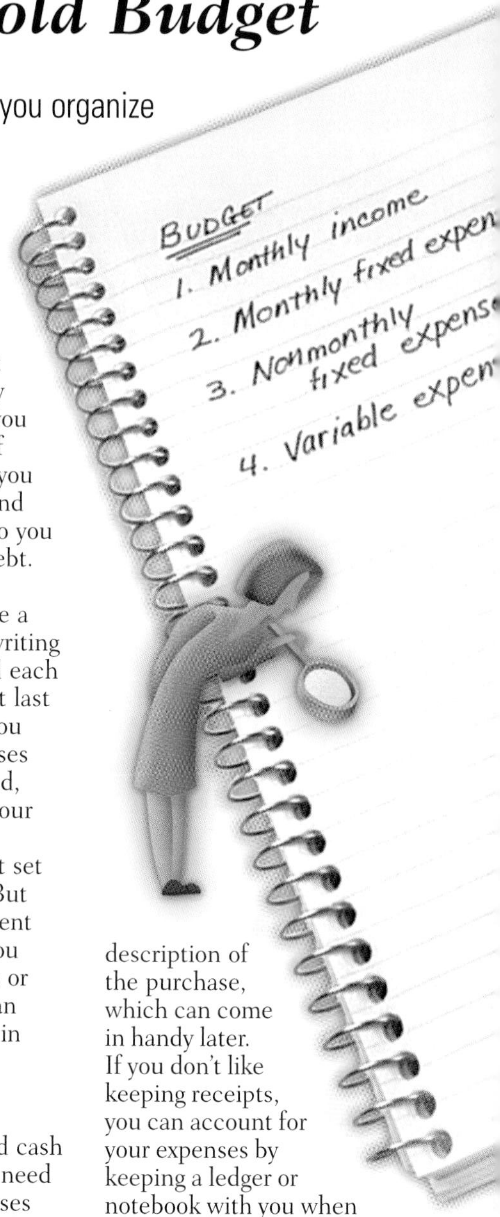

When you go to the grocery store, you usually take a list of the items you need to buy. That helps you shop more efficiently and economically.

Creating a household budget can help you in similar ways. By listing your monthly expenses, you can keep track of the amount of money you've spent, plan what you expect to spend in the future, and learn where you can cut costs so you can save, invest, or get out of debt.

Once you've assessed your monthly finances, you can make a projected budget for the year, writing down what you expect to spend each month based on what you spent last year. As the months progress, you can compare your actual expenses to what you thought you'd spend, and adjust your spending—or your budget—accordingly.

Of course, your budget is not set in stone. It's a working model. But you'll know where the money went when you've spent more than you wanted to in a particular month or on a particular expense. That can help you control your spending in the future.

GOING WITH THE FLOW

Keeping track of your household cash flow is an ongoing process. You need to track your income and expenses through accounting, analysis, and adjustments.

Accounting is basically keeping a record of your expenditures. Perhaps the simplest way to do your own accounting is to keep and file your receipts. That way, you'll have a record of the amount, date, and description of the purchase, which can come in handy later. If you don't like keeping receipts, you can account for your expenses by keeping a ledger or notebook with you when you shop. Every time you buy something, record it in your ledger, and note the purchase, amount, and date.

Once a month, you should analyze the record of your expenditures, and compare it to your projected budget. Analyzing will help you understand whether you're financially on track.

WHAT'S YOUR SITUATION?

To calculate your household cash flow, you need to have a handle on your monthly income and expenses.

1 Figure out your monthly income. List all your sources of income, including your salary, investments, rental property, alimony, and child support, as well as Social Security and pension payments, if you receive them.

2 List your fixed monthly expenses, or the expenses that are the same month to month. This category includes your mortgage, car payments, specific investment goals, and anything on a fixed monthly schedule.

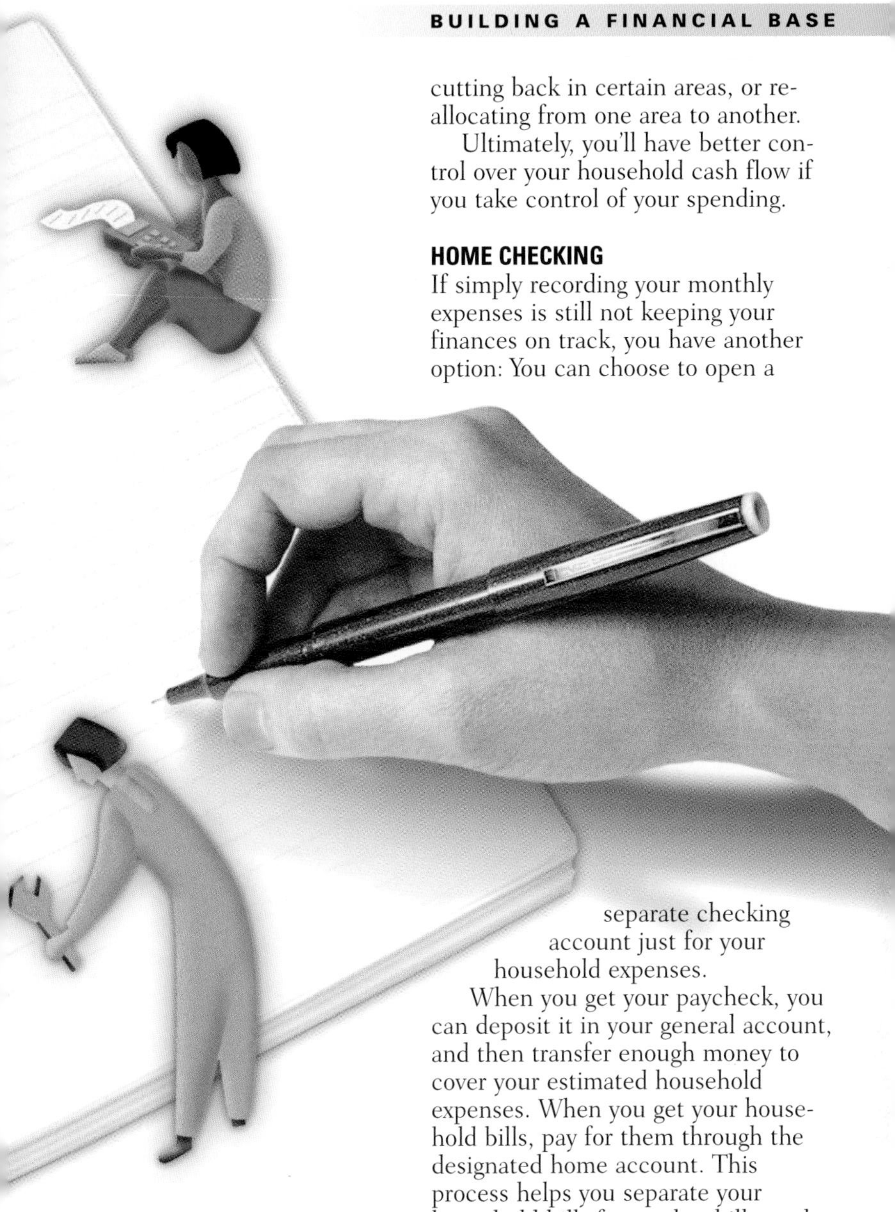

Of course, there are bound to be hanges in your life that will alter the ay you spend money. For instance, ou're likely to make adjustments to our budget if you get a salary ıcrease or you're buying a new home. f you have particular goals in mind ike getting rid of your debt), you ıay have to adjust your resources to ıeet your goals. That could mean cutting back in certain areas, or reallocating from one area to another.

Ultimately, you'll have better control over your household cash flow if you take control of your spending.

HOME CHECKING

If simply recording your monthly expenses is still not keeping your finances on track, you have another option: You can choose to open a separate checking account just for your household expenses.

When you get your paycheck, you can deposit it in your general account, and then transfer enough money to cover your estimated household expenses. When you get your household bills, pay for them through the designated home account. This process helps you separate your household bills from other bills, and also lets you deal with smaller increments of money in your personal checking account.

Opening a household account is also the perfect time to get a jump start on investing by opening an investment account. Each time you set aside money to pay your bills, pay yourself a percentage of your earnings too.

3 Calculate your nonmonthly fixed expenses, which are bills that don't rrive monthly but do come on a fixed basis every six weeks or biannually, for instance). 'ou might find it convenient to convert these nto monthly expenses. For example, if your uto insurance costs $800 every six months, hat's $133 per month. You can then add this mount to your fixed monthly expenses.

4 Compile a list of your variable monthly expenses. Basically, everything that doesn't fit into the earlier categories goes here, such as food, clothing, credit card payments, subscriptions, contributions, and medical expenses. If you don't have records of these expenses, you can look at your checkbook or credit card bill for a record of your major monthly expenses.

Reaping the Benefits

Getting a job means more than just bringing home a paycheck.

Whether you're starting your first job or moving up the corporate ladder, making the most of your employee benefits package makes smart economic sense. In fact, you should weigh the benefits that different jobs offer if you're choosing among them. For example, you may decide that the opportunity to get family healthcare coverage at a modest cost may be more valuable than a slightly higher salary.

FOR YOUR HEALTH

You may get health insurance as part of your employer's package of benefits. Some employers pay the full cost, and some require you to pay some or all of the cost. Most plans cover hospital care, medical treatment, visits to doctors, medical examinations, and similar expenses.

If you have a **fee-for-service plan** you can choose any doctor or hospital you want. You pay the full cost of care up to a certain amount, or **deductible**, before your insurance kicks in. Once you've reached the deductible, your insurance company will pay a percentage (often about 80%) of the medical costs that they approve, and you pick up the rest, known as your **copayment**.

Health Maintenance Organizations (HMOs) are the oldest of the **managed care** health plans. With an HMO, you choose a primary care doctor from a list of doctors or physician groups employed by the health plan. Depending on the HMO, you either make a small co-payment (usually $5 or $10) or pay nothing at all for medical visits. If you go to a doctor outside your HMO you'll have to pay the bill yourself.

Your employer may offer a type of managed care known as a **Preferred Provider**

)rganization (PPO)**. You can choose ny doctor you want, but you pay less : you choose a doctor who is includ- d in the insurer's preferred list.

OR YOUR FUTURE

'he chance to participate in your mployer's retirement savings plan is ne employee benefit you'll want to ake advantage of. A **salary reduction lan**, like a 401(k), 403(b), or 457, ets you accumulate money toward our retirement by contributing pretax ollars and deferring tax on any earn- ngs in your account. Tax deferral llows your earnings to compound at a faster rate than if you put money into taxable investments, and potential- y creates an important source of etirement income.

In certain salary reduction plans, our employer also contributes to your ccount, in some cases by matching art of your contribution. But with nany plans, you must choose to articipate to get these employer ontributions.

In all of the plans, you decide how he money you contribute is invested y choosing among the options your lan offers.

PREADING THE WEALTH

ome companies offer **profit sharing** lans. If your company has a prof- table year, your employer may add p to $41,000 in 2004, or 25% of our salary (whichever is less) to your profit sharing account. You won't owe income tax on contri- butions or ny earnings in the account until you vithdraw the money. And if your plan llows—and you meet certain crite- ia—you may be able to borrow from he account to pay for personal xpenses, like buying a home or pay- ng for medical expenses.

> **NEXT STEPS**
>
> 
>
> If you're married, and you and your husband have different health-care packages, you and your dependents are in a good position to be covered for most medical costs, using a technique called **coordination of benefits**. By settling a medical claim with your own insurance company and then submitting the settlement to your spouse's insurer, you may get broader coverage for your medical expenses, though never more than the actual cost. For example, some plans may offer dental insurance or pay a higher percentage of an approved expense than others.
>
> However, if one plan is significantly better than the other, you can cut costs by only participating in the plan that offers the best benefits. Some employers even offer a small bonus for not partici- pating in their plan.

You may also be able to participate in an **Employee Stock Ownership Plan (ESOP)**. With an ESOP, your employer contributes shares in the company to the plan, and they are allocated to employee accounts on a prearranged basis.

Some companies offer their employees **stock options** as a way of giving them a share in the company's potential success. As an employee with stock options, you have the right to buy shares of your company's stock during a specific time period at a pre- set price, usually significantly lower than the market price. However, most companies put restrictions on when you can exercise your options or sell the stock.

COVERING THE SPREAD

You may receive other benefits from your employer as well, or be able to purchase them at group rates. These include:

- Life insurance
- Disability insurance
- Employee assistance programs
- Childcare
- Health club membership
- Tuition reimbursement
- Flexible spending accounts
- Long-term care insurance

Getting a Handle on Debt

Keeping your debt in check is crucial to your financial health.

Most people assume that debt of any kind is harmful to their financial health. The reality, however, is that some debts aren't bad. A mortgage, for instance, is considered a good debt, since you've purchased an asset that may appreciate in value in the future. So are college loans, or money you borrow to start or build a business.

Bad debt is money you owe for things you no longer get any benefit from. These debts are the ones to try to eliminate.

SIDESTEP DEBT

Do you want to avoid debt altogether?

Make a weekly or monthly financial budget. As part of this budget, identify what your basic costs and extra expenses are. Don't forget to include your savings.

Avoid impulse spending. Try to limit your purchases to necessities. If you have credit cards, do your best to pay the bills in full each month.

Do your research before you buy anything. You can save money if you know where or how to get the best deal.

ELIMINATING DEBT

If you're in debt, there are ways to change your financial situation. One way is to create a **spending record** to chart how you are using your money. For a month or so, write down every penny you spend and where it goes.

Then break down your expenses into essential categories, including housing, gas, and groceries, and nonessentials, like video rentals, dining out, extra clothing, or anything else you spend money on.

To reduce your debt, take a close look at your nonessential expenses, and decide which of these you can live without. Cut them from your budget. Once you're out of debt, you can slowly reintroduce the things you've really missed, one at a time.

You may find that limiting the way you use credit

DON'T DELAY

The longer you put off dealing with debt, the longer it's likely to take you to get back in financial shape. If you owe more than you can reasonably repay, you may even have to consider filing for bankruptcy to get protection from your creditors. But that step seriously damages your credit history without wiping out all your debts.

RESOURCES

If you're having trouble getting out of debt, you can get advice from a credit counselor. These professionals offer financial advice, as well as create a personal system which can help you reduce your debt. For more information, you can contact the National Foundation for Credit Counseling (NFCC), which has a database of over 1,400 counselors in the US. You can contact the NFCC by phone at 800-388-2227, or online at www.nfcc.org.

ards can help you control spending. ome experts suggest getting rid of ll but one credit card and using it or emergencies only. While careful se of credit helps you build a good redit history, charging more than ou can afford) repay— specially you don't ıake at ast the ıinimum ayment ach ıonth— one of the ıstest ways) undermine your access to future redit and to get into potentially seri- us financial trouble.

SING YOUR SPENDING RECORD

)nce you've created a spending ecord, you can figure out where you ıay be able to cut costs. Here are ome hints to help you get started.

If your utility bills are eating away t your cash flow, try to remind your- elf to turn off lights when you're not ı the room, and to keep air condi- oning and heating under control.

Keep your eyes open for sales ı the newspaper, on the Internet, nd elsewhere.

If you live in a city with public ansportation but you're still driving car, consider your alternatives. ou can save money on gas and car ıaintenance by opting for the bus r train—and maybe avoid traffic eadaches as well.

TAKING ACTION

By resolving your financial problems before they overwhelm you, you can avoid legal consequences of bad debt, such as losing purchases you're paying for on credit, having creditors sue you, or even the possibility of bankruptcy. And if you get out of debt, you don't have to worry about a court ordering your employer to take a percentage of your salary to pay for what you owe.

Repaying the debts you've built up won't happen overnight. But if you get your spending in check and possibly get some professional advice, you can resolve your financial problems over time.

You can extend the time period you have to repay what you owe by asking your creditors to rewrite your loans. You'll probably be charged more interest if you get a loan extension, but having more time may help you pay off your debt.

If you have debts with several creditors, you can try to consolidate them into one loan so you're making only one payment instead of several each month.

The rates on consolidated loans can be high, and you may be hit with a prepayment fee if you pay the loan off ahead of schedule. So you'll want to make sure you have enough information before you try to put together a repayment package.

DIVORCE AND DEBT

If you are getting divorced, you may have to deal with debt incurred while you were married. If you signed any joint agreements or had joint accounts during your marriage, you're equally responsible for any debt that resulted.

You're also responsible for any unpaid taxes due on joint tax returns. However, you are **not** responsible for any taxes on income that your husband concealed from you during your marriage.

Creditors may also try to make you repay debts your husband ran up during your marriage. And laws vary from state to state about whether you are legally responsible for those debts, especially if you're separated but not divorced.

Credit Cards

Using a credit card is easy. But choosing one isn't always simple.

Shopping with a credit card is a snap, but shopping for the card that's right for you is another matter. Ask yourself these questions:

- Do you pay your credit card bills in full and on time each month?
- If not, do you spread out repayment over a fairly long period of time?
- Do you shop primarily at one store, or at many locations?

The answers can help you choose a card that will help you use credit at the lowest cost.

A WORLD OF OPTIONS

Not all credit cards are the same. With **traditional credit cards**, such as MasterCard, Discover, and Visa, you can charge up to a certain dollar amount, called your credit limit or spending limit. It's generally between $500 and $10,000, depending on your credit history. You have the choice of paying your bill in full each month, or paying what you owe over time. But you have to pay at least the minimum balance each month or you'll face a late charge, often $25 or more.

Charge cards, like the traditional American Express Card or Diners Club card, have no stated credit limit. However, you do have to pay your bill in full each month. If you don't, you'll be charged interest, and you may not be allowed to use the card again until you've paid your bill.

An **affinity card** is cosponsored by the card issuer, such as a bank or credit union, and another company, such as an airline, car manufacturer, non-profit organization, or website. The card issuer handles the billing, while the cosponsoring company offers perks, like travel points toward airline trips. Affinity cards usually have an annual fee and a high annual percentage rate (APR), and you usually have to charge a large amount before you get any benefit from using the card.

Many retail stores, from giants like Sears to specialty shops, offer charge cards, also called **retail credit cards**. Generally, these cards don't have annual fees, but the finance charges on unpaid balances may be higher than on other cards. The biggest problem may be having too many different bills arriving throughout the month.

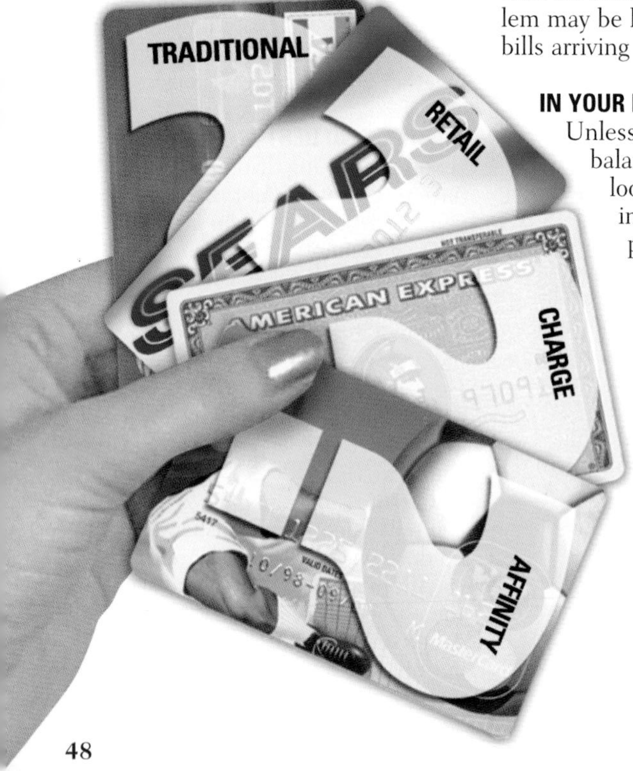

IN YOUR BEST INTEREST

Unless you always pay your balance in full, you should look first at a credit card's interest rate. The rate you pay is a major factor in determining how much credit costs you.

Some credit cards offer low initial interest rates, called teaser rates. But these apply for just a few months, and after that significantly higher rates apply. You have to look at the APR to get a true sense of cost.

Some interest rates, known as variable rates, change from time to time, either at the discretion of the card issuer or according to a formula created by the issuer. Fixed rates can change as well, but you'll be given at least 15 days' notice when your rates are going to change.

However, some rates go down with time, so you should always keep your eyes open for better deals. It may be a good idea to switch cards if you find a lower rate.

SECURED CARDS

If you're turned down for a credit card, investigate a **secured credit card**. Secured cards work the same way as regular credit cards, with one twist: You have to open an interest-bearing account, like a savings or money market account, or CD, with the bank that issues the card. If you don't make your payments on time, the bank will take the amount you owe out of your account. But if you use the card regularly and pay on time, you may become eligible for a regular credit card.

GRACE PERIODS

If you always pay in full, look for a card with a **grace period**. That's the amount of time (usually 20 to 25 days) you have between the date your bill is issued and the date the payment is due. If you've paid your previous balance in full and on time, no interest is charged on purchases you've made during the billing period. But if a card has no grace period, then you'll be charged interest from the moment you buy something until you pay your credit card bill, even if you paid your last balance in full.

CRACKING THE CODE

Understanding the lingo gives you an idea of credit card benefits and drawbacks.

WHAT IT'S CALLED	WHAT IT MEANS
Annual fee	The flat rate you pay per year to use the card. It's usually between $25 and $50, but some cards don't charge the fee at all.
Annual percentage rate (APR)	A finance charge expressed as a yearly rate. The lower the APR, the lower the cost of using credit.
Finance charge	What you pay to use credit, including interest, fees and other charges.
Grace period	The number of days you have to pay your bill without owing a finance charge.
Late payment fee	The fee you may be charged if you don't pay the minimum balance by the due date.
Minimum payment due	The amount you must pay by the due date. If you don't pay at least this amount, you may be charged a late payment fee on your next bill.
Over limit fee	The amount you must pay if you charge more than your credit limit.

Talking to Your Children about Money

Get an early start on teaching your kids the value of money.

Your kids go to school to learn grammar, multiplication tables, and history. But what about their financial education? As a parent, you play a crucial role in your children's education, and one area to focus on is teaching your children about money.

THE APPLE DOESN'T FALL FAR . . .

You probably know that children are excellent at the art of observation. Just as young children readily imitate words and gestures, older children are bound to pick up your financial behavior.

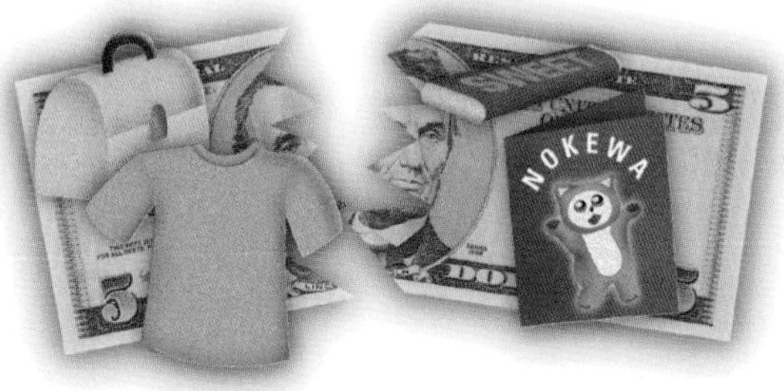

So a good first step in teaching your children about money is to make an effort to handle your money in a way you'd like them to copy. If your life shows that financial security comes from hard work, and that responsible spending is the result of thought and care, not impulse, your children will be more likely to take what you say about money seriously.

Some parents even involve their children in managing the family's finances, so the children know how much money is coming in every month, how it is being spent, and what financial choices have to be made. Their views on what's important may even help you revise your financial priorities.

START YOUNG

Letting kids make decisions about money at an early age can help them understand the concepts of earning, spending, saving, and investing. You can start these lessons by creating a minibudget with your children.

Start with two spending lists: one for essentials and the other for nonessentials. In the essentials category, you might include expenses like lunc money and clothing. In the nonessentials category, you can place anything that your children like to spend money on, such as snacks, comi books, or name-brand shoes or other clothing. Then, you can agree on a weekly or monthly allowance that cov ers the essential expenses and a fair amount of the nonessential expenses. That way, your children will have an allowance that helps them understan the difference between necessities and extras at an early age.

AN ALTERNATIVE TO SPENDING

Once you've established an allowance with your children, you can teach them an important lesson about saving. Try including a percentage for saving in the essentials list to show that planning for the future is a necessity if they want to be able to do the things they love.

And if your children have money left over at the end of a week, you can discuss the alternatives of spending it now on something they want, adding it to the savings account toward the purchase of a more expensive item, or spending it later on something they *really* want.

Many banks offer children's accounts that don't charge service fees for small balances. You can start your children off by opening an account with an amount you choose, and encourage them to add to it regularly. You might even add a savings bonus, matching any amount they put into the savings account.

If your children are working, and you can manage it financially, you might encourage them to set up an individual retirement account (IRA) and make a gift of the money they deposit. The maximum deposit is 100% of earned income up to $3,000. This gift can help them gain an understanding of the value you put on saving and investing money.

RESOURCES

Your family can learn more about money at these websites.

Kids Bank has both parents' and kids' sections, bulletin boards, interactive calculators, and a virtual money tour for kids. The website is www.kidsbank.com.

Planet Orange stands out for its solid but zany introduction to the essentials of earning, saving, spending, and investing. Both engaging in tone and thorough in content, the site also includes calculators, quizzes, and a teacher's resource center. The website address is www.orangekids.com.

Strong Kids is an interactive site with quizzes, calculators, articles on investing, setting goals, saving, and making money, as well as a dictionary of financial terms. You can visit Strong Kids at www.strongkids.com.

TAKING CARE OF BUSINESS

As your children get older, they may want to get jobs. Here are some reasons why getting a job can benefit your kids:

- A job can help your children learn what it feels like to *earn* money, not just receive it
- Your children can learn about the taxes taken out of a paycheck
- A job is a way for your children to excel in a certain area
- Working can boost self-confidence and help pave the way to a successful career

INVESTING 101

To help your children learn about investing, you can find a company that your children know and would enjoy following. Then, invest in a few shares of stock, reinvest any dividends the stock pays, and track the performance of those stocks with your children.

Another option is to invest in mutual funds directed toward children. The benefits of starting a fund are twofold: Your children can learn about the fund through education kits and activities that the fund provides, and you can start to build your children's financial security.

All in the Family

Helping your parents to plan their estate now may prevent headaches later.

Your parents probably helped you through tough decisions during your early years, and forced you to think about things you would have preferred to ignore. But as you get older, you may be in the sometimes uncomfortable position of urging your parents to make important financial decisions about managing their money and handling their estate plans. If your parents are elderly, in poor health, or if only one of them is living, your help may be even more essential.

THE REASONS

As strange and sometimes awkward as it may seem to talk about money with your parents, it's often a necessity. First of all, you and your siblings, if you have any, may need to manage your parents' affairs if they get sick or become incapacitated. Having a **durable power of attorney**—a legal document that gives you the right to act on your parents' behalf—is one of the only ways you can make financial or other decisions for them. And you should know where to find important legal documents such as their wills, as well as have a grasp of the size of your parents' estate. Because estate tax rates are high, it's important to plan ahead to avoid or minimize them as much as possible.

DOING IT RIGHT

One way to reassure your parents that you're not prying is to explain that you don't need to know the specific dollar details now, though someone will eventually. But you should insist that they create a list of their assets and liabilities and file it in a place that someone—you, an attorney, or a close family friend—can find if necessary. This information should include the locations of all insurance and retirement policies, legal documents, safe deposit boxes, financial statements, and personal assets. Remind them that keeping the list in a safe deposit box is a bad idea, since the box will be sealed and inaccessible if one of them dies.

GETTING IT ON PAPER

You may have to encourage your parents to decide what they want to happen to their estate after they die. If they don't leave the required documents, the courts will determine what will happen to their assets. Here are some things to be sure they've done or to suggest that they should do.

Each parent should write a will to designate who should inherit his or her assets. They might also set up one or more trusts, so they can pass assets on to others without having to include

hose assets in the wills. Trusts can e especially important if they own roperty in more than one state or if heir individual estates are larger than he amount they can leave tax free. In 2004 and 2005, it's $1.5 million at he federal level.

Be sure that the names of the eneficiaries on pension funds, nsurance policies, IRAs, and certain ther investments are current. The ssets in each of those accounts go irectly to the named beneficiary.

Review which property they wn jointly. If one parent dies, the urviving parent will own all of the roperty they had owned jointly.

AKING INVENTORY

o find the value of an estate, you eed to identify and add up what the assets are worth, and then subtract the costs of any outstanding debts, such as income taxes or mortgage payments. From there, you can begin to settle the estate.

An asset's worth is determined by figuring out the **fair market value**, which is the price someone would be willing to pay for property under current market conditions. That can be especially important if they've owned certain assets—such as a home or stock purchased as part of a retirement savings plan—for a long time.

When you create an inventory of your parents' estate, be sure to include any of the following that apply to them:

- Real estate
- Securities, such as stocks, bonds, and mutual funds
- Interest and dividends that are owed
- Bank accounts, including money-market savings accounts
- All physical personal property
- Life insurance policy face values
- Annuities paid by contract or agreement
- Income tax refunds due
- Payments from IRAs and other retirement plans
- Claims paid for pain and suffering, even after death (except in cases of wrongful death)
- Custodial accounts of which one of your parents is the custodian

GET AN EXPERT

If sitting down with your parents to talk about financial matters seems too difficult, or if you meet resistance, there is another route you can take: Get them in touch with an estate-planning attorney.

The advantage of talking with an expert is that your parents can keep their financial matters personal. You can breathe easier knowing that your parents' finances are in order, and you can minimize conflicts over the more personal aspects of their wills and trusts.

However, the major drawback is the cost, since lawyers' fees can be hefty. One alternative is to purchase software, such as Nolo program software, which gives step-by-step instructions to creating a will.

The Ins and Outs of Ownership

When it comes to ownership, you can go solo or take partners along for the ride.

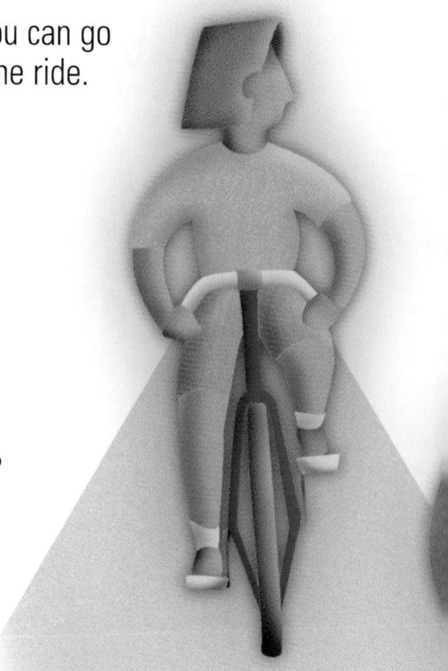

You have several options when it comes to owning bank accounts, real property, and investments. You can own everything the same way, or you can choose specific types of ownership for different assets. Certain rules govern your rights to the property and the decisions you can make about it, depending on the type of ownership you have.

MARRIAGE, DIVORCE, AND OWNERSHIP

Ownership can become slightly complicated when you get married or divorced. Generally, anything you owned before you got married—and keep in your own name—is yours even in the event of divorce.

However, any money that you and your husband earn during your marriage, as well as any investments and property you bought, is considered **marital property**. If you get divorced, that property is divided between you and your former husband, though it's not necessarily divided evenly unless you live in one of the nine community property states. In those states the law says that each of you gets half your assets, no matter who earned the money or bought the property.

SOLE OWNERSHIP

If you have sole ownership, you are the only owner of the property and have the power to decide what happens to it. You can sell it, give it away, or leave it to someone in your will, as long as you own the property outright.

JOINT DIFFICULTIES

Joint ownership has many benefits, but there's no guarantee that your ownership share is completely protected. If you have a joint checking or savings account, or a joint investment account, and signatures from both owners aren't required to authorize a transaction, you (or the other owner) are entitled to take all assets out of the account on your own.

In some cases of joint tenancy, your share is automatically passed on to the other owner or owners if you die. That's called having **rights of survivorship**.

INVESTING WITH A PARTNER

If you're in a long-term relationship, but you're not married, you and your partner have several options for owning property and investments together. Joint tenancy, for instance, works the same way for unmarried people as for married people. If one of the owners dies, the other automatically gets the joint property.

However, if you're not married, you can't pass property to each other free of tax, as married couples can. The total value of whatever you own jointly is legally considered part of the estate of whoever dies first. As a result, that person's estate may be taxed if its value is more than the

WAYS TO OWN PROPERTY

There are four ways to own property, including investments.

JOINT TENANTS
If you own property with two or more people, you may be joint tenants. Any one of you can sell your share, but in most cases, you have to get the consent of the other owner or owners first. And if you sell, the proceeds must be shared equally with the other owners.

TENANTS IN COMMON
If you're a tenant in common, you own property with two or more people. Each of you has the right to sell or give away your share of the property and to keep the profit if you do sell. The surviving owners are not automatically entitled to inherit the shares of an owner who dies.

TENANTS BY THE ENTIRETY
If you're married, you and your husband may own property as tenants by the entirety. Neither of you can sell without the other's permission, nor can you leave the property to someone other than your spouse in your will.

mount that's exempt from tax—$1.5 nillion in 2004 and 2005. And the urviving partner may end up paying nheritance taxes.

One alternative in a case like this to set up a **trust**, which is a legal ocument that transfers ownership to trustee, who distributes the assets ccording to your wishes when you ie. Passing property to your partner nrough a trust may be a way to nsure that your intentions for the roperty are acted on. That's because is more difficult for unhappy family nembers to contest a trust than a ill. But if you're considering a trust, e sure to consult an attorney who pecializes in that area of the law.

COMMUNITY PROPERTY
The nine community property states are Arizona, California, Idaho, Louisiana, Nevada, New Mexico, Texas, Washington, and Wisconsin.

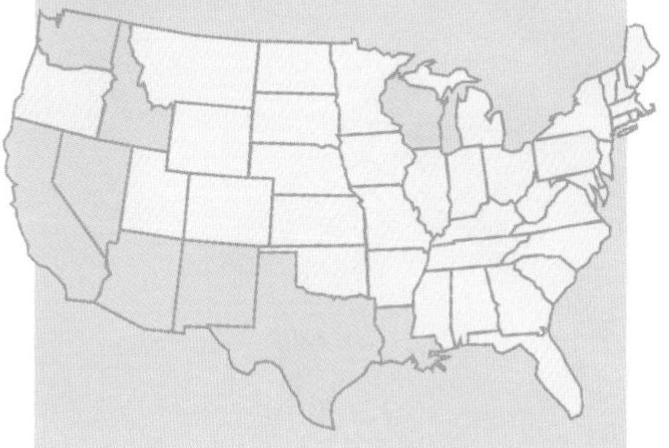

The Basics of Investing

Investing can seem very complicated. But it doesn't have to be.

Investing is about putting your money to work so that your **principal**, or the amount you start with, increases in value. If you choose your investments wisely, they can make the difference between being able to achieve your financial goals or being forced to postpone them.

Investing isn't the same as saving. When you save, you usually put some of your money in a safe place where it earns interest—a bank savings account, for example. Savings accounts are ideal as emergency funds, or for holding money you expect to spend in the near future. But the interest you earn on bank savings accounts doesn't usually grow much faster than the rate of inflation. That means the money you save won't be worth much more in the future than it is today, leaving you short on buying power. Factor in the cost of taxes and that sets you back another step. To come out ahead, you must earn more.

WHAT THE INVESTMENTS ARE

Whether you're a new or experienced investor, the investments to concentrate on are:

- Stocks and mutual funds that invest in stocks
- Bonds and mutual funds that invest in bonds
- Cash and cash-equivalent investments, such as certificates of deposit (CDs) and US Treasury bills

In general, you choose stocks and stock mutual funds for **growth**, bonds and bond mutual funds for **income**, and cash and cash equivalents to hold the money you're planning to use in the fairly near future or are accumulating to invest.

The longer your time frame, the more you need to focus on growth. That might include investments you make to pay for your children's education while they're still quite young, and certainly includes what you're investing for retirement.

THE STEPS TO TAKE

Finding the right investments isn't hard, but it won't happen if you don't make up your mind to get started. The biggest investment mistake you can make is to procrastinate.

Unless you have a lot of money on hand, perhaps from an inheritance or a pension payout, you'll be building your investment portfolio over time. That means you can begin small and learn as you go.

The first step is to define your investment goals. If you know what you want to achieve and the time frame you have to do it, you can narrow the field to the type of investment that best matches your goals.

Next, get a grasp of the basics. Go o your library and start reading maga-ines and newspapers. Then branch ut to more advanced books on the conomy, stock market, and investing.

Check out investment seminars hat are being sponsored by reputable inancial institutions, look at websites n finance, stocks, and mutual funds, nd talk to friends and family who are lready investors.

Finally, look for a financial adviser vho can help you select specific nvestments. It's one of the best ways o get the expertise you need to make nportant decisions.

HE INVESTMENT PROCESS

t's smart to set up an investment ccount that's separate from your hecking account. It can be an nsured savings or money market ccount, a money market mutual und, or an account with a brokerage irm. Or you can plunge right in and nake your investment account a stock nutual fund. Compare the costs to pen and maintain each type of ccount, and find out what the cur-ent earnings are. You may find that noving right to the stock fund makes he most sense.

You can add a specific mount to your account very week or every month, s part of managing your ousehold accounts. Or you an have the money deposit-d directly from your pay-heck or transferred from our checking account.

HELPFUL HINTS

There's no rule about how much you should be investing, but experts suggest a goal to aim for is 10% to 15% of your gross income. If you're contributing to a retirement savings plan at work, the percentage you're putting in your account counts toward the total. And whenever you get a bonus, a gift, or other unexpected cash, it's a good idea to put some or all of it into your investment account as well. That extra boost can make a big difference.

RECYCLED EARNINGS

Reinvesting your investment earnings is one of the easiest and most reliable ways to build your portfolio.

If you invest in a mutual fund, you can select the reinvestment option when you open the account. Then the fund will automatically use your earnings to buy more shares instead of sending you the money. You can also choose to reinvest any dividends you earn on stocks that offer **dividend reinvestment plans (DRIPs)**.

The Power of Time

Time can be your most powerful investment ally—or your fiercest opponent.

It's true that it's never too late to start investing. But it's even more true that it's never too soon. Consider this example of two investing styles:

Karen starts saving money at age 25, investing $200 a month in a tax-deferred retirement plan earning 9%. Tricia starts saving in the same plan at 45, but she puts away $400 a month, twice as much as Karen. At 65, both Karen and Tricia have invested a total of $96,000, but Karen's investment has grown to $850,000, while Tricia's investment is worth only $258,000, even though she invested the same amount of money.

How does Karen end up with so much more money? Because her investment has the advantage of an extra 20 years of **compounding**, a financial phenomenon that makes time work in her favor. Basically, compounding means you have earnings on your earnings, which increase the size of your investment base. The more years your earnings compound, the greater your investment's value.

HOW COMPOUNDING WORKS

Each time your earnings are paid, they're added to your **principal**, which is the amount you invested. As time goes by, you earn both on the original amount you invested and on the previous earnings. The best way to take advantage of compounding is to start investing as soon as you can, even if you start with a small amount. Given enough time, compounding can turn it into a sizable sum.

Base amount
+ Earnings

= New base amount
+ Earnings

= New base amount
+ Earnings

= New base amount
+ Earnings

= Value over time

TIME AND RISK

Over the course of a day, a month, or a year, most investment prices fluctuate, sometimes dramatically. They go up and down repeatedly in response to changing market conditions, investor attitudes, and other factors. This constant movement, known as **volatility**, varies from investment to investment, with some investments being significantly more volatile than others.

Stock prices, for example, tend to be more volatile than bond prices. So the shorter the period that you own a stock, the more risk you take that its price will be down if you need or want to sell. That's why most financial advisers recommend you don't put money into stocks if you know you'll need it in the next year or two.

But over every 15-, 20-, or 30-year period since 1926, stock prices as a group—though not the price of every stock—have increased in value.

THE INVESTING RACE

The younger you are when you start investing, the more you benefit from compounding. If you begin at 25, you can contribute less each month and still come out ahead of someone who starts at 45, even if she invests more than you each month.

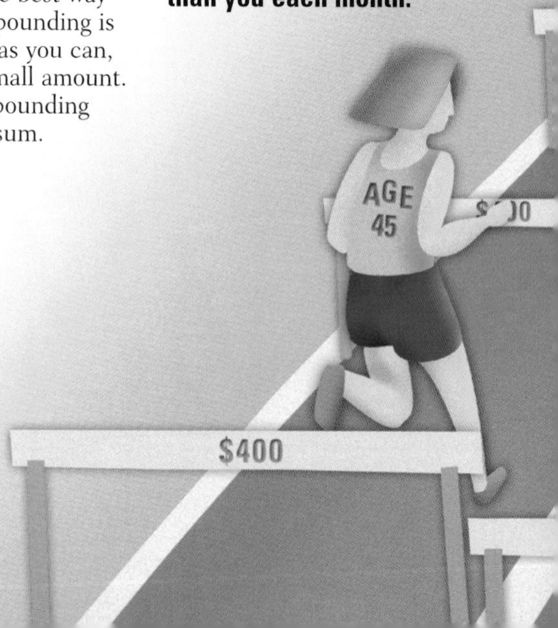

DOLLAR COST AVERAGING

One way you may be able to take advantage of volatility is by using an investment strategy called **dollar cost averaging**. That means you invest the same amount of money in a specific investment on a regular schedule no matter what it costs. For example, you might add $100 to a mutual fund every month.

When the price goes up, your $100 buys fewer shares. When the price goes down, you buy more shares. If you stick with the plan for an extended period, you may be able to lower the overall price of your investment, since your average cost per share will be less than the average share price. But you do have to buy when prices drop for the strategy to work.

One word of caution: This strategy won't protect you against market losses or guarantee a profit.

VERY RISKY BUSINESS

Market timers and day traders, who buy and sell investments very quickly, try to take advantage of market volatility by buying when prices move down and selling when prices move up. The problem is that stock movement isn't predictable. There's no way to make money consistently.

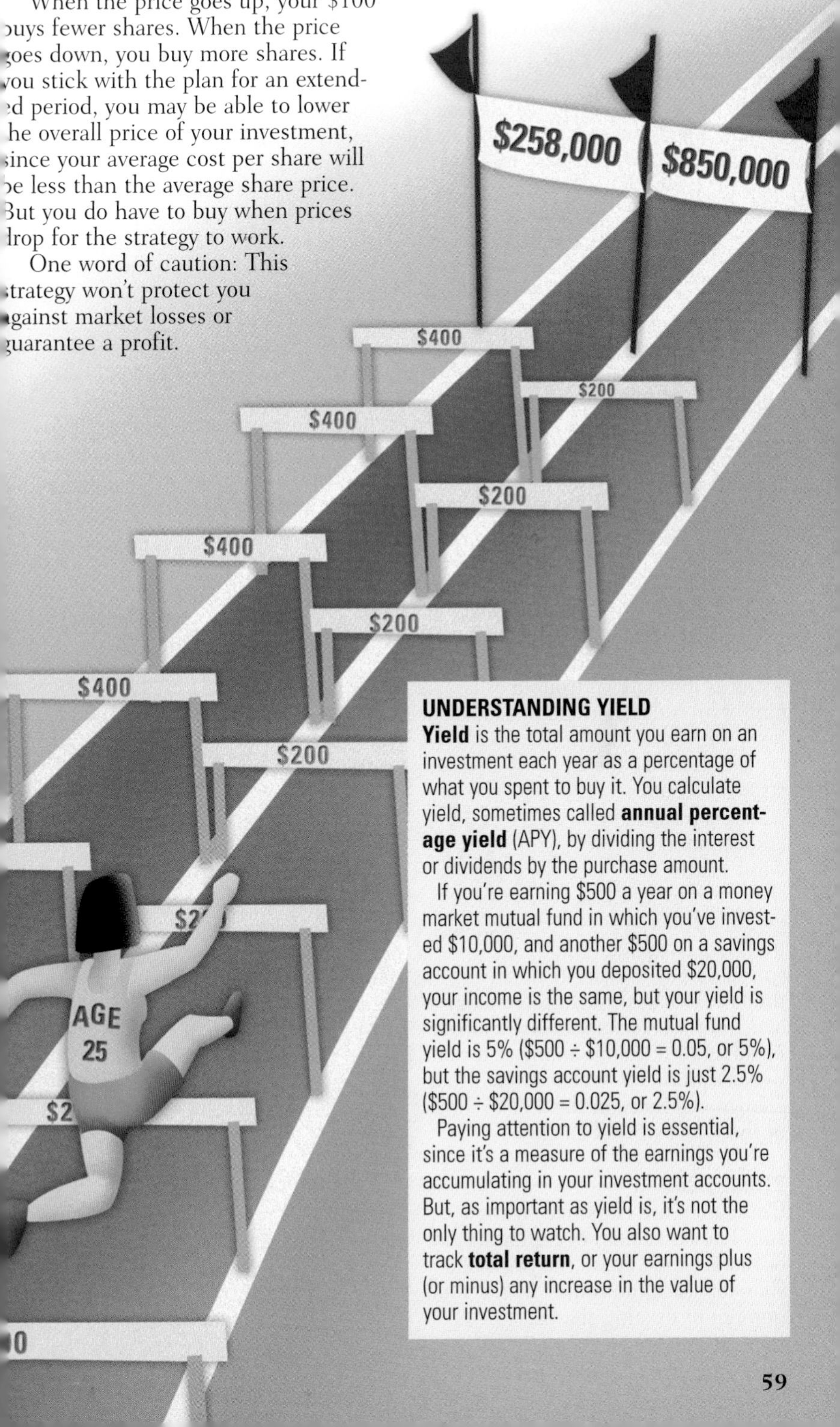

UNDERSTANDING YIELD

Yield is the total amount you earn on an investment each year as a percentage of what you spent to buy it. You calculate yield, sometimes called **annual percentage yield** (APY), by dividing the interest or dividends by the purchase amount.

If you're earning $500 a year on a money market mutual fund in which you've invested $10,000, and another $500 on a savings account in which you deposited $20,000, your income is the same, but your yield is significantly different. The mutual fund yield is 5% ($500 ÷ $10,000 = 0.05, or 5%), but the savings account yield is just 2.5% ($500 ÷ $20,000 = 0.025, or 2.5%).

Paying attention to yield is essential, since it's a measure of the earnings you're accumulating in your investment accounts. But, as important as yield is, it's not the only thing to watch. You also want to track **total return**, or your earnings plus (or minus) any increase in the value of your investment.

Stocks

Stocks have an important place in an investment portfolio.

When you buy stock, you're buying a small part of a publicly traded company. Your **equity**, or ownership, means you're in a position to profit from the company's success. That's usually measured by its earnings or by an increase in the price of its stock, or both.

When you buy stock, you do take a certain amount of risk that it will drop in value and be worth less than you paid for it. If you sell when the price is down, you can lose money.

Despite that potential risk, stocks continue to be popular investments with people trying to meet their long-term financial goals. That's because, over time, stocks have provided significantly higher returns than any other type of investment.

STOCK PRICES

A stock doesn't have a fixed value the way some other investments do. Its price can go as high as you and other investors are willing to pay to own it—usually because you expect it to be worth even more in the future. Similarly, a stock's price can drop, sometimes significantly, if the issuer is in financial trouble or is part of an industry that's out of favor with investors.

Traditionally, the stronger a company's earnings and the more consistently they have increased, the more investors have been willing to pay for the stock. In the late 1990s, though, technology and Internet stocks increased rapidly in value even though many of them weren't profitable. What impact that change will have on the stock markets in the long run isn't clear.

STOCK SIZES

Companies are classified by their size, known as market capitalization, or market cap. That's the price of a share of stock multiplied by the total number of existing shares.

For example, a company with 100 million shares of stock priced at $34 each would have a market cap of $3.4 billion.

Since a company's capitalization is a factor in its growth potential and how vulnerable it is to financial stress, size is something to take into account as you choose stocks for your portfolio.

The largest US companies—there are about 500 of them—have market caps of $5 billion or more. Many of the **blue chips**, or the oldest and most financially stable companies, pay dividends and grow at a steady but modest pace.

Midsized companies—another 500 or so fall into this category—have market caps between $1.5 and $5 billion. If a mid-cap company prospers and its stock price increases, it may displace a company in the large-cap group that has grown slowly or slipped in value.

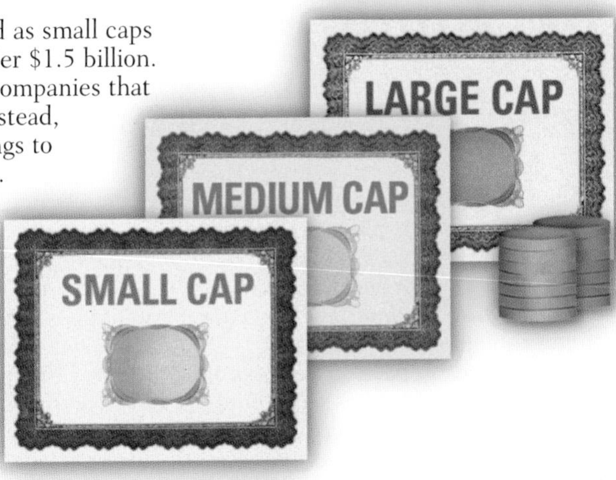

Companies classified as small caps ıave market values under $1.5 billion. They're often younger companies that arely pay dividends. Instead, hey reinvest any earnings to ɜxpand their operations. While some compa-ıies in this group fail ɔr are bought by arger companies, ɔthers are the large caps of the future.

NVESTMENT STRATEGIES

ou can use a num-ɔer of different strategies to invest in stocks.

A **buy and hold** approach means ou look for stocks you expect to ncrease significantly in value over a ıumber of years. When you buy, you keep the stocks for the long term. Typically you don't sell when the ɔrice drops and may even buy more shares during such periods.

If you **trade**, you buy stocks you ɜxpect to increase in value in the short term and establish a set of guidelines to help you decide when o sell. For example, you might always sell a stock whose price has increased 20% and use the gain to make another investment.

You can look for **value stocks**, or bargains, whose prices are lower than the company is worth. When the price goes back up, you can sell at a profit. This type of investing is known as buying low and selling high, and although it sounds pretty basic, history shows that most investors tend to follow the crowd and do just the opposite. Instead of buying low, most investors buy popular stocks when prices are going up and sell unpopular stocks as prices are falling.

You can look for **growth stocks** in industries that seem likely to have a powerful role in the future. Investors who bought computer stocks in the 1980s and Internet stocks during the 1990s are normally described as growth investors.

CAPITAL GAINS

If you own stock that increases in value, you get a double bonus. First, your net worth increases, which helps you become more finan-cially secure. If you need cash to reach a particular goal, you can sell some of the stock to pay for it. If not, it has the potential to continue to increase in value.

In addition, you don't owe tax on any increase until you sell the stock and **realize**, or pocket, the **capital gain.** Any tax you owe at that point is figured at the capital gains rate, which is always lower than your current income tax rate.

Bonds

If you're looking for income, bonds may be the right choice.

Bonds are **debt securities**. When you buy a bond, you're really lending money, called your **principal**, to a company or government for a certain **term**, or period of time. The company or government—known as the **issuer**—agrees to pay you **interest** on the loan principal, just as you would pay interest if you borrowed money from a bank. And the issuer promises to repay the principal when the bond matures at the end of the loan period.

THE VALUE OF BONDS

The bond's **par value** is the amount that the issuer borrows and the amount that's repaid at maturity. In most cases, that par value is $1,000. But market forces and investor attitudes affect bond prices just as they do stock prices, though with bonds the increases and decreases are always in relation to par value.

Changes in the interest rate have the biggest single impact on bond prices. As rates go up, the prices of existing bonds drop because they provide a smaller return. For example, if interest rates increase from the 7% on an old bond you bought to the 8% on a new bond you're buying, you'd get 1%, or $10, more per $1,000 investment on the new bond than on the old one. As a result, you and other investors would be willing to pay less to buy an old bond than a new, higher-paying one, and the price of the old bond will drop below $1,000. Bonds selling for less than par are said to be **selling at a discount**.

Similarly, if rates drop, older bonds become more desirable because they provide a higher return. So investors will pay more than $1,000, or what's known as a **premium**, to own them.

BUYING TO HOLD

If you buy a bond when it is issued and hold onto it until it matures, it's a simple transaction. You pay your money up front, and know exactly how much you're going to earn and when you'll get your principal back. That appeals to investors who want to be able to count on a steady stream of income.

Inflation poses a potential risk. Since the interest a bond pays is usually fixed, the amount you receive over time will buy less. That's a particular problem with long-term bonds, which is one of the reasons they typically pay at a higher rate than short-term bonds. For that reason, you need some incentive for tying up your money.

HELPFUL HINTS

Some bonds require large initial investments of $10,000 or more, putting them out of range for the average investor. You might want to investigate bond funds, which own a number of different bonds, as a way of diversifying your portfolio. Or you might open a Treasury Direct account and buy US Treasurys, which you can purchase in increments of $1,000, whether you want one or a thousand.

TYPES OF BONDS

Corporate bonds are issued by companies who want to raise money—to fund expansion or modernization, for example. Corporate bonds tend to pay the highest interest, but the interest is taxable unless you hold the bonds in a tax-deferred or tax-exempt retirement savings plan.

US Treasury bills, notes, and bonds are issued to raise money for running the federal government. These bonds tend to pay lower interest than corporate bonds, but you have to pay only federal taxes on the interest, not state or local taxes.

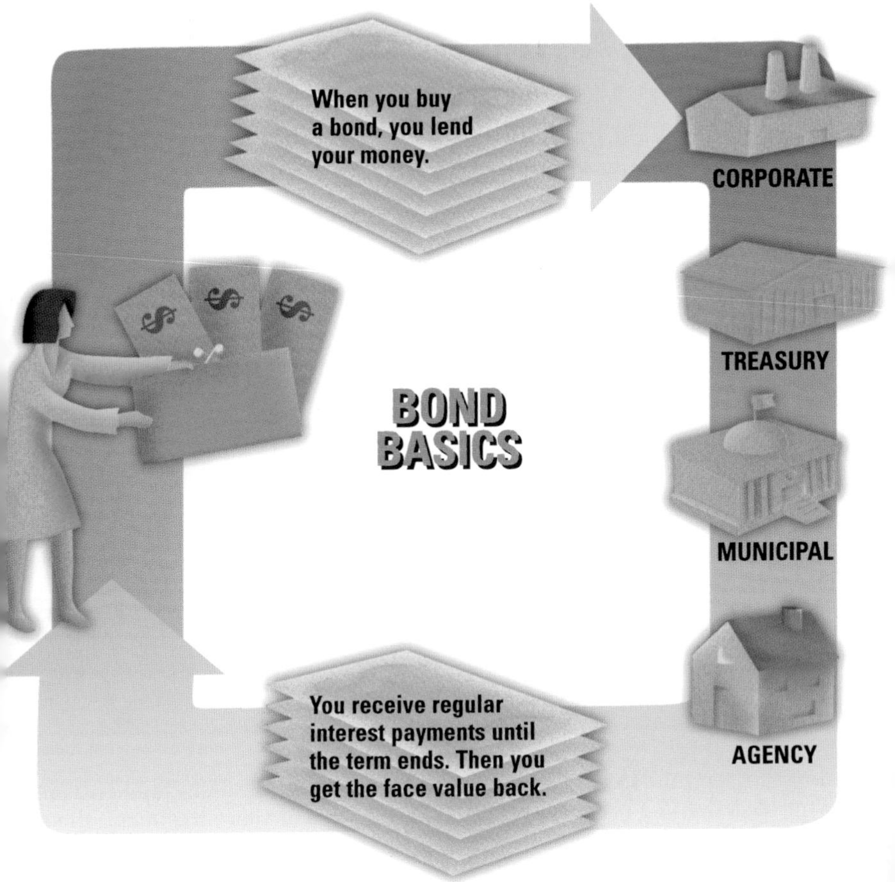

BUYING TO TRADE

You can also trade bonds through a broker on the **secondary market**. That means you buy bonds that another investor is selling—or sell bonds you own to investors who are interested in buying. Some investors trade bonds as they would stocks, with the goal of making money on price fluctuations and interest rate changes.

THE BIG ZERO

Zero-coupon bonds work a little differently than most other bonds. You buy them at a **deep discount**, or much less than their par value. For example, you might pay $11,000 for a $20,000 zero-coupon bond. You receive no interest during the bond's term, but when the bond matures, you get the face value plus the interest that accumulated over the years.

The relatively low cost and big payout on zero-coupon bonds makes them popular with people investing for big-ticket items with predictable time frames. Remember that you have to pay taxes on the interest you earn each year, even though you don't receive it until the bond matures. And zero-coupon prices are extremely volatile in the secondary market.

Municipal bonds, known as munis, are issued by state and local governments to raise money for projects and expenses. If you buy municipal bonds from the state you live in, the interest is tax free. If you buy bonds issued by another state, you have to pay state and local (but not federal) taxes on the interest.

Agency bonds are issued by various government agencies for specific projects. For example, GNMA, or Ginnie Mae, bonds are issued to raise money to help provide affordable mortgages. Rates tend to be slightly higher than on Treasury bonds because they pose a marginally higher risk. The interest is taxable.

Mutual Funds

To conduct a good fund performance, a mutual fund manager must know the score.

When you invest in a mutual fund, your money is pooled with the money of other investors to give the fund enormous buying power. As money comes into the fund, the fund's manager decides how to invest it, based on the fund's investment objective, his or her approach to investing, and what's happening in the financial markets.

You can redeem your shares at any time by selling them back to the fund. The price you get when you sell is determined by the fund's current value.

SOMETHING FOR EVERYONE

Whether your investment goal is growth, income, or a combination of the two, there's a mutual fund for you. Each fund states its investment objective in a **prospectus**, which is a document that describes the fund's performance, investment style, fee structure, and key investments. You can request a prospectus from the fund or ask your financial adviser for a copy.

FUND FACTS

Mutual funds fit into three basic categories: stock funds, bond funds, and money market funds.

Stock funds focus on increasing the value of your investment, though the rate of growth they seek may vary significantly. Some also invest in dividend-paying stocks to provide some current income. Funds tend to be more price stable than individual stocks, since weak performance by some holdings may be offset by strong performance from others.

Bond funds invest to provide income, though if your share of fund earnings is reinvested, your fund may also grow in value. One big advantage of bond funds over individual bonds is that you can invest significantly smaller amounts and get greater diversification. But bond funds aren't bonds. There's no maturity date, no fixed rate of interest, and no promise that you will get your original investment back. Instead, the value of a share of a bond fund goes up and down to reflect what's happening in the market.

Money market funds buy debt investments, such as short-term corporate and government bonds. They provide regular income, usually at about the same rate as CDs. You can put your money in a money market fund while you decide where to invest it, use the fund to hold your emergency cash, or use it as a checking account.

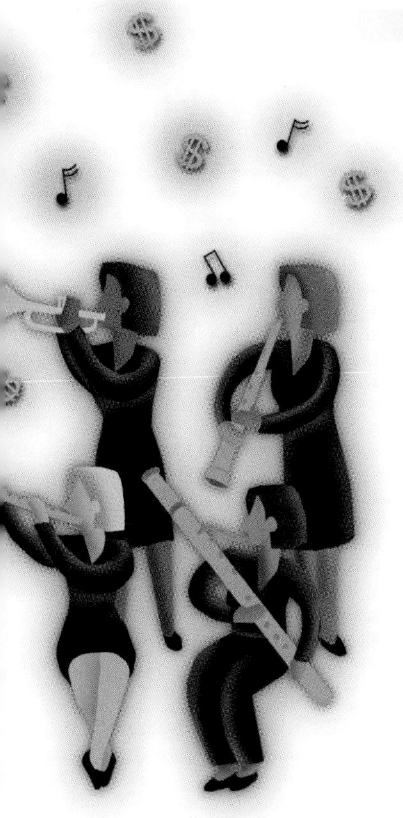

THE GOING PRICE

Each mutual fund has a **net asset value (NAV)**, which is found by dividing the total assets of the fund by the number of existing shares. The fund's assets are the investments it owns, called its **underlying investments**, and their value is determined by their current market prices.

When you sell shares back to the fund, it pays you the NAV. It's figured at the end of every trading day.

CLASSES OF SHARES

When you buy a mutual fund through your financial adviser, you may have to choose among several share classes.

With Class A shares, you pay a percentage of your investment when you buy. That's known as a front-end load. With Class B shares, you pay the sales charge if you sell the shares during the first few years. That's a back-end load. If you buy Class C shares, you pay a percentage of your account value every year you own the fund. That's a level load. And with Class D shares, you pay both a level load and a back-end load.

In making your choice, you can compare the costs for the different classes and consider how long you plan to hold on to your shares.

HELPFUL HINTS

There are two types of mutual funds: load and no-load. A **load fund** charges a load, or sales commission, when you buy or sell shares or once a year, depending on the fund. Usually, you buy a load fund through a broker or financial adviser.

A **no-load fund**, which you can buy from the investment company that sponsors the fund, doesn't charge a sales commission—but some do charge a 12b-1 fee, which covers some of the fund's marketing costs.

MAKING MONEY WITH A FUND

A mutual fund pays you and other shareholders two types of distributions. **Income distributions** are based on dividends or interest the fund earns on its investments. **Capital gains distributions** are paid from profits the fund makes from selling investments it owns.

You can take these distributions as income or you can reinvest them to buy more shares in the fund. The advantage of reinvestment is that it's designed to help you build your principal. Remember, though, that you have to pay income tax each year on your distributions even if you reinvest them, unless you own them in a tax-deferred account such as a 401(k) plan or a traditional IRA.

Choosing Alternative Investments

There are lots of ways to put investment money to work.

You can build your investment portfolio without looking further than stocks, bonds, and cash. But there's a range of other investment opportunities you might want to investigate to help meet your financial goals.

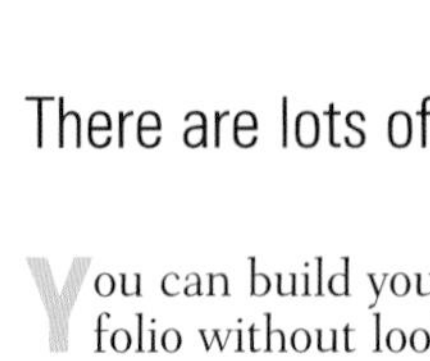

Some of them, like buying real estate, may have the added advantage of providing you with a place to live. Others, such as futures contracts, are higher-risk choices that may not be something you're ready to consider. But having a sense of the possibilities can help you make informed decisions.

Choices like **certificates of deposit** (**CDs**) are insured cash-equivalent investments that typically provide a stronger return than the return on savings accounts. And, at the other end of the spectrum, you might consider investing in start-up companies or companies that aren't publicly traded. To do that, you may have to have a significant net worth—often over $1 million.

REAL ESTATE

Whether it's the place you call home or property you rent to someone else, real estate is an investment. Better yet, real estate investments have historically increased in value and may have tax advantages, such as deducting property taxes and mortgage interest. Further, if you make a profit on the sale of your home, there's no capital gains tax on up to $250,000 of that profit if you're single, or $500,000 if you're married and file a joint return, provided you've lived in your home for two of the previous five year

Of course, there's no guarantee you make money. Real estate is not liquid, which means it can take time to conve your investment to cash, especially if you try to sell the property in periods high mortgage rates or limited demand

As an alternative, you can buy shar in publicly traded **Real Estate Investment Trusts** (**REITs**), which invest pools of money in a variety of real estate ventures. Though they have risks as well, REITs offer you greater diversification than you could get buying property on your own.

COLLECTIBLES

Collectibles include objects such as fine art, antiques, stamps, coins, fine wine, and basically any other possession that people consider valuable. You can make a good deal of money if you have an eye for collectibles, or if the right buyer is interested in what you're selling. But unlike publicly traded securities or mutual funds, which usually

ve a market, there's no guarantee at anyone will want to buy what u've collected when you're ready to ll it. And there's no way to anticipate whether or not you can sell at the price you want.

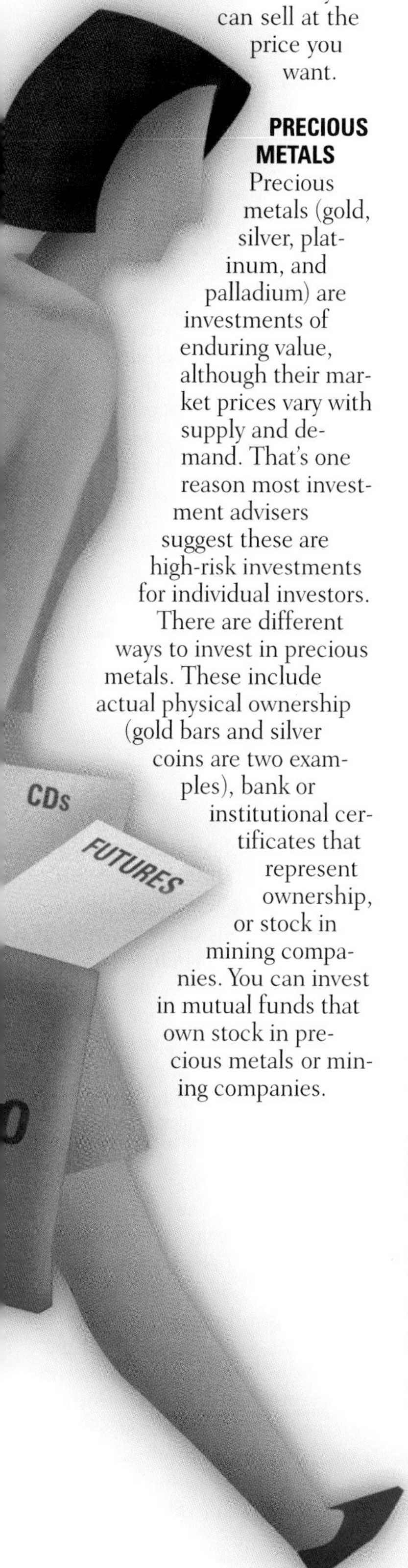

PRECIOUS METALS

Precious metals (gold, silver, platinum, and palladium) are investments of enduring value, although their market prices vary with supply and demand. That's one reason most investment advisers suggest these are high-risk investments for individual investors.

There are different ways to invest in precious metals. These include actual physical ownership (gold bars and silver coins are two examples), bank or institutional certificates that represent ownership, or stock in mining companies. You can invest in mutual funds that own stock in precious metals or mining companies.

DERIVATIVES

A derivative is an investment, such as a futures contract or an option, whose value depends on the value of an **underlying investment**, such as a stock or commodity. (Commodities are the raw materials in consumer products.) One appeal of derivatives is that you can use **leverage**, or a small amount of your own money, to buy something of greater value. But derivative prices are volatile, which means you can make or lose a good deal of money very quickly.

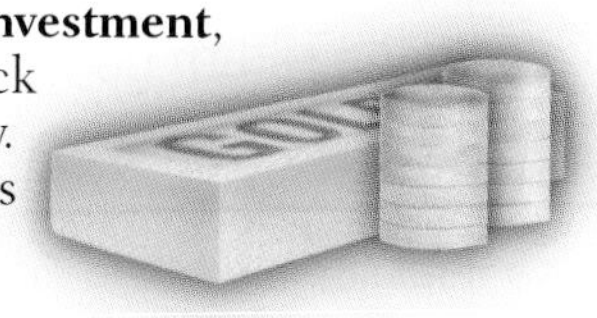

When you buy or sell a **futures contract**, you're agreeing to carry out an obligation to close the deal on a certain amount of the underlying investment by the **expiration date**, which is a specific date in the future. But what most investors do instead is buy an offsetting contract—for example, one that obliges them to sell if their original contract obliged them to buy, hoping to make money on the changing value of the contract.

When you buy an option, you pay a **premium**, or a fraction of the value of the investment, for the *right* to buy or sell a specific quantity of the underlying investment at a set price, known as the **strike** price, within a particular time frame. Unlike a futures contract, a buy option puts you under no obligation to do anything before the contract expires. But it can be an opportunity to profit if your analysis of the market is correct.

When you sell an option, though, you collect the premium but you must fulfill an obligation to buy or sell the underlying investment at the strike price if the option is exercised. The biggest risk occurs if you sell an option on stock you don't own, because it means you'd have to buy it at market price to meet your obligation to sell. That could cost you a bundle.

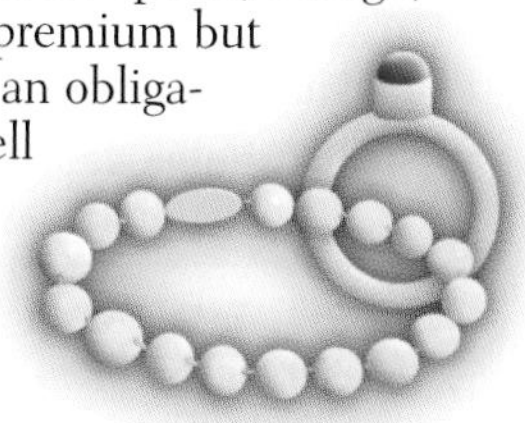

Risk and Return

On the trail to meeting investment goals, risk and return go hand in hand.

For your principal to increase enough in value to meet your financial goals, you have to learn to live with a certain amount of **risk**. Risk includes the chance that your investments might, at certain times, be worth less than you paid for them, and even the chance that you might lose some or all of the money you have invested.

What you're looking for in exchange for taking those risks is known as **return**. It includes any income you get from an investment and any increase in its value.

TOTAL RETURN

Total return measures the increase or decrease in value of an investment, including any reinvested dividends. For example, if a $1,000 investment paid you $50 in dividends before you sold it for $1,200, your total return would be $250 ($50 + $200). But if you earned the $50 and sold for $900, you'd have a negative total return of –$50 ($900 – $1000 = –$100 + $50 = –$50).

TOTAL RETURN INCREASE
The initial investment is $1,000.

	+$200	**Value increases**
+	**$50**	**Dividend paid**
=	**$250**	**Total return**
÷	**$1,000**	**Investment**
=	**.25**	**or 25% percentage return**

TOTAL RETURN DECREASE
The initial investment is $1,000.

	–$100	**Value decreases**
+	**$50**	**Dividend paid**
=	**–$50**	**Total return**
÷	**$1,000**	**Investment**
=	**–.05**	**or –5% percentage return**

A WORD TO THE WISE

Avoiding what you think of as risk is one of the biggest investment gambles you can take. For example, chances are that you won't lose money you pu in checking or savings accounts and other federally guaranteed bank deposits. But the rate of return you realize on these accounts is so low that you risk falling victim to **inflation**, the gradual decline in the purchasing power of the dollar.

In fact, there's no such thing as a completely risk-free investment. The only way that phrase is ever used accurately is when it's applied to 13-week US Treasury bills. Since they're backed by the federal government, there's virtually no chance that the principal won't be repaid. And since the term is so short, there's no real danger from inflation.

A RISK CONTINUUM

One approach to dealing with risk is to rank investment choices by risk level. The riskiest choices include futures contracts and speculative stocks, while the least risky are US Treasury bills and insured CDs.

The other perspective classifies risk by the kinds of investment decisions you make. Then the riskiest choice is to put all your money into just one or two investments and to concentrate on investments that are vulnerable to inflation. The least risk is investing for long-term growth and building a diversified portfolio.

TIME OF YOUR LIFE

The younger you are, the more you can afford to make higher-risk investments. That's because you have the time to wait out market fluctuations.

If you're retired or nearing retirement, you may be counting on income from your investments. Losing principal at that point poses a much higher risk because you'll have a smaller base to produce the income you need. And you have less time to wait for a market rebound.

Your life situation also plays a role
ı the amount of risk you're willing to
ıke. If you have children you plan to
ɜnd to college or aging parents who
ɜpend on you for financial support,
ɔu may be unwilling to put any
ıoney at risk, even if those invest-
ıents were likely to produce signifi-
ınt returns in the future. Or if
ɔu're taking the risk of building your
vn business, you might want other
ıvestments you can be sure of.

Your personality matters as
ell. Most experts agree it's
ɔunterproductive to make
ıvestments that make you
ɔ nervous you can't sleep.
ut they also encourage
ɔu to learn more about
ıe long-term rewards of
ıoughtful risk-taking.

ECOGNIZING RISK

Iarket risk and interest rate
sk are two of the major invest-
ıent risks you have to anticipate,
though you can't predict when
ıey will occur.

Market risk is the chance
ıat the financial markets as a
hole will drop in value and
eate a ripple effect on your
ɔrtfolio. For example, if the
ock market loses value,
ıances are your stock or
ock fund will decrease in
ılue as well until the market
turns to a period of growth.
Iarket risk exposes you to
ɔtential loss of principal,
nce some companies
ɔn't survive market
ɔwnturns. But the
eater threat is the loss
principal that can
sult from selling
hen prices are low.

Interest rate
sk is the possibili-
that interest
tes will go up.
that hap-
ɜns, the value of existing bonds and other fixed-income investments drops because they provide a smaller return than newly issued bonds. Rising interest rates also tend to mean lower stock prices, since investors put more money into interest-paying investments.

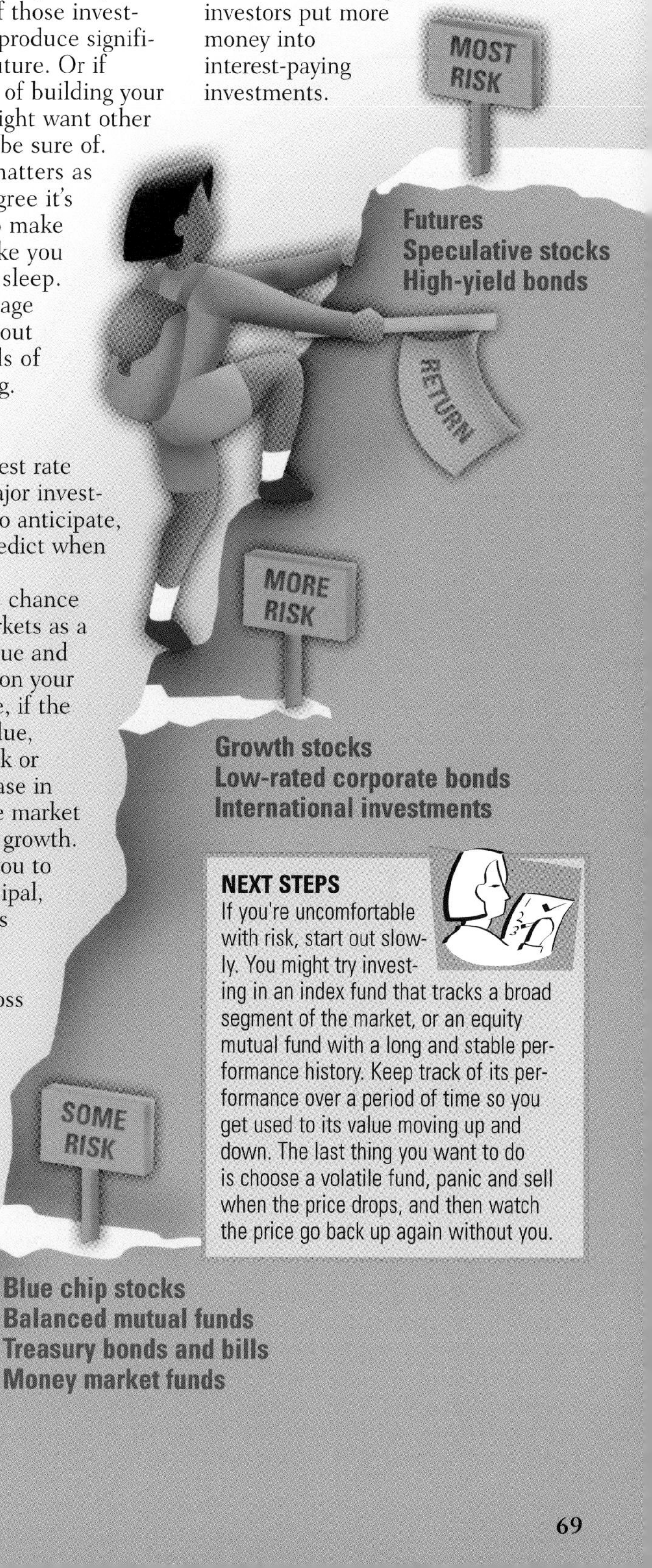

NEXT STEPS

If you're uncomfortable with risk, start out slowly. You might try investing in an index fund that tracks a broad segment of the market, or an equity mutual fund with a long and stable performance history. Keep track of its performance over a period of time so you get used to its value moving up and down. The last thing you want to do is choose a volatile fund, panic and sell when the price drops, and then watch the price go back up again without you.

Diversifying Your Portfolio

Variety isn't just the spice of an investor's life. It's an essential ingredient.

As logical as it might seem to look for the perfect stock, bond, or mutual fund and make it your investment of choice, that's not the best approach to meeting your financial goals. No single investment, or type of investments, provides a strong return year in and year out.

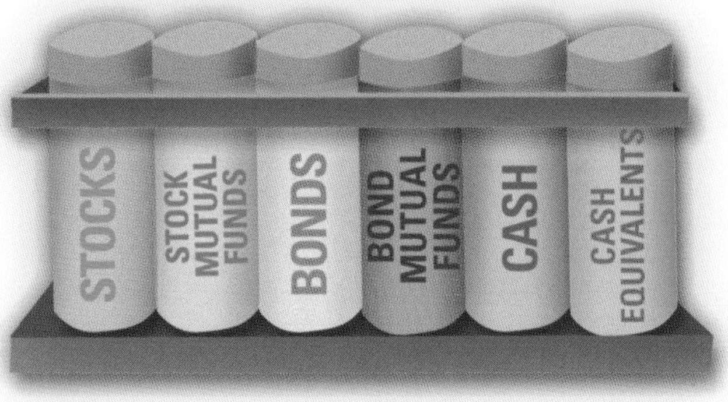

The saving grace is that each **asset class**—stocks and stock mutual funds, bonds and bond mutual funds, and cash and cash equivalents—tends to perform differently in different economic markets. When stocks falter because interest rates are high, bonds often provide a strong return, and vice versa. Rather than risk being invested in the wrong asset at the wrong time, the solution is to divide your portfolio among the various classes so you are always in a position to benefit from whatever is doing well.

THE RIGHT ALLOCATION

There's no one right allocation for everyone. But there are some general allocation guidelines you may want to think about. Perhaps the most important is that every portfolio needs some **growth**, typically from stock and stock mutual funds, some **liquidity**, typically from cash equivalents including US Treasury bills and CDs, and, in many cases, some **income**, typically from bonds.

Most financial advisers suggest that younger women allocate a greater percentage of their portfolio to growt than older women, since they have more time to recover from a potentia drop in value. If you're in your 30s, you might have as much as 85% of your portfolio in stocks and stock mutual funds and the rest in cash. But if you're 65, you may choose to reduce your stock holdings 60% or even les and allocate 30 or more to bonds.

The old rule of thumb was that if you subtracted your ag from 107, that number was th percentage you should put into stocks. But in the bull market of the 1990s, advisers became more aggressive, suggesting that all investors increase their stock holdings.

STAYING ON TRACK

Every time the value of the investments in your portfolio changes, the asset allocation you have chosen is affected as well.

For example, you may have decide that you want to keep 70% of the val of your portfolio in stocks. If the stoc market soars, the value of your stocks may increase so much that they are worth 90% of your portfolio. To keep your allocation on track, you should review your portfolio annually, and yo might want to sell some of your stock and reinvest the money in bonds or cash. If the stock market falls, howev er, you'd have to move more money into stocks to get back up to 70%.

Sticking with your chosen asset allocation mix over time can be difficult, since it often seems to go again common sense. Who wants to sell when the stock market is booming, or buy when it seems to be on its 'ay down? One solution may be to ›balance only when one asset class xceeds the allocation you've assigned › it by 15%. Using such a benchmark an help reduce the stress of wonderng whether or not to make portfolio hanges and cut trading costs too.

And remember that changes in our personal life, or a major change ı your financial goals, may call for a evised asset allocation. Adopting a aby, for example, might mean you 'ant to put new emphasis on building college savings account. Or taking n early retirement may accelerate our need for regular income.

FINER CUT

he other part of controlling risk is alled **diversification**. Since there's o one perfect investment, your goal to invest in a combination of indidual investments across the asset lasses that complement your objecves and risk tolerance. For example, ›u might soften the risk of ıvesting in an aggresve-growth mutual fund y putting some money ıto a blue chip fund. he first mutual fund likely to keep you well head of inflation, but an expose you to intense olatility at times. The econd is more likely to otect your principal ut won't grow as raply in value.

NEXT STEPS

There are some guidelines to keep in mind as you begin to allocate your portfolio. These include:

- **Growth**. You'll want to stay ahead of inflation with investments that increase in value over time. Stocks, stock funds, and real estate are typical growth investments.
- **Income**. You may need regular income from your investments, especially if you're retired. Bonds, bond funds, and CDs are typical income investments.
- **Liquidity**. You never know when you might need cash quickly. In case of an emergency, you want to have some liquid investments, such as money market funds and short-term CDs.
- **Risk**. There's no such thing as a risk-free investment. Higher growth and income come with more volatility and the risk of losing your principal. Higher liquidity comes with the risk of falling behind the rate of inflation. Owning a number of investments with different types of risk can help protect you from losing out on any one of them.

Investment Clubs

When it comes to investing, you don't have to go it alone.

Joining an investment club can be a great way for beginners to get an introduction to investing and for experienced investors to share sophisticated analysis and research. The camaraderie of working together as a group to realize common goals is an added plus, whatever your personal situation may be.

Best of all, many clubs regularly realize returns that beat market indexes, rewarding their participants with a profit on their investments.

HOW CLUBS WORK

Most investment clubs have between 10 and 20 members, so they're small enough to allow real interaction but large enough to build up a diversified portfolio. You and the other members decide on your investment goals, how much and how often you will contribute to the investment pool, and how to invest your combined assets. You may want to hire an adviser, or have experts from the financial community speak to your group, and you'll probably want to develop an educational program to explore investment principles.

Here are some reasons to conside[r] starting or joining a club:

- You can invest a modest amount, say $50 or $100 a month
- You experience the ups and downs of investing without putting a lot of your assets at risk
- You benefit from other members' research and knowledge
- You typically pay lower brokerage commissions on club transactions than individual investors pay

IS A CLUB RIGHT FOR YOU?

It usually doesn't make sense to join an investment club unless you plan to stick with it for several years. Plus most clubs don't want to waste their time on uncommitted members or those who want to drop out at the first sign of trouble.

Since you're in for the long haul, make sure the other members of a club are people you trust and enjoy working with. Remember that they'll share in the decisions that will affec[t] your money, so make sure you're comfortable not being in total contro[l]. It's a good idea to find people with

ıvestment philosophies and risk
›lerances similar to your own.

Successful clubs require their ıembers to pull their own weight, oth by researching companies and erforming administrative duties. Iany clubs rotate administrative ›sponsibilities among members › that no one has too many duties r too much power. And remember, y joining a club you're agreeing to ›llow their rules, which are often ritten down as a charter or bylaws.

ECIDING WHAT TO BUY AND SELL

Iost investment clubs work the same ay. The majority focus on equity ıvestments and buy individual stocks ıther than stock mutual funds. An verage club portfolio might include nywhere from 10 to 20 stocks at any ne time—enough to provide diversity ut not so many that it's hard to keep ack of how they're doing.

Each club member, or team of ıembers, researches a number f companies and reports on them t monthly meetings. Then everyone otes on which stocks to buy and sell ith the combined funds.

Everyone profits from this division f labor. Plus, there are people around › keep you motivated and answer our questions.

GETTING STARTED

If you're serious about starting an investment club, here are some of the topics you'll want to discuss with your fellow members.

- **Accounting methods**: What software package will you use?
- **Broker**: Whom will you use to complete your transactions?
- **Bylaws**: What basic rules do you want to lay down for membership, participation, and other policies?
- **Club officers**: How will you decide who's going to fill which offices, and how long will each office term be?
- **Funding**: What will the initial investment be?
- **Dues**: How much will each member contribute each month?
- **Stock research**: How will you go about researching companies?

FINANCIAL ADVISERS

The convenience and low cost of online trading has its appeal, but new investment clubs might want to consider using a broker for guidance and advice. A broker is someone to call with technical questions, especially as you're just getting started. And brokerage accounts may offer useful services, such as free check writing or discounted trading rates for clubs.

You should meet with several brokerage firms before deciding which one to use. One of the questions you might ask is whether the broker has worked with clubs before. And you should be sure to establish which members are authorized to place orders or speak for the club.

HELPFUL HINTS

The best way to find the right investment club is probably to start your own, though you might find a local one by asking friends or searching online. Starting a club is not as difficult as it sounds, but it does require a serious commitment. Remember that costs tend to be higher for new clubs since members are still learning the ropes.

A number of organizations, most notably the National Association of Investors Corporation (NAIC), offer step-by-step information to help get you started. You can check out the NAIC website at www.better-investing.org, or contact them at 248-583-6242.

Investment Income

The key to a comfortable retirement is investing early and wisely.

According to the 1999 Women's Retirement Confidence Survey conducted by the Employee Benefit Research Institute, 59% of working-age women don't know how much money they need to save for retirement. But having a steady source of income in your 70s and 80s is essential if you want to maintain your financial independence, be able to afford the things that are important to you, and avoid feeling that you're a burden on your family.

The good news is that you can start saving today—through an employer sponsored retirement plan, a personal retirement plan, and a portfolio of personal investments.

QUALIFIED EMPLOYER PLANS

One of the most effective ways to invest for retirement is to participate in an employer sponsored, tax-deferred retirement plan. If your employer offers this type of plan, it's smart to sign on, since tax-deferred plans have the potential to provide faster compounding of your earnings.

When you contribute pretax salary to a qualified plan, you don't pay taxes on that money, or on any earnings in the account, until you start withdrawing. You can contribute up to a set limit each year, plus catch-up contributions if you're 50 or older, and you put your money into the investments offered through the plan.

PERSONAL TAX-DEFERRED PLANS

You can also create a personal retirement plan, taking advantage of other tax-deferred investment opportunities, including traditional IRAs, Roth IRAs, and fixed and variable annuities. A major difference between a personal retirement savings plan and an employer sponsored plan is that you often have to pay taxes on the money you contribute *before* you invest it. But there may be cases when you can deduct your contribution to a traditional IRA.

However, you can defer taxes on investment earnings with a personal retirement plan, just as you can with an employer sponsored plan. That means you don't have to report any earnings on your tax return until you start withdrawing money.

TAXABLE INVESTMENTS

Since women receive less from Social Security and pensions than men do, it's even more essential for women to make wise personal investments.

You'll pay tax on the money before you invest it, and you have to pay taxes on your annual earnings, such as your mutual fund distributions or

DID YOU KNOW?

A woman earns between 72 and 84 cents for each dollar a man makes. Women are generally in the workforce for fewer years than men, often because they are raising children or caring for elderly parents. And 80% to 90% of women will be completely responsible for their finances at one point in their lives. For these reasons alone, saving for retirement is crucial to every woman's life.

tock dividends. But one incentive for uying stocks or mutual funds is that f you hold them for more than one ear and make a **capital gain**, or proft, when you sell, your gain is taxed at lower rate than withdrawals from a ax-deferred plan.

One strategy you can use is to ook for investments that don't pay lividends but are likely to increase n value. And it's also a good idea to einvest your earnings. Before you egin, it might be wise to consult a inancial adviser who can lay out your hoices and provide guidance on what nvestments may be right for you.

OCIAL SECURITY

Over 44 million Americans now enefit from the monthly income ocial Security provides to retired vorkers and their spouses.

While you're working, you autonatically contribute 6.2% of your nnual salary—up to a set salary limit, vhich is $87,900 in 2004—for Social ecurity, and 1.45% of your total alary to Medicare. Your employer natches the amount you put in each ay period. When you retire, the mount you get from Social Securty is based on your total earnings adjusted for inflation), divided by he number of months you worked, o get what's known as your **averaged ndexed monthly earnings**.

RESOURCES

If you'd like more information on issues specific to women and retirement, there are several resources on the web that you can consult.

The Women's Institute for a Secure Retirement offers information on pensions, health care, and more. Their website is www.wiser.heinz.org.

Access America for Seniors has a retirement planning section that includes information on medical coverage and financial planning. Their website is www.seniors.gov.

Women's Financial Network has a section devoted to retirement planning for women, which can be found at www.wfn.com.

If you're married, you're entitled to receive 50% of whatever your husband receives when he begins taking his benefits. So if you work but earn less than your husband, or you don't work outside the home, you can still receive Social Security payments. However, most financial advisers suggest that Social Security will only provide a portion of the money you will most likely need during retirement.

Salary Reduction Plans

Salary reduction plans are one of the most convenient ways to save for retirement.

Planning for retirement can seem daunting, confusing, and sometimes downright exhausting. But putting money into retirement investments can pay off, literally, in the long run.

One of the most popular ways to invest for retirement is through an employer sponsored **salary reduction plan**. These plans let you contribute pretax income, or income from which taxes haven't been withheld. Your contributions and any earnings they produce are tax deferred. You don't owe taxes on your retirement savings until you start withdrawing money from your account.

Your untaxed investments **compound**, since your earnings are added to your principal. That creates an even larger base to produce the next round of earnings. In turn, you can accumulate money in your account more quickly than in taxable accounts earning at the same rate.

As an added bonus, you owe less current income tax because your taxable income is reduced by the amount you contribute to the plan. The money you save on taxes can be invested in an IRA or other account to help you move even closer to achieving your financial goals.

HOW SALARY REDUCTION WORKS

The way a salary reduction plan works is that your employer creates a plan that lets you set aside a certain percentage of your salary each pay period. You then invest by choosing from the options your plan offers, which may include fixed-income, equity, and money market mutual funds, and annuities. You also get to choose how much of your contribution goes to each investment.

Your employer may match, or add to, your retirement account. One method employers use is to match 50% of whatever you contribute to the fund, up to a certain percentage of your salary, often 6%. So if you earned $45,000 and contributed 6%, or $2,700, to the plan, your employer would contribute an additional $1,350, or 50% of your amount.

MOVING INVESTMENTS

One advantage of salary reduction plans is that you have control over how your money is invested within the plan. And you can transfer your money from one investment to another if one isn't performing as well as you expected or if more attractive choices are added to your plan. Depending on what your plan's rules are, and how frequently your account is valued, you can transfer money quarterly, monthly or even daily.

Most experts advise against frequent switching, arguing that it makes it harder to reach your goals. But making certain changes can help you to diversify your portfolio or let you rebalance your allocation to improve your account's long-term performance.

THE 400 CLUB

The most common salary reduction plans are named after the sections of the federal tax code that describe them—**401(k)**, **403(b)**, and **457**. There are also thrift savings plans that don't have numbers, and two types of plans identified as **SIMPLEs**.

While each plan is a little different, they share some important characteristics:

- You can contribute a percentage of your pretax income, up to an annual limit established by Congress
- The contribution reduces your current taxable income
- Any earnings in your plan accumulate tax deferred
- There is generally a penalty on withdrawals before you reach age 59½
- Withdrawals are taxed at your regular income tax rate

IT'S YOUR CALL

If you work full-time for an employer who offers a plan, you're eligible to participate if you're at least 21 years old.

Retirement savings plans, unlike most pension plans that employers offer, are **portable**. That means if you leave a job, you can take the amount you've contributed with you, either by transferring it to a rollover IRA or to a plan your new employer offers. Any amounts your employer has matched may be moved as well, provided you've been at the job long enough to qualify.

And while there's usually a penalty for withdrawing early, you may be able to borrow from your plan. There's no penalty for borrowing, though you must pay interest on the loan as you repay it. The drawback of borrowing is that the money you take out of your account can't grow, so you are likely to limit the rate at which your retirement savings accumulate. That could mean you wouldn't meet your long-term goals.

HELPFUL HINTS

If you work for a company with 100 or fewer employees, your employer may offer a Savings Incentive Match Plan for Employees, known as a **SIMPLE**. If you participate, you can add pretax income each year, and your employer is required to contribute a set amount based on one of two formulas. The amounts you can add have increased each year, and reach $10,000 in 2005. Whatever you add to the account is vested immediately and grows tax free until you withdraw it.

Tax-Deferred Benefits

You can get a break from Uncle Sam as you build a tax-deferred retirement plan.

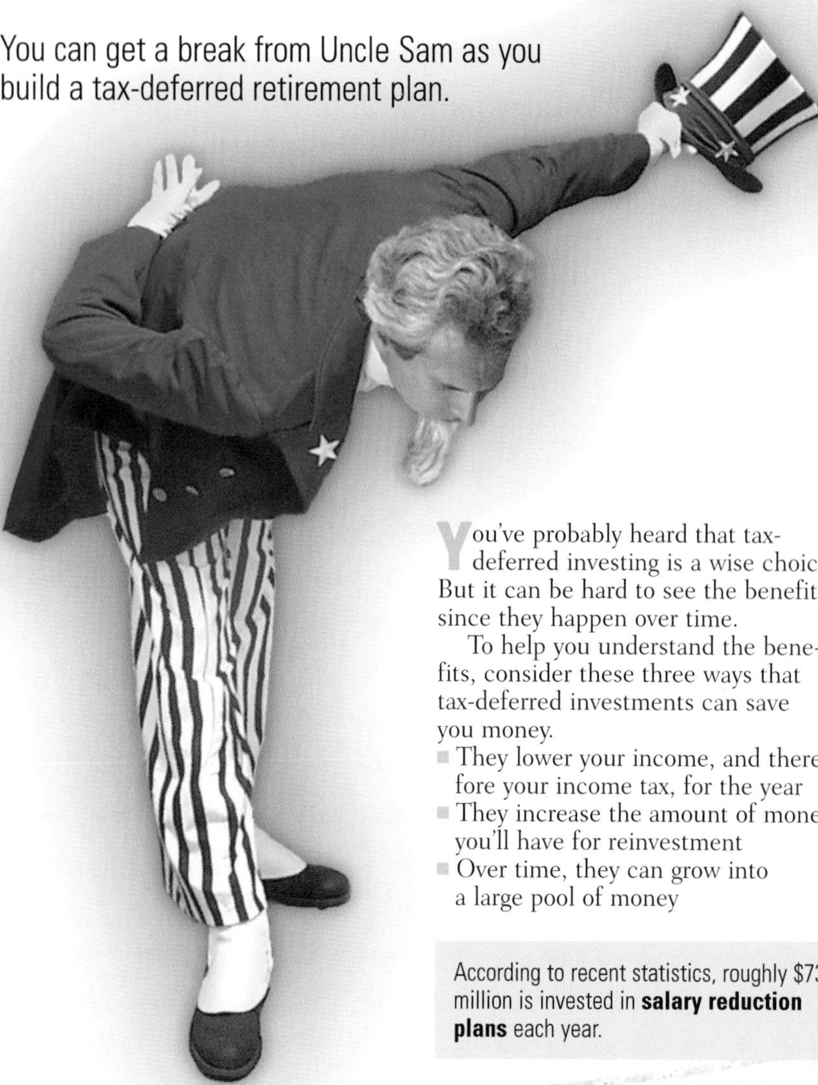

You've probably heard that tax-deferred investing is a wise choice. But it can be hard to see the benefits, since they happen over time.

To help you understand the benefits, consider these three ways that tax-deferred investments can save you money.

- They lower your income, and therefore your income tax, for the year
- They increase the amount of money you'll have for reinvestment
- Over time, they can grow into a large pool of money

According to recent statistics, roughly $73 million is invested in **salary reduction plans** each year.

SALARY REDUCTION ADVANTAGES

There's another tax advantage to a tax-deferred salary reduction plan. Since you contribute part of your paycheck to the plan, the money you contribute lowers your salary, which in turn reduces your current income tax.

So if you earned $70,000 in a given year and contributed $7,000 to your salary reduction plan, the wages reported to the Internal Revenue Service would be $63,000. That means you'd pay less in tax.

Salary	**$70,000**	**Tax on $70,000**	**$14,353†**
– Contribution	**– $ 7,000**	**– Tax on $63,000**	**– $12,566†**
= Taxable Income	**= $63,000**	**= You save**	**= $ 1,787**

†Based on single taxpayer, one exemption, 2003 rate

HOW INVESTING WORKS

If you participate in a tax-deferred retirement plan, you don't pay taxes until you withdraw. But do you save money on a year-to-year basis? In most cases, you do.

TYPE OF INVESTMENT	ANNUAL INVESTMENT		10% EARNINGS		TAX* (IF ANY)		REINVESTMENT AMOUNT
Tax deferred	$4,000	+	$400	–	$0	=	$4,400
Taxable	$4,000	+	$400	–	$124	=	$4,276

*Tax based on combined state and federal tax rate of 31%

EARLY CONTRIBUTIONS

'here's normally a limit on what our employer will contribute to our salary reduction plan each ay period. If you spread out your ontributions throughout the year, ou have a better chance of getting ll the matching funds you're entitled) than if you added large amounts few times a year.

If your employer matches your ontribution to a certain percentage, 's also smart to contribute at least nat percentage. If you don't, you're iving up money you're entitled to.

THE LIMITATIONS

Keep in mind that federal regulations govern the contributions to all tax-deferred plans, including employer sponsored salary reduction plans, and plans you set up yourself, including IRAs.

For example, if you participate in a 401(k), 403(b), or 457 plan, the amount you can contribute is capped each year, though the ceiling will increase from time to time.

However, if you invest in fixed or variable annuities, there's no federal cap on the amount you can contribute.

MAKING THE COMPARISON

If you're trying to decide which type of retirement plan would work for you, consider the following hypothetical example in which earnings are 8% before tax:

EMPLOYER PLAN
You invest $2,000 pretax dollars in an employer's plan, such as a 401(k) or 403(b). You don't pay taxes on your contributions or earnings until you start to withdraw.

TAX-DEFERRED PLAN
You invest $1,380 aftertax dollars in a tax-deferred plan, such as an IRA or an annuity. You don't pay taxes on the earnings until you withdraw.

TAXABLE INVESTMENTS
You invest $1,380 aftertax dollars in taxable investments. You pay taxes every year on the earnings.

After 30 years your account balance is:

Even after you pay the taxes you'll owe on your tax-deferred account, you'll come out ahead if you invest in a tax-deferred plan.

*Tax figured at 31% combined rate for a single payer reduces $2,000 income to $1,380

The World of Annuities

When you're buying annuities, the choice is yours.

Are you deciding what to include in your retirement savings plan? Are you considering ways to invest for retirement on your own? In either case you might consider **annuities**, which are tax-deferred products that many employers offer as part of a salary reduction plan or that you can buy individually. In both cases, the earnings the annuity produces accumulate tax deferred until you withdraw them.

QUALIFIED OR NONQUALIFIED

If you buy an annuity that is offered in an employer sponsored retirement savings plan, the annuity is considered a **qualified annuity**. You contribute pretax income, and the same contribution limits and withdrawal rules apply to it that apply to other choices within the plan.

An annuity you buy with aftertax income is considered a **nonqualified annuity**. The contribution and withdrawal rules are flexible. Often you can postpone taking money out until you are 85 or older. You can contribute income from any source to the individual account. It doesn't have to be money you earned. But the amount you put into the annuity is not tax deferred and doesn't reduce your current taxes.

RIGHT AWAY

If you buy an annuity, you have the choice of receiving income from it right away, or building your account over time and eventually converting the money that has accumulated into a source of income.

If you buy an **immediate annuity**, you make one lump-sum contribution and pick a date to start receiving payments. You can choose how long you want to get payments, either for your lifetime (a **life annuity**), for your lifetime and that of another person (a **joint and survivor annuity**), for a set period that you choose (a **fixed-period annuity**), or some combination of those options.

The actual amount you get depends on how much you contribute to the annuity, the payout option you choose, whether you have a fixed or variable annuity, and how old you are (and if it's a joint annuity, the age of the person you're sharing it with). Is an immediate annuity the right choice for you? It depends on your personal situation. Many people of retirement age decide to purchase this type of annuity because of the steady stream of income it will provide during retirement.

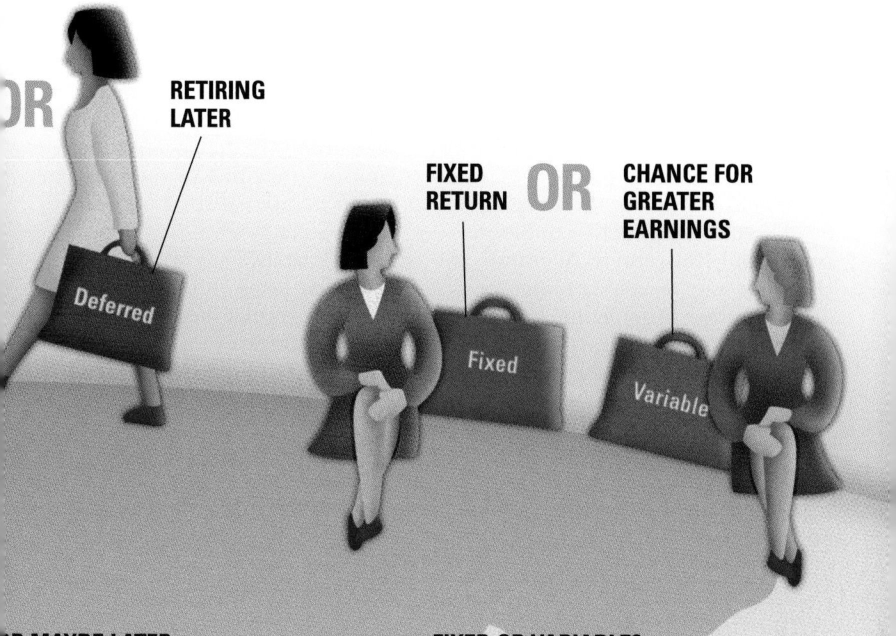

)R MAYBE LATER

)n the other hand, if you aren't ready o retire yet, you can choose a **leferred annuity**, which lets you uild up savings over a series of years n a tax-deferred account. To open a leferred annuity account, you can uy an annuity contract with a lump um of money, make a series of pay- nents over time, or sometimes both.

After your account's investments ave **accumulated**, or grown for a umber of years, you can convert your ccount value into a source of income. As you collect money, you owe taxes n the amount that has been pro- luced by earnings. The return on our principal is not taxed because t was taxed before you put it in.

You can either receive regular ayouts based on your annuity con- ract, use the money you have in the ccount to buy an immediate annuity, r opt for a lump-sum payment.

Since a deferred annuity doesn't ave an annual contribution limit and s a tax-deferred retirement option, it nay be a viable choice for you. Iowever, keep in mind that you'll ace penalties if you withdraw early, nd that annuities may have higher ees than some other retirement avings options.

FIXED OR VARIABLE?

Do you want to earn a fixed rate of return and be able to convert your annuity account so you get regular income for the rest of your life? Then a **fixed annuity** may be right for you, because it gives you a guaranteed rate of return. When you're ready to withdraw, you can choose a payout method that meets your current financial needs. And with some fixed annuities, you get a **bailout clause**, so if the interest rates drop below a certain level, you can give up your policy without fines or penalties.

If you want a choice of investment portfolios, then a **variable annuity** may suit you better. You can choose from a number of equity or fixed-income funds offered through the annuity. What you earn is based on the performance of the funds you choose. Your income may increase over time, although there is no guarantee it will.

Don't confuse **annuity**, the retirement savings plan, with **pension annuity**, the retirement income your employer pays. An annuity is a plan you can use to accumulate savings and provide income after you retire. A pension annuity is usually a regular monthly check paid out of your employer's retirement fund.

IRAs: The Basics

Creating an IRA gives you a palette of retirement choices.

If your employer doesn't offer a retirement savings plan, you may have to shoulder the responsibility of building a retirement account on your own.

Not having an employer sponsored retirement plan makes you eligible to deduct contributions to a traditional **Individual Retirement Account (IRA)**, as long as you earn income or are married to someone who does.

Before you jump in, you have some choices to make, starting with which type of IRA best suits your needs.

BRUSHING UP ON IRAs

If you have a choice of which IRA to open, you can weigh the pros and cons.

	ROTH	TRADITIONAL IRA	
		Nondeductible	Deductible
PROS	■ Tax-free income ■ No required withdrawals	■ Tax-deferred earnings	■ Immediate tax savings on tax-deferred investment ■ Tax-deferred earnings
CONS	■ Not deductible ■ Account must be open five years to qualify for tax-free provision	■ Not deductible ■ Tax paid at regular rates at withdrawal ■ Required withdrawals begin at 70½	■ Tax paid at regular rates at withdrawal ■ Required withdrawals begin at 70½

HOW TO SET UP AN IRA

To open an IRA, you fill out an application, provided by the brokerage firm, bank, mutual fund company, or other financial institution. You can choose any of these to be **custodian**, or trustee, of your IRA.

You have the power to choose which types of investments to include in your plan. That means you're also responsible for following the rules of the IRA account, such as only contributing the amount you're entitled to each year, and making investments that have been approved. And you must remember to report traditional IRA contributions to the IRS.

TRADITIONAL IRAS

A traditional IRA is a personal, tax-deferred retirement account. You can put up to $3,000 each year—but no more than your total earnings if you earn less than $3,000—in your choice of investments, and you can defer income taxes on your earnings. That means you won't owe taxes on earnings in the account until you start to withdraw money.

All traditional IRAs have three things in common:

- Your earnings are tax deferred
- You pay taxes on the earnings at your regular income tax rates once you start to withdraw
- You are required to withdraw beginning at age 70½

Your contributions to a traditional IRA may be **deductible** or **nondeductible**. Whether you qualify to deduct your contribution depends either on your **adjusted gross income (AGI)**, which is your total income minus certain deductions, like medical expenses or alimony, or on whether you are eligible for an employer's plan.

Keep in mind, though, that if your employer doesn't offer a retirement plan, you can always deduct the entire amount of your contribution up to $3,000 for a single year, no matter what your AGI is.

ROTH IRA

Like traditional IRAs, the earnings in Roth IRAs accumulate tax deferred. And earnings are totally tax free if you follow the rules for withdrawal. That means your account must have been open at least five years and you must be at least 59½ when you withdraw.

The most you can contribute in one year is $3,000—or the total amount you earned if it's less than $3,000. But there are income limits on eligibility. Basically, you qualify if you're single and make less than $95,000, or if you're married, file a joint tax return, and your combined income is less than $150,000. You can make partial Roth contributions for incomes up to $110,000 if you're single, and up to $160,000 if you're married and file jointly.

THE INVESTMENTS

You have a great deal of flexibility when you choose your IRA investments. You can put your money into low-risk investments, such as a savings account, a certificate of deposit (CD), or a US Treasury bill. However, you also have the choice to invest in more volatile investments like futures and options.

The only things you can't buy for an IRA are gems, non-US coins, fine art, or other collectibles.

SPOUSAL IRA

If you're not earning income but your husband is, he can open a spousal IRA in your name and contribute up to $3,000 a year to your account—the same amount he can contribute to his own IRA.

If you're working and your husband isn't, you can do the same for him. You must file a joint tax return any year either of you puts money in a spousal account.

Your family income will determine if you can select a Roth IRA. And your income—or whether the working spouse's employer offers a retirement plan—determines whether you can deduct the contribution to a traditional IRA on your tax return.

The great appeal of a spousal IRA is that you don't have to sacrifice your long-term financial security by taking time off from the workforce—whether to try something you've always wanted to do, spend time with your children, or care for older parents.

Expect the Unexpected

Knowing your finances can help you weather the unexpected.

What would you do if you lost the job that provides most of your income, or were disabled and couldn't work? What if your partner died or you were divorced and could no longer count on your husband's income? How would you handle a poor investment decision that cost you a large amount of money? What if you had elderly relatives who needed your financial help to cover their health costs?

You can't plan fully for these emergencies, but you can prepare for the unexpected by knowing exactly where you stand financially.

FOR THE RECORD

It's important to have a firm grasp of your short-and long-term living expenses. To find out how much money you need to maintain your lifestyle, you can review your checkbook, credit-card records, bank statements, loans, and mortgage payments.

Identify all the costs that are essential—food, shelter, transportation, healthcare—and total those amounts. Then figure out the percentage of those expenses that your income covers and the percentage that comes from various other sources.

While it can be a little frightening for people to realize how threatened their financial security would be if their income was suddenly cut in half or if their expenses doubled overnight, it can—and does—happen.

> If you're single, most advisers suggest that you keep up to a year's worth of funds, unless you have family who can help you financially.

INFORM YOURSELF

You should know which of your accounts are in your name alone, and which, if any, you hold jointly with your partner. You should also look at your pension plans—and your husband's pension as well, if you're married—and your retirement investments. When will you have access

to those funds? What amount can you expect them to provide?

It's a good idea to know what your health and insurance plans cover in case of an emergency, and whether you need authorization to get emergency treatment. Also be sure you know where copies of life insurance policies are and whom you must call to file a claim.

Finally, you and your partner hould both know where all your legal ocuments are, and how to access hem. That can include your keys r codes for a lock-box or safe, your ousehold computer passwords, and our PINs to all bank, retirement, nd investment accounts.

IFE'S BUMPY ROAD

Now that you have grasp on your urrent situation, you'll be eady if you

iit a bump in the road. No matter vhat you might face, having money et aside during these rocky times vill be essential.

For instance, what if the furnace n your home has to be replaced, or he roof of your house springs a major eak? Or what if you're facing a more ong-term challenge such as providing or a disabled child?

HELPFUL HINTS

While you're creating a financial plan for emergencies, it's also a good idea to do the following:

- Buy a notebook or looseleaf to organize your records
- Look for computer-based software to save your financial records electronically
- Write out a list of emergency numbers, including your financial adviser and lawyer, in case someone else has to take over your finances

EMERGENCY FUNDS

One thing you can and should do is build your own emergency fund. Financial advisers encourage people to set aside three to six months' worth of income in a readily accessible account, which you can tap into when you have unforeseen expenses. These expenses may be large, such as funding your elderly relative's healthcare or putting some extra cash into your small business. Or some might be smaller, like replacing your car's transmission or buying a new refrigerator.

You and your financial adviser can decide where it's best to park that money, whether it's in a relatively risk-free money market fund, US Treasury bills, or a savings account at your bank.

ANOTHER VIEW

Some experts argue that its better not to keep too much of your emergency money in low-risk accounts. They suggest you may want to keep your funds in a variety of investments, such as stocks, bonds, and mutual funds, since you can sell those investments if you are ever in need of emergency cash. Otherwise you risk losing too much buying power to inflation.

Avoiding Fraud

Staying alert is the best defense against fraud.

The best way to prevent fraud is to stay informed, aware, and on top of your finances. The nature of fraud is to deceive, so it's often difficult to recognize when you've gotten involved in a fraudulent situation. Unfortunately, getting out of the resulting mess can be made more difficult by the false, missing, or misleading paper trails that fraud may leave in its wake.

IDENTITY THEFT

If you have to give out your name, credit card number, or Social Security number (or you've had them stolen), others can use that information to assume your identity, spend your money, or make you liable for debts or charges. Unfortunately, almost 10% of Americans have been subject to ATM, debit, or credit card fraud, according to The Wall Street Journal.

With credit cards in particular, your cash liability is limited and relatively easy to resolve. For instance, both Visa and Mastercard have created zero-liability policies, so you're protected in cases of identity theft. But your creditors may assume you are at fault for unpaid bills until you can prove otherwise. That takes time, as does straightening out the records. And you may have to reestablish downgraded credit ratings. To prevent that, keep the following tips in mind:

- Be very cautious about giving people—even friends—your key numbers and information, since they might be less careful than you
- Don't make theft easy—choose unique PINs, and avoid using your Social Security or other easily identifiable number combinations
- Don't write PINs on cards or keep them in your wallet
- Check your credit card bills carefully to be sure you authorized all of the charges
- If you do lose your cards or codes, make sure you have a list of the relevant numbers in a secure place, along with ways to invalidate missing cards, passwords, and other important information
- Written or printed records or notes can be found by anyone, so make sure you tear up receipts before you throw them away

INTERNET FRAUD

Complaints of online fraud have been on the rise for several years. But you can escape the fraud trap by being clear about who you're working with, what you're being offered, and when and how you can get out of any quick commitments. Hard sells that demand instant action or payment should be treated with caution.

One way to ensure your safety is to read through any online pitches very carefully. If something seems too good to be true, it may very well be.

TELEMARKETING

You're probably familiar with phone calls offering you free trips, discounted magazine subscriptions, and other special offers. These calls are the most common form of **telemarketing** and they're extremely common in the US. Many telemarketing calls are completely legitimate. But according to the National Consumers League, at least 92% of Americans have received a fraudulent telemarketing call—and older women are often the targets.

How do you avoid illegal telemarketing schemes? First, try to deal only with companies you're familiar with or have done business with in the past. If you get a call from a company you don't know, ask them to send you information in the mail regarding their products or the specific offer. Before you agree to buy anything over the phone, it's a good idea to have the offer in writing.

And, perhaps most importantly, experts advise that you don't give out the following information over the phone to anyone except companies you trust, and only for necessary transactions:

- Bank account information
- Credit card numbers
- Social Security number

If you receive a telemarketing call that you suspect is fraudulent, you can report it to the Federal Trade Commission (FTC) by filing a consumer complaint form. For more information, you can call the FTC at 1-877-FTC-HELP.

YOUR FINANCIAL ADVISER

Most financial advisers want to help you achieve your goals and are willing to answer any questions you have about their advice. But some advisers may be impatient, pressuring, or simply dishonest. It's possible that they can work against you by:

- Doing unauthorized transactions
- Not executing transactions you specifically request
- Trading to increase their commissions but not your investment portfolio growth
- Making impossible promises or giving you misleading information

The best defense is to keep close tabs on your accounts to be sure you've authorized every transaction. If you have a complaint, spell it out in writing, first to your adviser and perhaps your adviser's supervisor. And always keep a copy.

NEXT STEPS
If you want to learn more about fraud and how it can affect your financial security, check out the National Consumer League's Fraud Information Center's website at www.fraud.org.

The Cost of Divorce

It's important to know what you might face during a breakup.

According to recent statistics, one in two marriages ends in divorce. So if your marriage doesn't stand the test of time, you're far from alone.

Women often bear the larger financial burden that results from divorce—regardless of who initiates the split. So knowing the cost of divorce, as well as the state of your finances, is very important.

CONSEQUENCES

The financial downside of divorce can be substantial. For starters, simply getting a divorce can cost a bundle if you hire a lawyer to represent you. But unfortunately, that's often an unavoidable cost.

After the marriage is severed, you're likely to run a separate home and be solely responsible for the mortgage or rent, insurance, utilities, and other expenses. There might be car payments, credit card debt, and other obligations to assume as well, particularly if you have children. And you continue to be responsible for any joint debts.

These costs add up to increased financial burdens for you. That means you may have to adjust your goals to fit your new circumstances.

GETTING FINANCIAL HELP

You might be tempted to economize by not turning to a professional whose fees seem high. But ultimately, good financial advisers, lawyers, and other professionals can save you money by informing you about approaches you might not have been aware of, or providing you with strategies for getting back on a solid financial track once the dust settles.

WHAT YOU OWN, WHAT YOU OWE

It's smart to keep track of your finances throughout your marriage. However, the moment you feel that your marriage is getting rocky, it's important to start putting together your own record of where you and your spouse stand financially. Make sure you have copies of:

- Recent tax returns, wills, and salary statements
- Savings, checking, brokerage, and credit card statements, and any other relevant transactions and status reports
- All insurance policies—such as life, homeowner's, disability, medical, and car
- Retirement plans or accounts, such as a 401(k), IRA, SEP, Keogh, employment pension, or privately held annuity
- Real estate documents, like ownership and occupancy certificates, mortgages, and home equity loans
- Employment benefit plans—stock options, bonuses, insurance, or guaranteed wage increases
- Appraisals and photos of valuables

It's also smart to know what pen-
ɿion and Social Security benefits
'ou're entitled to, which may include
ı portion of your husband's benefits.

The more extensive your knowl-
ɘdge of your financial situation, the
ɔetter your chances will be of mini-
nizing the cost—both emotional and
inancial—of your split. And if you
ɛnow both your own financial status
ınd your husband's, you're more likely
o get what you feel you deserve in
'our divorce settlement.

ƆIVIDING YOUR ASSETS

ƽtate laws determine much of the
ɔrocess of sharing possessions and
vealth upon divorce. Some states use
he rule of **equitable distribution**.
Ƭhat means the amount you get in your divorce settlement depends on certain factors, such as your salary when you got married, the length of your marriage, your age and your husband's age, and the expenses you might have as a custodial parent. Unfortunately for many women, it's quite common that the more affluent partner—usually the man—gets a larger share of the family assets.

If your home is in a **community property state**, then the law requires a fifty-fifty split of jointly owned property and of everything either of you earned during the marriage. However, there are often major disputes about what was earned, what is owned, and so on. So keeping records and copies of essential information can be just as valuable to you in a community property state.

Wherever you live, you can save money and headaches by trying to work out your divorce settlement outside of the courts, with a lawyer present to document and record whatever you and your ex decide.

MEDIATORS AND ARBITRATORS

Mediators and arbitrators can also help head off a trip to court. **Mediators** are facilitators who participate in your negotiations but cannot make decisions. **Arbitrators** also advise and facilitate, but they are often given the power to enforce a settlement, known as a **binding decision**, which they may outline themselves. Unfortunately, many women feel that they get short-changed when their divorce is arbitrated, and have to live with the financial consequences of that binding decision.

RESOURCES

There are websites that provide divorce advice, guidance, and other types of resources. Here are a few to check out:

www.women.com has a life and money section with financial planning hints for women going through divorce.

www.divorcenet.com has articles and columns written by divorce experts, and a state-by-state resource center.

www.divorcecentral.com has weekly expert chats, frequently asked legal questions, and various links to state laws on divorce.

Dealing with Illness

Keep your fingers on the pulse of your financial health.

Serious sickness can strike both suddenly and unexpectedly. And its effects can be devastating to your emotional health, your financial resources, and your long-term plans. But if you're prepared, it's possible to weather an illness.

HOW ILLNESS HITS

Remember that when you or someone you love gets sick or is injured seriously, the effects are emotional as well as financial. In fact, the two are often linked. Can you afford to spend hours a day tending to a sick person in your home? Are you willing to do it? Will you need help? Where can you find help and at what cost?

While there is no way to accurately predict the effects of illness, you can create a plan that gives you flexibility.

WHAT TO DO

The cost of healthcare continues to soar, so you need to be sure you can pay the bills. At the same time, whoever is ill may not be earning as much as in the past, and whoever is providing care might lose income as well. It's smart to anticipate what you cutbacks in income might be, along with the likely expenses you will face.

While it's impossible to predict what your financial situation might be it helps to consider these questions:

- If somebody got sick or hurt, where would you find money to pay the healthcare bills?
- What portion would your insurance policy cover?
- Would you have to cash in some of your investments or ask your family for help?
- Could you take time off from work to care for a loved one who has become ill?

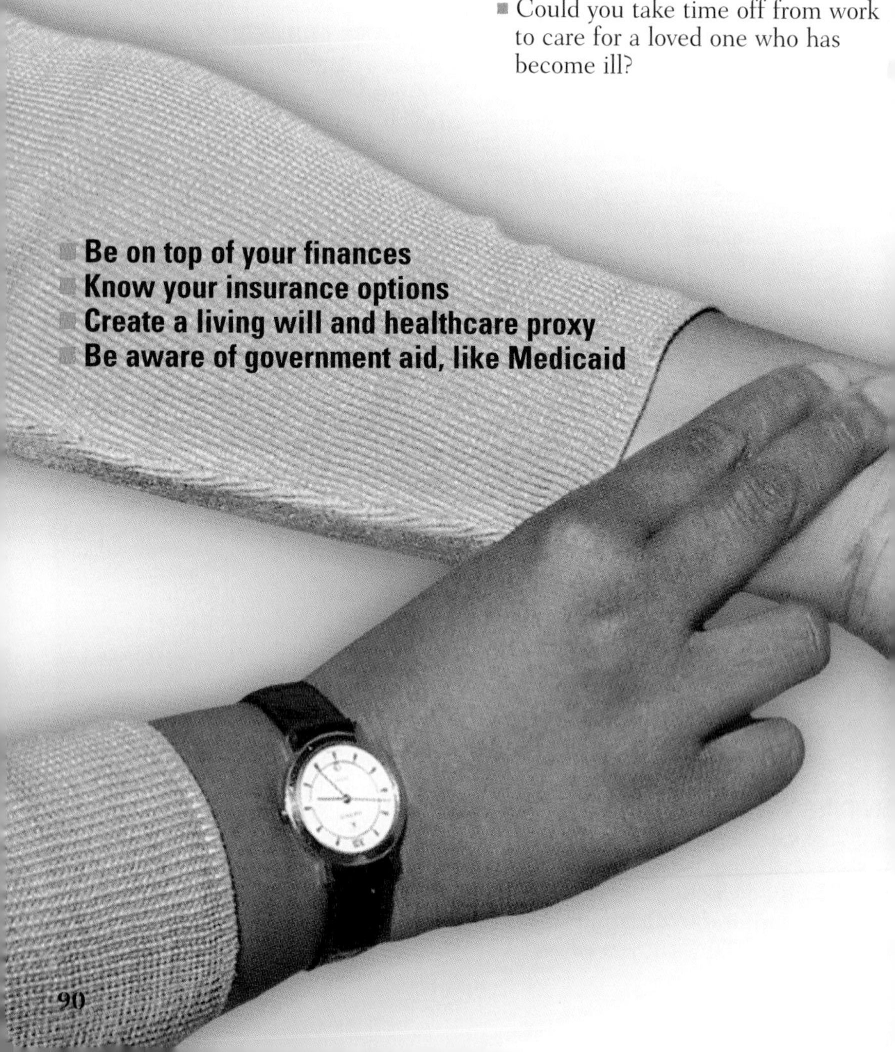

- **Be on top of your finances**
- **Know your insurance options**
- **Create a living will and healthcare proxy**
- **Be aware of government aid, like Medicaid**

ꞁNSURANCE

ꞁnother key part of planning for a ıedical emergency is to examine ·our insurance coverage.

With healthcare costs constantly rowing, it is important that you rotect yourself and your amily from the catastrophes hat all too often strike—not ıst sickness or injury, but he financial setbacks hat can follow from the ost of treating them.

For these reasons, you ıight want to look into **ong-term care insurance**, /hich typically covers some f the costs that may follow serious illness, like homecare r time in a nursing facility. You ıay be able to purchase this type f insurance through a group plan t work, but private coverage is avail- ble as well. Most experts suggest hat you purchase long-term care ısurance in your mid to late 50s, ince the costs get much higher if ou're older than that age.

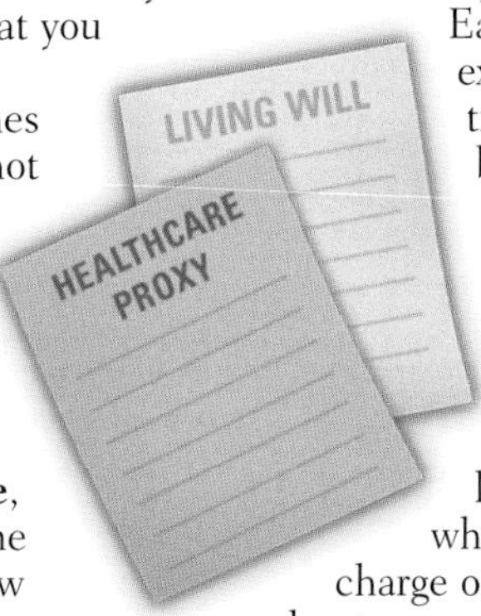

ꞁVING WILLS AND PROXIES

·e aware that sudden illness or injury ıay severely incapacitate the person strikes—so severely that the person annot take part in deciding how to andle his or her care, treatment, or rehabilitation. And the nature of such emergencies typically requires quick, decisive action.

That's why a **living will** and **healthcare proxy** can be essential. Each is a document that explains what medical treatment you want if you become ill and can't communicate your wishes directly. The living will details the procedures you want or don't want in these situations.

The healthcare proxy lets you name someone whom you want to be in charge of any further decisions about your care or treatment. Requirements and forms for these documents vary from state to state, so be sure yours are valid and up to date.

Your lawyer and healthcare providers can usually advise you on what to do in this regard. And once you have the right documents prepared, you should give them to someone who might need quick access to them—your partner, adult children, attorney, or doctor.

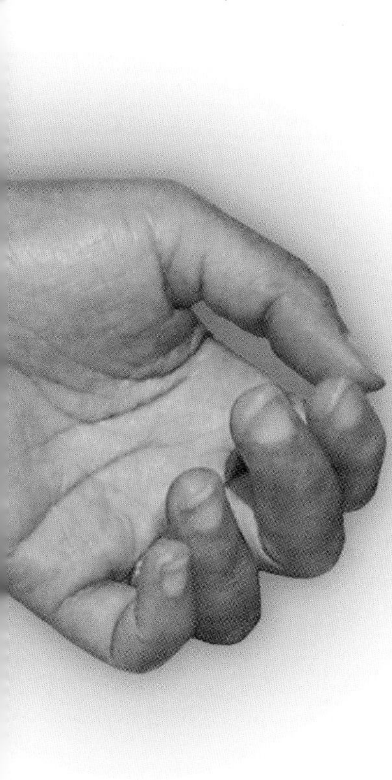

MEDICAID

If you or someone you love is very ill, you may be able to get some help from the government. **Medicaid**, which is state-run and administered by the US government's Centers for Medicare and Medicaid Services (CMS), provides insurance to low-income people who have large health-care costs, particularly nursing home bills. If you qualify, Medicaid may pay for the cost of a nursing home or adult daycare facility.

There are strict limitations concerning who qualifies for Medicaid, and the rules for eligibility vary from state to state. In general, Medicaid recipients are those people who can afford little of the costs of professional care. Medicaid then pays the rest of the bills.

You should also be aware that some nursing facilities don't readily accept Medicaid patients. And Medicaid itself only pays for nursing homes that meet specific standards.

For more information on Medicaid, you can go to the CMS website, www.cms.hhs.gov.

Coping with Death

Talking about your finances now can help keep your future secure.

Of the 13 million widowed people in the United States today, 11 million are women. Over half of women age 65 and older are widows, and the average age they become widows is 56. So chances are good that you'll have to deal with living alone at some point in your adult life. By facing this fact now, you can put yourself in a much better position to cope, should someone you love die early or unexpectedly.

Although you can't prepare yourself emotionally for the death of a partner, you can do certain things now while you're both healthy to create financial stability in the future. In preparation, the first step is to talk to your partner about your money and plans. While this will probably be a difficult conversation, it can help you to assess what you know and can handle. Being financially aware can help you avoid many roadblocks later.

KNOWING THE BASICS

If you feel uncertain about understanding your finances, now is also the time to begin to look into the basics. Schedule a meeting with your family's financial adviser, accountant, or lawyer. Your local school or library might provide seminars on money management and financial planning, and there are plenty of books, websites, and magazines that can be useful as well.

It's also possible that other members of your family will be in a position to help, should your partner die. But if they don't have the expertise you are seeking, consider a professional financial adviser who can be an impartial and unemotional guide.

DOCUMENTS

It's important to create a **will** for each partner. If you don't have them yet, it's a good idea to take care of that now. If you do have wills, make sure you and your lawyer know where they are.

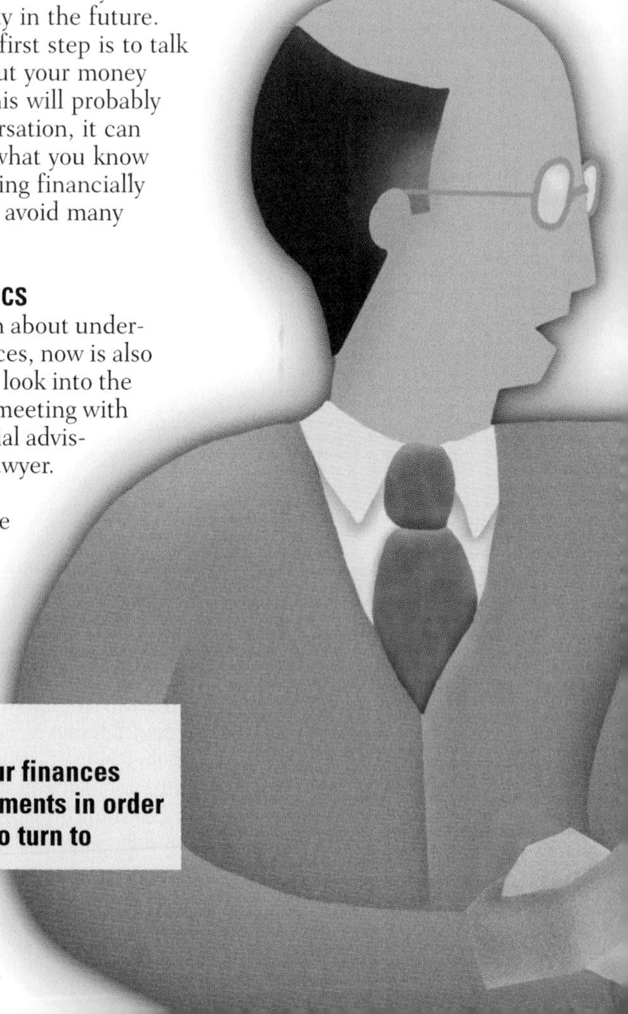

Remember to:
- **Talk about your finances**
- **Get your documents in order**
- **Know whom to turn to**

The same goes for bank account
tatements, investment balance
heets, and passwords to your major
nancial accounts. These documents
eed to be kept where you or your
artner can find them. And you
hould also decide on a location
or insurance policies, retirement or
ension plan statements, mortgage
nformation, and any other records
f substantial amounts of money
ou have or are entitled to.

AKING THE ADJUSTMENT

f you have a solid financial plan in
lace already, you can focus more of
our energy on working through your
rief than worrying about making
nds meet.

There will be several issues to
hink about in the period after your
artner has passed away. You'll need
o provide a death certificate to col-
ect from the insurance and retire-
nent plans. You must have a lawyer
ead and execute the will. You may need to change joint bank, brokerage, and mutual fund accounts into your name alone, as well as pay off your partner's bills and income taxes.

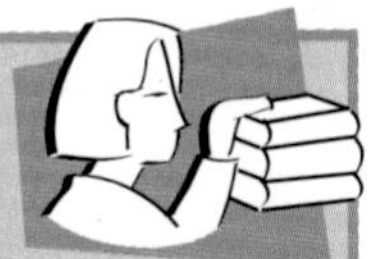

RESOURCES

Although family and friends are often a valuable outlet for expressing your grief, you may also want to investigate the many professional support groups for widows. Contact the following organizations for more information on coping with loss:

AARP Grief and Loss Programs
601 E St, NW
Washington, DC 20049
202-434-2260
www.aarp.org/griefandloss/

Grief Recovery Online
www.groww.org

GriefNet
www.griefnet.org

You'll have to contact Social Security to report the death—and confirm your status as a widow, if you were married. If you're at least 60 and were married at least nine months, or if you're younger than that but taking care of a child under 16, or a disabled child, then you are eligible for survivor benefits.

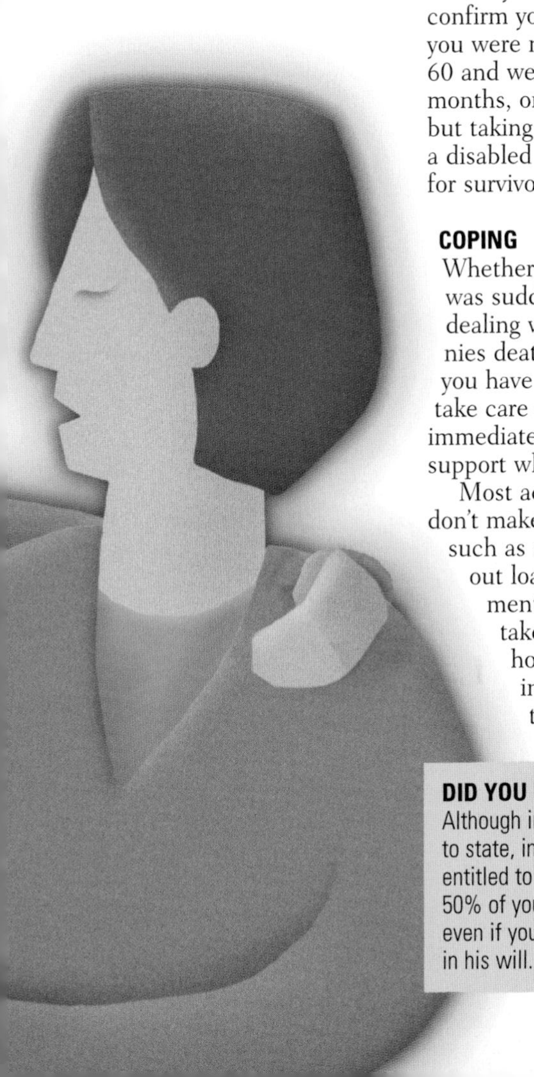

COPING

Whether the death of your loved one was sudden or somewhat expected, dealing with the grief that accompanies death is never easy. Hopefully, you have friends and family who can take care of the issues that need immediate attention—and provide support when you need it most.

Most advisers suggest that you don't make any huge decisions—such as selling your home, taking out loans, or selling off investments—immediately. Instead, take the time to figure out how you can deal with your immediate grief in a way that's best for you.

DID YOU KNOW?

Although inheritance laws vary from state to state, in general it's likely that you're entitled to receive approximately 33% to 50% of your husband's estate. That's true even if your husband didn't leave it to you in his will.

Aging Parents

Caring for parents as they age is something many adult children must face.

One in four households in the US includes someone over 50 who needs care. With people over 85 now the fastest growing segment of the US population, the Census Bureau projects that the elderly dependency ratio—the number of people aged 65 and over per 1,000 adults aged 18 to 64—will nearly double in the next fifty years. More than 20 million of these adults are likely to need assistance of some kind.

Committed to careers and children, families struggle to help their parents maintain their quality of living as they age or become ill. And today the costs—in terms of money, time, and emotions—seem higher than ever before.

And as parents live longer, not only their health but also their financial resources may fail and increase the burden on their children.

GETTING HELP

Dealing with aging parents is not easy for anyone. Financial advisers, lawyers, and other professionals can help. Turn to your financial adviser in particular to figure out cash flows, sensible tax plans, and investment decisions for your parents if they are open to your help.

Your attorney can review wills and other estate planning documents. Investigate a **durable power of atto ney**, which allows you or someone you trust to handle your parents' affairs with their permission. Otherwise, you might be faced with having them declared legally incompetent by the court. Having power of attorney can greatly speed and simplify the management of health emergencies and the like.

There are also a number of goverr ment programs that can play a crucia role in helping you care for older par ents. Medicare and Social Security provide benefits to most people over 65, and Medicaid may be available if your parents have limited assets. A parent may also qualify for veteran benefits, Supplemental Security Income (SSI), local public housing, or elder daycare assistance. Be sure

ou know what your parents might be ligible for and how to arrange for it.

Finally, geriatric care managers can e particularly useful for helping older eople handle their daily lives, such s paying bills, grocery shopping, nanaging home health support, and eporting to family members on a egular basis. That's especially helpful f you don't live near your older parent r relative.

HOICES

f you have an ailing parent, you have everal choices when it comes to his r her healthcare.

First of all, you could investigate he option of a **nursing home**, which s a living facility that provides profes-ional medical treatment. If your par-nt or parents can no longer live on heir own, and require medications, herapy, or constant medical atten-ion, then a nursing home may be a ood choice. Keep in mind, though, hat Medicare only covers the cost if our parent requires skilled medical are that only a nursing home can rovide, and only if the facility is pproved by Medicare. If your parent oesn't fit those criteria, and doesn't ualify for Medicaid, you and your amily may end up having to pay the ıll expense.

You can also look into an **assisted iving** facility if your parent needs help with daily activities, but is not necessarily in need of medical attention. Many assisted living facilities help senior citizens with laundry, housekeeping, and dressing. Some offer medical care as well, though not as extensive as nursing homes.

Finally, many people choose **homecare**, which lets you hire someone to care for your ailing parent in his or her home. According to the National Association for Home Care, over eight million people currently use homecare services, and there are over 20,000 homecare providers throughout the United States.

The main advantage to homecare is that your parent can continue to live at home, and you can be sure that he or she is receiving care when it's needed. And since Medicare provides over 40% of medical homecare expenses each year, the costs of providing homecare for a parent who needs medical attention may not have to come out of your pocket.

BEING A CAREGIVER

You may choose to be your ailing parent's primary caregiver. This decision may be a financial one, if you and your parents can't afford nursing homes or homecare. Or it may be a personal decision, depending on your relationship with your parents. However, it's important to consider the financial and emotional sacrifices you might have to make.

You might have to take a leave of absence from your job to care for a parent who's ill. And seeing the day-to-day suffering of a sick parent may not be an ideal situation for a child. So you may choose to pay for professional care for your parents, both for their well-being and yours.

Planning for Your Health

Know your choices before you pick an insurance policy.

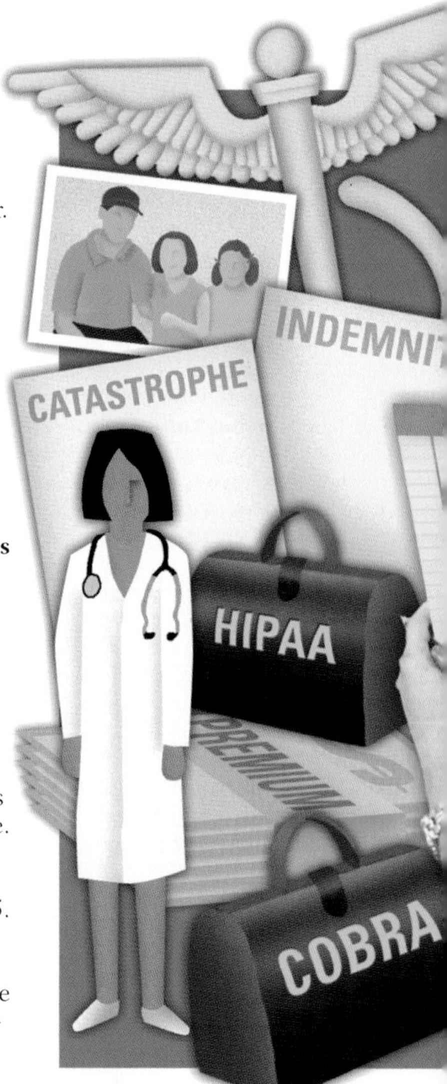

Health insurance can help you pay for the medical expenses you and your family might encounter. In general, most health insurance plans cover the cost of doctor and hospital visits. Some also include dentist visits, physical therapy, and alternative care.

HEALTH INSURANCE OPTIONS

The biggest choice in health insurance today is between **managed care** and **fee-for-service coverage.**

Managed care, which includes **Health Maintenance Organizations (HMOs)** and **Preferred Provider Organizations (PPOs)**, requires you to choose healthcare providers that participate in your plan and have agreed to accept a specific fee for their services. You choose a **primary care doctor**, often called a gatekeeper, who will refer you to specialists if your medical problem is outside his or her sphere of expertise. You pay a small charge, called a **copayment**, for each visit. The payment usually ranges from $10 to $15.

Fee-for-service medical plans, sometimes known as conventional health insurance, allow you to choose the healthcare providers and specialists you want to use. You pay your medical bills until you reach your **deductible**, which is a predetermined amount of money, usually set around $250. After you reach your plan's deductible, your insurance company begins to pick up part of the cost. Generally, you pay the bill first and then submit a claim. Your plan reimburses you a portion—typically 80%—of the amount the plan approves for the particular service you've had.

ADDITIONAL COVERAGE OPTIONS

Catastrophe plans will keep you covered in the event that your medical expenses exceed your **cap**, or the upper limit on your health insurance policy. Though health insurance caps are often $1 million to $2 million, you could reach that amount if you have a major accident, serious illness, or other unexpected medical needs.

Indemnity plans will pay a benefi amount for every day you spend in the hospital. These plans are most often used as a supplement to a broader health insurance plan, enabling you to cover nonmedical costs of your hospitalization. Indemnity plans usually contain many restrictions, and aren't typically used as your only health insurance.

PAYING FOR HEALTH INSURANCE

Buying insurance as an individual means you pay a premium on a fixed schedule, usually monthly or quarterly. You will pay significantly less if yo can participate in a group plan offere

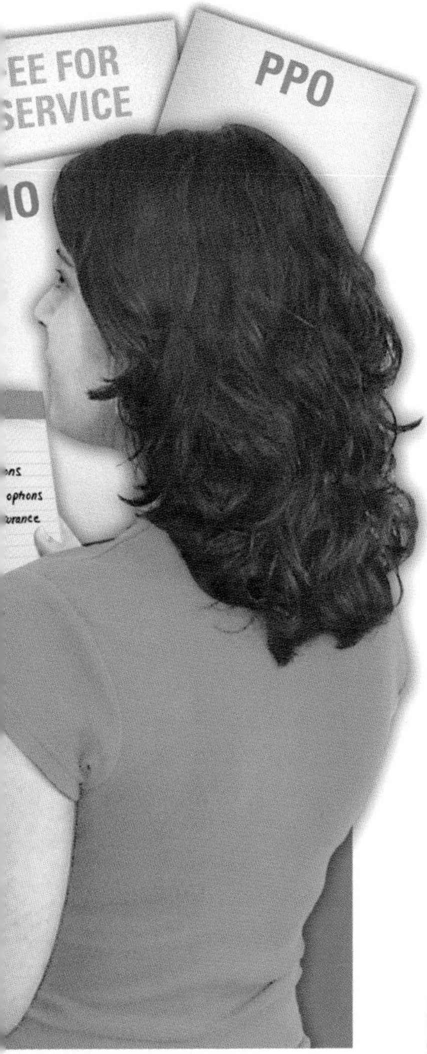

y your employer or a professional ssociation that you belong to. ome employers pick up the entire remium for your coverage.

An advantage of receiving group nsurance is that you are often ble to insure family nembers under your plan, hough you may have to ay the premium for that overage. But, as part of a roup, you may not have he flexibility to choose etween joining a managed are or fee-for-service plan. If you are narried and your husband is covered nder a separate plan, you have the ption of choosing the better plan and eclining the one with fewer benefits.

SWITCHING JOBS

If you are changing jobs, and both the old and new jobs provide health insurance options, you qualify immediately for full coverage through **portable insurance**. As of 1997, with the passage of the **Health Insurance Portability and Accountability Act (HIPAA)**, a waiting period is no longer required for **preexisting conditions**, which are medical problems treated prior to your coverage under the new plan.

The **Consolidated Omnibus Budget Reconciliation Act (COBRA)** of 1985 established another safety net for the period when you're between jobs. If you leave a job, you have the right to continue the insurance that's been provided by your employer for 18 months (29 months if you are disabled) through COBRA.

If your employer has been paying your health insurance premiums, the cost of COBRA coverage can be surprising. You are responsible for the full premium plus up to 2% in administrative costs. Usually, COBRA will be less than what you'd pay to buy insurance independently—and could save you lots of money in case of an accident or illness. COBRA coverage is also available for your adult children or your former husband for three years after they are no longer eligible for coverage on a family policy.

THE BIRTHDAY RULE

If you and your husband have separate insurance plans—for example, if you have policies from separate employers—will covering your children under both plans give them double insurance? If you do choose to cover them under both plans, the insurance companies will designate one plan as the primary plan and the other as the secondary plan. The primary pays the cost of claims first.

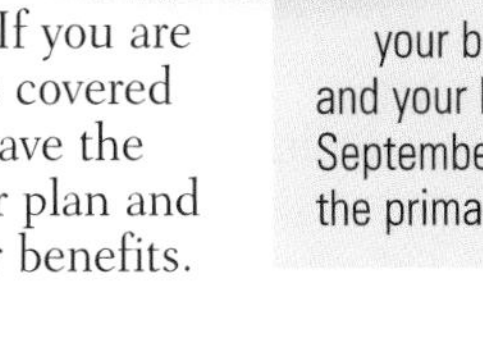

The spouse with the first birthday of the calendar year, but not necessarily the older spouse, becomes the primary plan holder. For instance, if your birthday is on January 5, 1958, and your husband's birthday is on September 10, 1955, you would hold the primary plan.

Insuring Long-Term Health

Educate yourself about the cost of extended medical care.

Over 40% of all Americans older than age 65 will spend some time in a nursing home due to a prolonged illness or disability. The expense of long-term care, which includes the cost of an extended stay in a nursing home or receiving homecare, can be overwhelming. In such cases, neither managed care health insurance, fee-for-service health insurance, nor Medicare is likely to provide financial assistance. You need specific long-term care insurance to ease the strain of paying for your future medical needs. Beyond your own needs, long-term care insurance can prove very worthwhile if you're caring for an elderly parent or a disabled child.

Like health insurance policies, long-term care policies can vary greatly in cost and coverage. While some policies may cover cognitive diseases, such as Alzheimer's or senility, many do not. You can find the policy that best suits your needs by looking closely at the various options.

HOW COVERAGE WORKS

Long-term care insurance typically pays part of the cost of a nursing home or a homecare provider. You choose the **daily benefit** of the policy, which is the maximum amount your policy will pay for each day of care you receive. Most policies allow benefits from $40 to $250 a day.

Once you qualify to receive benefits, the plan will pay that amount. You are responsible for the balance of the charges, if any.

HOW LONG WILL COVERAGE LAST?

The length of time you will receive benefits is called your **benefit period**. Insurance companies usually offer plans that can cover you for anywhere from two to five years, or for your lifetime. Keep in mind that the average length of a nursing home stay is just under three years.

Before you receive benefits, you will have to meet a **deductible**, which is a predetermined amount of money you pay for your medical bills. For long-term care insurance, this amount is measured in terms of the number of days you agree to pay on your own. Long-term care policies call this your **elimination period**. Among the most common choices are 30 or 90 days.

WHEN TO BUY

Long-term care insurance is typically a costly investment, so you want to

COST BY STATE

One factor in the cost of long-term care is location. The price of care varies according to where you live or where you plan to retire. For example, in Louisiana the average cost of care is $90 a day, but in Alaska you could pay as much as $413 a day. That means one person could face anywhere from $82,000 to $375,000 for a typical nursing home stay of two and a half years.

CHOOSING THE RIGHT TIME

Timing is an important issue when you're buying long-term care insurance. The following chart shows how quickly the yearly premiums and total costs of long-term care insurance escalate as you get older.

AGE AT PURCHASE	YEARLY PREMIUM		YEARS UNTIL AGE 84		TOTAL COST
45	$746	x	39	=	$29,094
50	$945	x	34	=	$32,130
55	$1,255	x	29	=	$36,395
60	$1,719	x	24	=	$41,256
65	$2,580	x	19	=	$49,020
70	$3,723	x	14	=	$52,122
75	$6,734	x	9	=	$60,606

be sure that you weigh the cost of premiums over an extended period versus the chance that you'll eventually need this type of insurance.

Buying coverage too young has certain risks. Due to inflation, the cost of living and the cost of healthcare go up each year. Assuming a 5% increase in the cost of care per year, a stay in a nursing home 30 years from now could cost more than four times as much as it does today. Long-term care policies with an inflation protection rider will increase the amount of your daily benefit each year.

Most experts agree that the best time to buy long-term care insurance is between the ages of 55 and 60. That way, you avoid the extremely high premiums you would pay if you waited until you were older, and reduce the consequences of inflation that would result from buying when you are younger.

INFORMATION PARTNERSHIPS

California, Connecticut, New York, Indiana, Illinois, and Washington have established partnerships with insurance companies. These partnerships meet special Medicaid requirements to give you more control over your healthcare. Having this type of partnership allows you to keep a portion of your assets. For example, if you buy a policy that will eventually cover $100,000 in long-term care costs, but your bills exceed that amount, then you can apply for Medicaid assistance and still protect $100,000 of your total assets.

These partnerships also distribute free written material on long-term care insurance and answer specific questions over the phone. For more information or to find out if you live in a partnership state, contact your state's department of health or your financial planner to talk about participating in a partnership program.

HELPFUL HINTS

To understand long-term care, it helps to learn the lingo.

- **Benefit amount**—How much your policy pays for each day of care that you receive
- **Benefit period**—The length of time you receive insurance payments for your care
- **Elimination period**—The amount of time you have to wait before you can begin receiving benefits

Disability Insurance

You can replace a part of your salary while you're unable to work.

How would you support yourself if you couldn't work? Living with a disability can increase your daily expenses, because you're likely to have more medical costs. Since most employer health plans replace only a portion of your salary if you become disabled, making ends meet can be a challenge. Whether you are responsible for a family or only yourself, disability insurance is a good way to ensure that those who depend on your income won't be at financial risk.

DEFINING DISABILITY

What qualifies as a disability? Insurance companies create their disability policies based on their definitions of disability, but these definitions can vary drastically. Some require you to be under a doctor's continuing care and unable to do work in your own occupation. Others say you're disabled only if you are unable to do any job that you could qualify for.

For example, if you were a computer programmer and lost the ability to type, you would qualify under the first definition but not the second. Many policies will not cover disabilities caused by suicide attempts, drug abuse, war, or attempts to commit a crime. Preexisting conditions are also frequently excluded.

COSTS AND BENEFITS

The cost of disability insurance depends on three factors: the amount of money you receive each month during the period of disability, the amount of time the payments last, and the waiting period between the time you become disabled and when the benefits begin.

The most common periods of coverage are two years, five years, and until age 65. The longer the coverage and the shorter the waiting period, the more expensive the insurance. The usual waiting time is 90 days, but 30-day and 180-day periods are also generally available.

Like health insurance, group disability plans are significantly cheaper than individual coverage. And if you're married, some group plans will allow your husband to purchase coverage as well. That can be especially helpful if he is not able to participate in a group coverage plan on his own.

REPLACEMENT SALARY

Most disability policies pay a percentage of your basic monthly salary, up to a specific **cap**, or limit. You might, for example, receive 60% of your salary each month, with a payment cap of $10,000. So if your monthly salary were $5,000, your disability check would be 60% of that amount, or $3,000. Your salary would have to exceed $200,000 a year to reach your payment cap.

If you don't know exactly how much money you need from your insurance policy, you can calculate your monthly spending to come up with a reasonable figure. You can then use that information to help choose the disability plan that will allow you to support yourself.

HOW TO CALCULATE YOUR DISABILITY NEEDS

Add up your regular expenses using the following list of monthly costs:

- Mortgage or rent (with property tax)
- Food
- Clothing
- Medical expenses
- Car payments
- Credit card payments
- Bank loans
- Utilities
- Home, car, health, and life insurance
- Investments and monthly savings

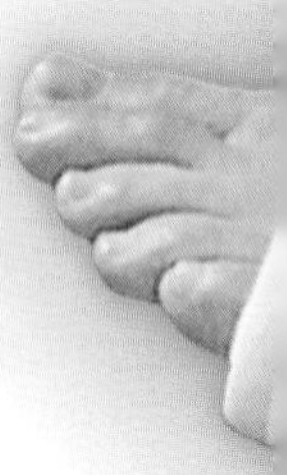

From that total, subtract any additional money you might receive each month, perhaps from your husband's ncome or your investments. The esult is the amount of money you need from a disability plan.

If the amount you calculate is greater than your current income, nsurance won't provide it. Most disability policies will pay only a percentage of your basic monthly salary.

COVERAGE QUESTIONS

There are a few important elements o consider when you compare lisability insurance policies.

Renewability. If you decide to keep your disability insurance longer han initially planned, you need to make sure that it's renewable. Many plans allow you to maintain coverage up to age 65, as long as the premium payments are up to date.

Cost of living adjustments (COLA). Many salaries increase when the cost of living increases. Your disability insurance should do the same. Some policies provide he option of buying cost-of-living protection so that you are eligible or increased benefits.

Waivers of premium. It's a good idea to choose a policy that ncludes a waiver of premium, which allows you to stop paying premium payments when you are collecting benefits.

Residual or partial disability. If you are only partially disabled and you have residual coverage, you will be able to collect a portion of your benefits. For example, if your salary drops 50% because of your disability, you would be able to collect 50% of he benefits.

HELPFUL HINTS

Social Security may not be enough to cover you in difficult times. Qualifying for disability benefits through Social Security can be difficult because of the rigorous standards used to define disability. For example, you must be disabled for more than five months to apply, and be unable to earn more than $800 a month—or be terminally ill—to be eligible.

ARE DISABILITY PAYMENTS TAXABLE?

If you pay for your own disability insurance, it's not taxable income. But if your employer pays the premiums, the payments are taxable when you receive them.

Property Insurance

Protect yourself from threats to your home.

Your home is an investment, one of the largest you'll ever make. Having property insurance, also called **homeowner's insurance**, means that your financial security will remain intact even if you must replace or significantly repair your house or belongings. In a sense, property insurance assures that your family will always have their home.

WHAT MAY BE COVERED

Homeowner's insurance has different levels of policies, labeled H01 to H08, to cover different amounts of personal property. The most limited policies, labeled H01, provide payment only when your house is damaged by an explicit list of **perils**, usually fire, wind, hail, and others. With higher levels of coverage, you can obtain insurance on all of your belongings to protect against damage or theft. In addition, you may choose to cover your liability in case someone is injured on your property.

Basic policies rarely cover common disasters, including earthquakes and floods. These threats must be covered by their own specific policies or by special **riders**, or amendments to your policy purchased individually.

You may also have the option to purchase **loss of use** coverage, which provides for your family's housing if you are unable to occupy your home for a period of time because of damages covered by your insurance policy.

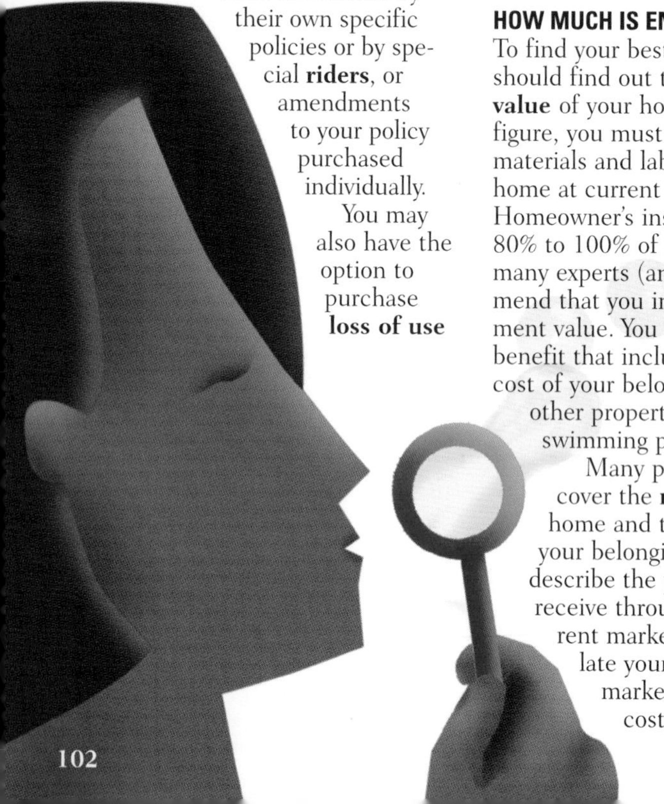

PREMIUM VS. DEDUCTIBLE

Like other forms of insurance, property insurance charges you annual payments, called **premiums**. In this case, too, you agree to pay a **deductible**, which is the amount of your loss that you are responsible for before insurance coverage kicks in. Larger deductibles make for smaller premiums, but also for higher costs at the time you have a loss.

You may be eligible for reduced premiums. Groups of employees or alumni, for example, may be able to negotiate attractive rates. Senior citizens also generally enjoy a discount. And careful planning can significantly cut your bills. Many insurance providers offer discounts if you hold more than one kind of policy (your property and automobile, for example) with them, and if you maintain your affiliation for a long time.

HOW MUCH IS ENOUGH?

To find your best premium rate, you should find out the **replacement value** of your home. To calculate this figure, you must research the cost of materials and labor to replace your home at current market prices. Homeowner's insurance will cover 80% to 100% of this figure, although many experts (and insurers) recommend that you insure the full replacement value. You may also choose a benefit that includes the replacement cost of your belongings and of any other property, like toolsheds or swimming pools.

Many providers prefer to cover the **market value** of your home and the **cash value** of your belongings. Both figures describe the price you would receive through sale in the current market, and both miscalculate your coverage. Home market value includes the cost of your land, which

ısurance can shield you from ·otential disasters.

arely needs insurance but inflates ·our premiums. And the cash value f most appliances depreciates over ime. Getting a new refrigerator, for xample, costs much more than you ·ould get from selling your old one.

While the privilege of replace-nent-cost coverage may come at a ·rice, it protects you from the volatili-y of real estate markets and, to some egree, the pressure of inflation.

ENTAL AND CONDO HOUSING

Most insurance companies offer enter's insurance as a standard policy. .evels of coverage are similar to those f homeowner's insurance, but you ormally don't need to cover any part f the building. Instead, renters may hoose to insure their belongings or over their personal liability in case hey are considered at fault for other ·eople's injuries.

Many insurance companies now lso offer specific insurance for those vho own condominiums or co-ops. n this case, levels of protection are imilar to those offered to renters, but ou can purchase additional coverage ɔ include the unit walls, floors, and eilings. The owner association should till keep a separate policy to cover he external walls of the building.

WHEN DISASTER STRIKES

It's much easier to file a claim if you've kept good records all along. Save a room-by-room inventory of valuable property, including purchase price and date, manufacturer and vendor, serial number if applicable, and even receipts and photographs when possible. A video of your belongings and home is an even better supplemental record. If harm occurs, photograph the damage as soon as it is safe to do so. The more reliably you can show your losses, the easier it will be to gain compensation.

NEXT STEPS

There are several features that can qualify your home for a reduced "low-risk" premium. Be sure to tell your insurance company about:

- Houses less than five years old
- Durable construction, such as bedrock foundations and plaster walls
- Location—near a fire station or hydrant
- Geographical region, especially inland and away from severe-weather zones
- Installed features, such as intrusion and smoke alarms

Life Insurance

Buying life insurance now will protect your loved ones in the future.

Life insurance is a way to provide financial security for the dependents who outlive you. Without that protection, the loss of your contribution could devastate your household. That's true even if you don't work outside the home, because the cost of hired childcare and home maintenance could easily equal the loss of a supplemental income.

With life insurance, you can cover yourself and your loved ones, and can rest assured that your family will be financially taken care of after you die.

HOW IT WORKS

A life insurance policy ensures that when you die, your **beneficiary** (a person or people you name) receives a specified lump sum of money, known as the **death benefit**. You purchase your policy through your annual **premiums**. These premiums can usually be made on a flexible schedule, and you are required to make payments in order to keep your existing coverage in force.

TERM INSURANCE

Term insurance covers you for a specific span of time, often 1 to 20 years. If you die in that period, your beneficiaries receive the **face value** of the policy, known as a death benefit. The insurance coverage ends when the term ends, unless you choose to renew your policy. For instance, a ten-year term contract will terminate after ten years if you don't renew it.

While term insurance is almost always reasonably priced, be aware that your premium might increase. Your payments can change on three schedules:

Annual renewable policies are continued each year by paying another premium. Since insurance costs increase with age, these premiums rise steadily over time under this plan.

Level term policies fix the premium for a specified term, usually five or ten years. Policies generally cost less in total, although the earliest payments exceed those of an annually renewable policy.

Decreasing term policies charge small level premiums and provide benefits that decrease with time. They provide the most coverage in the short term.

VHAT IT COVERS

ife insurance benefits cover the xpense of final arrangements and our outstanding financial responsibil-ies. Your beneficiary may invest the est to produce long-term income.

VHICH TO CHOOSE

erm insurance is generally cost effec-ve during your early years of coverage. But it can become more costly as you get older, especially if you become ill or need medical attention.

Cash value products offer many payment options, access to cash, and life-long protection. However, premi-ums tend to be higher than term insurance costs.

Before you choose the type of cov-erage you want, you might want to consult a qualified insurance adviser who can help you figure out what your needs and goals are.

ASH VALUE INSURANCE

ash value policies combine insurance vith cash accumulation. Part of your premi-m is set aside in a tax-deferred account eld by the insurer and called a **cash ccumulation**. You can borrow from the ccount, but any amount you don't repay efore your death is subtracted from your eath benefit.

The three main types of cash value poli-es differ in the premium, the benefit, and e way the cash value accumulates.

Whole life insurance has a fixed premi-m, paid for a specified amount of time, nd the policy covers you until your death. he insurers control the cash value.

Universal life insurance offers flexibility. ou can use part of your cash reserve to ary your premium, and you can change e death benefit. Policies also often guar-ntee a rate of return on your cash value, ut these privileges mean high commis-ons and fees.

Variable life policies let you put a por-on of your premium in one of the plan's vestment packages. The death benefit epends on how well the investments ou've chosen are performing. For that rea-on, variable life policies are normally the skiest form of insurance. They also usually ome with the highest sales charges.

If you end your policy, you get back the **ash surrender value**. Any amount eater than the total you paid in premiums considered taxable income before you each $59\frac{1}{2}$.

INCOME TAX ISSUES

Death benefits are tax free to recipi-ents. But, if you own the policy on your own life, the death benefit is included in your estate when you die. If your estate is large enough to be subject to federal estate taxes, you may choose to have someone else—a husband or partner, perhaps—own your policy. That transfer of owner-ship removes the asset from your estate after three years.

RISK AND COST

Insurance companies set their premi-ums based on life expectancy, and describe young and healthy applicants as **preferred risks**. Since these people are more likely to pay more annual premiums before the insurer has to pay a death benefit, they enjoy lower costs than higher-risk applicants.

LIVING BENEFITS

You can purchase a **living benefits** clause to provide you with access to some portion of your death benefit during an extended illness or a cata-strophic disability. The rest of the benefit remains intact for your benefici-ary to eventually cover your final expenses.

The Tax Seasons

Income taxes aren't just a springtime hassle.

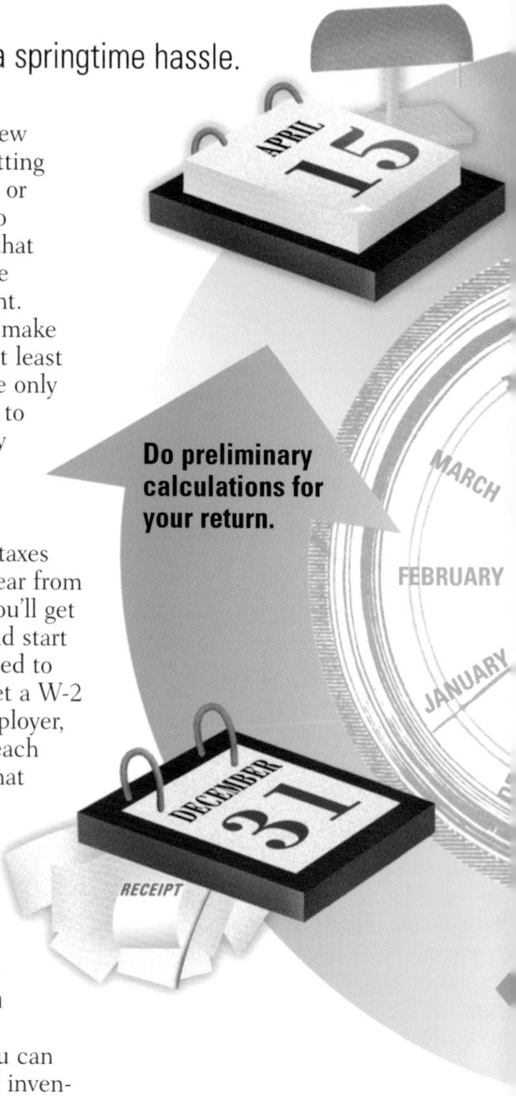

Whether you're buying a new home, changing jobs, getting promoted, starting a business, or raising children, you'll run into income tax implications. But that doesn't always mean you'll owe more to the federal government.

If you plan ahead, you can make decisions that will reduce or at least postpone the tax you owe. The only catch is that you usually need to get everything taken care of by December 31.

WINTER/SPRING

As anyone who has ever filed taxes knows, tax season is in high gear from January to April. In January, you'll get a tax package from the IRS and start receiving the documents needed to complete your return. You'll get a W-2 wage statement from your employer, as well as a Form 1099 from each bank or financial institution that paid you interest, from any brokerage firm where you have earnings or losses, and from the corporations and mutual funds in which you own shares. As you get these documents, it's smart to file them in a place where you can find them easily.

As April 15 approaches, you can use the information from your inventory to do some initial tax calculations. That will let you predict whether you're going to get a refund or will owe money. And remember that the earlier you file your return, the sooner you receive a refund, if you're owed one.

April 15 is also your last opportunit to contribute to your Individual Retirement Account (IRA) for the previous year. After that, the contribu tions you make will count toward the next year. Contributions to Simplified Employee Pensions (SEPs) and Keog plans are also due by April 15, unless you have an approved filing extension

DID YOU KNOW?

As you think about your yearlong tax concerns, it's smart to keep the following things in mind.

Try not to make investment decisions just to escape taxes. For instance, just because a municipal bond pays tax-free interest doesn't mean it will help you meet your financial goals.

Be sure you understand the difference between tax-deferred and tax-exempt investments. **Tax deferred** means that you postpone paying taxes on investment earnings until you withdraw them, while **tax exempt** means you will not owe federal tax on the earnings.

And finally, don't overlook any tax saving you're entitled to.

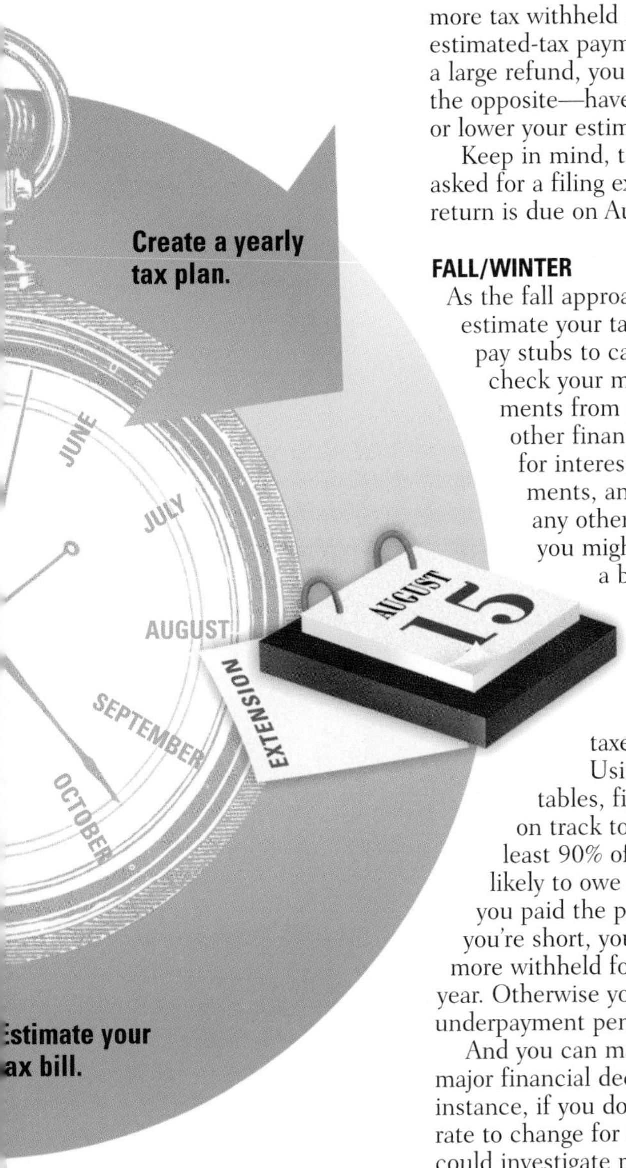

SPRING/SUMMER

After you file your return, it's time to review what you paid and to evaluate your long-term tax goals.

Financial advisers suggest that you use your most recent tax return as a starting point to create a yearly tax plan. If you had high taxes on last year's return, you might want to consider what you could do to ease the tax strain for the current year. It's also a good way to check that you're taking advantage of all the deductions and credits for which you qualify.

If you owed more than a few hundred dollars, you can consider having more tax withheld or increasing your estimated-tax payments. Or if you got a large refund, you might want to do the opposite—have less tax withheld or lower your estimated-tax payments.

Keep in mind, too, that if you asked for a filing extension, your return is due on August 15.

FALL/WINTER

As the fall approaches, you should estimate your tax bill. Use your pay stubs to calculate your salary, check your most recent statements from your bank and other financial institutions for interest and dividend payments, and try to anticipate any other taxable income you might receive, such as a bonus or commissions. Then figure out how much has been withheld and any estimated taxes you've paid. Using last year's tax tables, figure out if you're on track to have prepaid at least 90% of the tax you're likely to owe or 100% of what you paid the previous year. If you're short, you may want to have more withheld for the rest of the year. Otherwise you may face an underpayment penalty.

And you can make some other major financial decisions. For instance, if you don't expect your tax rate to change for the next year, you could investigate postponing some of the income you expect until after the first of the year. That lets you postpone the tax on it as well. Or you might try to bunch certain expenses, such as medical bills that aren't covered by insurance, into one year so they total enough to deduct.

If you know that you have large capital gains, you may want to sell off some investments at a loss to offset those gains.

INCOME TAX HISTORY

Income taxes were first introduced by the US government in 1862 to finance the Civil War. They were repealed in 1872, but eventually reenacted under the 16th Amendment of the Constitution in 1913.

Getting Tax Help

When it comes to taxes, it never hurts to get expert help.

As most Americans know, filing a tax return can be time consuming and frustrating. It's possible to miss out on major tax benefits and pay more than you actually owe, or make yourself vulnerable to an audit.

However, you can turn to tax professionals, published guides, the Internal Revenue Service (IRS), and computer programs to ease your stress and get sound tax advice.

THE PROFESSIONALS

You may want to ease the complexity of your tax return by seeking out professional tax help. And since almost half of all taxpayers turn to a professional tax preparer or accountant to help with their tax return, you won't be alone if you decide to seek assistance. Professionals can find strategies to get the most from your tax return, as well as simplify the sometimes confusing language of the IRS's instructions.

In addition to paid professionals, there are also a number of volunteer organizations that can offer advice and counsel during tax preparation.

RESOURCES

Despite the negative feelings some people have toward the Internal Revenue Service, there are many ways the IRS can help you. For instance, you can get free information on at least 140 topics from **Tele-Tax**, the IRS's toll-free information service. If you call 800-829-4477, you can choose from a list of topics that could be helpful as you prepare your tax return.

If you want to read more about specific tax subjects, you can contact the IRS to receive their printed publications. For more information, contact the IRS by phone at 800-829-3676 or go to their website, www.irs.gov.

And if you are hearing impaired or have vision problems, you can get tax assistance in person at most IRS offices. Check out the IRS website to find an office near you.

COME PREPARED

You want to make sure that the professional you choose has the credentials you're looking for. So start by asking your potential tax preparer some or all of the following:

- Are tax preparations and returns a major part of your business?
- What are your professional credentials in this field?
- How much experience do you have?
- Have you worked with clients who have similar tax situations to mine?
- Are you available to answer tax questions throughout the year?
- Would you identify yourself as conservative or aggressive when it comes to interpreting tax laws?
- What do you charge for your usual services?
- What help can you provide in the event of an audit?

TYPES OF TAX PROFESSIONALS

When you look for professional help, consider the following tax experts:

AGENT
- Licensed by the IRS
- Certified by the Treasury Department
- Able to represent you during an audit or appeal
- Typically charges a modest amount for service

TAX PREPARATION SERVICE
- Prepares returns for middle-income people
- Can join you at audits, but can't represent you
- Usually charges a modest amount for service

CERTIFIED PUBLIC ACCOUNTANT (CPA)
- Usually hired by executives or professionals
- Often works year round with clients
- Can represent you during audits
- Charges by the hour

ATTORNEY SPECIALIZING IN TAX LAW
- Acts as adviser, rather than preparer
- Expert in tax interpretation and litigation
- Can represent you before the IRS and in court
- Charges by the hour

ON YOUR OWN

If you don't want to hire a professional, or you can't fit it into your yearly budget, there are still many ways to get advice and instructions on filing your tax return. If you go to your local bookstore, you'll probably find an entire section devoted to tax guides and instruction manuals. You can choose from books published by tax companies, like Ernst and Young or H&R Block, or opt for a book geared toward a specific demographic, like single women or married couples. When you choose a book, look for one that is updated yearly and provides clear explanations of tax topics.

You can also purchase a computer program for calculating your own tax return. It can help you figure out your taxes and avoid math miscalculations. A typical program usually costs under $40. Microsoft, Quicken, and Kiplinger's are among the many companies that offer software.

In addition, there are a number of websites that offer free advice and guidance on taxes. For general information, you can go to www.ustreas.gov, www.moneycentral.msn.com/tax/home.asp, or www.quicken.com/taxes/. If you're looking for websites that address women-specific tax issues, you can check out www.womenswire.com, www.ivillagemoneylife.com, or www.ka-ching.com.

Tax Rates

The one drawback to earning more is that you pay income tax at a higher rate.

Federal income taxes in the US are progressive. That means that as you earn more, you pay a higher percentage of your income in tax.

Each rate applies to a different range of income, known as a **tax bracket**. The portion of your income that falls into a particular bracket is taxed at the rate for that bracket. For example, if your taxable income were high enough, you might pay at three of the six possible rates or even at all six.

The highest rate at which you pay is known as your **marginal tax rate**. But your effective, or average, tax rate is lower than your marginal rate if your income falls into more than one bracket.

FILING STATUS

It's not just how much you earn that determines the rate at which you owe income tax. Your **filing status**, or your identity as a taxpayer, also matters.

You choose one status from the five Congress has identified: single, married filing jointly, married filing separately, head of household, or qualifying widow with dependent child. But you must choose the one that describes you accurately as far as the IRS is concerned. For example, long-time partners who are not legally married may not file a joint return. And a widow who lives alone and has no dependent children must file as a single taxpayer, even if she was married for 50 years.

STATUS QUESTIONS

Choosing one filing status over another may save you money. For example, a head of household pays less tax on the same amount of income than a single filer does. The same is true of a married couple filing a joint return.

If you're not sure which filing status to use, you can read the descriptions in IRS Publication 17 or consult your tax adviser. If you have a choice about whether to file a joint or separate return, as married couples do, you can calculate what you owe each way and choose the one that saves you money.

Remember, though, that if you file separate returns, you may not qualify for certain other tax-saving options. For example, if you're married but file a separate return, you're not eligible to roll over a traditional IRA to a Roth IRA. Or, if you're married and pay someone to watch your children, you can take the dependent-care credit only if you file a joint return.

If you discover these limitations after the fact, you may be able to file an amended return, changing your filing status from filing separately to filing jointly. But you must do it within three years.

DEPENDENT ISSUES

If you support someone—or provide at least half of his or her support—you may be able to name that person as a dependent on your tax return. But there are some fairly strict rules about who qualifies. A dependent has to:

- Be related to you or live in your home for the entire tax year
- Be a resident or citizen of the US, Mexico, or Canada for at least part of the tax year
- Not file a joint return for the tax year with anyone

- Have less income than the limit set by Congress unless he or she is your child and younger than 19 (or a full-time student and younger than 24)

If you're divorced or separated, there are special rules for determining who claims the children as dependents. That's also true if you share the expense of supporting your parents with your siblings. Check with the IRS or your tax adviser for more detailed explanations.

CHILDREN WITH INCOME

If you have children who earn income or receive interest and dividends over the limit that Congress sets for the year, you'll have to report that income and pay the tax that's due.

If your child is younger than 14, you can file Form 8814 with your own return. Children younger than 14 owe tax at your rate, but children older than 14 owe at their own, usually lower, rate.

ALTERNATIVE MINIMUM TAX

If you have tax-sheltered income—from municipal bond interest or as a result of large charitable gifts, for example—you may be subject to the **alternative minimum tax (AMT)**. This method of calculating what you owe was instituted to ensure that wealthy taxpayers weren't able to escape income tax. But, by 2007, it will affect up to nine million taxpayers and account for almost one third of what the IRS collects. If you're vulnerable to the AMT, it may be smart to get the help of a tax adviser.

There are six federal income tax brackets. The lowest rate is 10% and the highest is 35%.

Tax Withholding

Your taxes keep the government running.

Imagine how hard it would be to manage your household if you were paid just once a year. The federal government would find itself in the same situation if you—and every taxpayer—paid your tax bill on the day you file your tax return. So to ensure a steady stream of income throughout the year, the government requires your employer to **withhold** a percentage of what you earn from each paycheck and deposit it with the government.

If you're not employed, or if you have lots of income from investments or other sources, you must estimate the amount of tax you'll owe and pay it in installments during the year.

WHAT'S WITHHELD

The government requires withholding on many types of income:

- Tips and commissions
- Many job perks, like a company car
- Sick, vacation, and severance pay
- Bonuses, including retirement bonuses
- Some retirement income, including pension, annuity, and some IRA payments
- Gambling winnings

HOW WITHHOLDING WORKS

Your employer is responsible for withholding the tax you owe, but you're responsible for providing the information your employer uses to calculate the correct amount. You do that by filling out the IRS Form W-4, which your employer will give you when you start a new job. Ideally, the amount that's withheld will equal what you owe when you figure your tax bill, give or take a few dollars.

You report your filing status on the W-4 by choosing either single, married filing jointly, or one of the other options. You list the number of allowances you are claiming, usually based on the number of dependents you have, and other factors, such as a second job, that will influence the amount of tax you'll owe. You can estimate the number of allowances by using the worksheets that come with the W-4. But you'll find it helps to have your most recent tax return and the stub of your most recent paycheck handy to get it right.

The IRS can charge you a penalty if you've had too little withheld, which they can detect if you owe

The federal government is fueled by two tax sources:

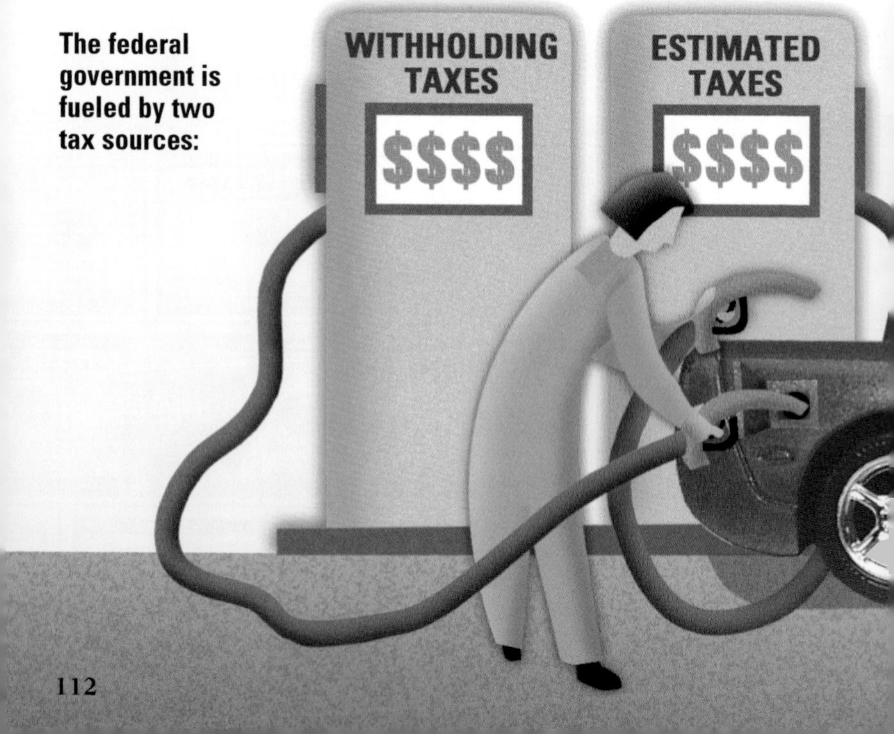

a substantial amount when you file your return. And there are more serious consequences if you knowingly give false information to reduce your withholding.

UPDATING YOUR W-4

Your employer probably won't ask you to update your W-4 after you've been on the job, but will plug in the new information you provide.

It's a good idea to review what you're having withheld from time to time, especially if you owe a substantial amount when you file your return or if you get a big refund. Any major change in your life—having a child, buying a new home, losing a dependent, getting a raise—will affect your taxes.

The more allowances you claim, the smaller the amount that will be withheld. So if you're in a situation that's likely to decrease your taxes—filing as a single head of household or jointly as a married couple, paying mortgage interest and real estate taxes, or qualifying for childcare credits—you can increase your allowances.

Or, if you have more than one job, your income is high enough to limit deductions and exemptions, or you have substantial investment earnings, you may want to decrease the number of allowances you could take to increase what's being withheld.

ESTIMATED TAXES

If you must pay estimated taxes, you use Form 1040-ES to calculate what you owe. That amount is due on a quarterly schedule, in April, June, September, and January. You can choose to pay off your whole bill at any time. But if you pay less than you owe in any quarter, you may owe a penalty, even if you pay the difference later in the year.

Unless your income for the year is fairly predictable, as it may be if you're collecting Social Security or interest on a certificate of deposit, it's probably wise to work with a tax adviser to do your calculations.

A BAD WAY TO SAVE

Many people increase their withholding to get a big refund in the spring. That's the money they use for vacation or some other luxury. But using withholding as a savings plan is like giving the government an interest-free loan, or the equivalent of hiding money in your mattress. What you get back is what you put in.

If you're afraid you won't save regularly on your own, ask whether your employer will deduct money from your paycheck and deposit it directly in a mutual fund or other investment account you've chosen. Or you can have part of your check directly deposited in a checking account and the rest in a savings account.

ESTIMATED TAXES APPLY

The government expects you to pay estimated taxes on:

- Self-employment wages
- Personal contract income
- Substantial investment income
- Unemployment benefits
- Alimony
- Some monetary awards

Income and Adjustments

Your tax return tests your math, reading, and comprehension skills.

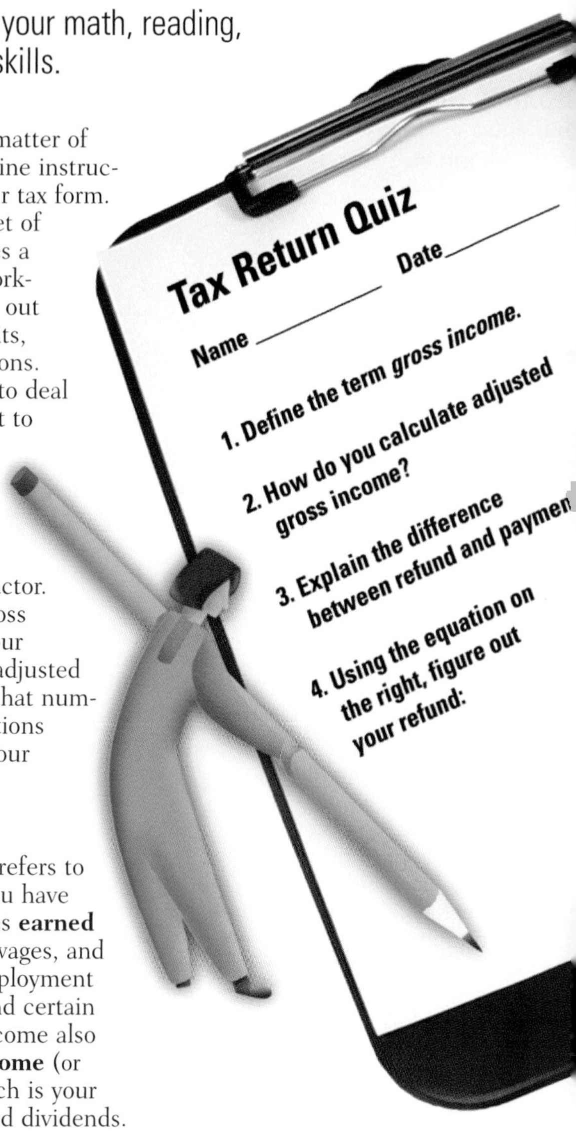

Filing a tax return is a matter of following the line-by-line instructions that come with your tax form. Each form has its own set of instructions, and includes a number of charts and worksheets to help you figure out if you're eligible for credits, deductions, and exemptions.

But before you begin to deal with a tax form, it's smart to understand the ins and outs of your yearly income. The first lesson to learn is that taxes are figured by reducing your income, factor by factor.

You start with your gross income, then subtract your adjustments to get your adjusted gross income, and from that number subtract your exemptions and deductions to find your taxable income.

GROSS INCOME

The term **gross income** refers to all the taxable income you have in one year. That includes **earned income**, such as salary, wages, and tips, plus sick pay, unemployment wages, strike benefits, and certain fringe benefits. Gross income also includes **investment income** (or **unearned income**), which is your capital gains, interest, and dividends.

If you have farm income, rents, retirement and Social Security payments, and gambling earnings, they all might be included in your gross income as well.

SPECIAL CONSIDERATIONS

If you lose your job, you'll still be taxed on the **unemployment income** you receive. At the end of January, you'll receive a Form 1099-G, which shows your unemployment income for the previous year.

Tips are also taxable income. You have to pay taxes if your employer doesn't withhold on your tips.

Calculating your tips is not an easy task, unless you keep very detailed records of the amounts you receive. The IRS projects the estimate you're likely to receive based on the type of job you have, and expects you to report and pay tax on at least that amount. If you keep careful records and calculate a smaller total than the one the IRS expects, you can dispute the IRS assumptions.

KNOWING YOUR AGI

Once you've figured out your annual gross income, you'll need to calculate your **adjusted gross income**, or **AGI**. You do that by subtracting adjustments, or certain amounts you have spent, from your gross income. The

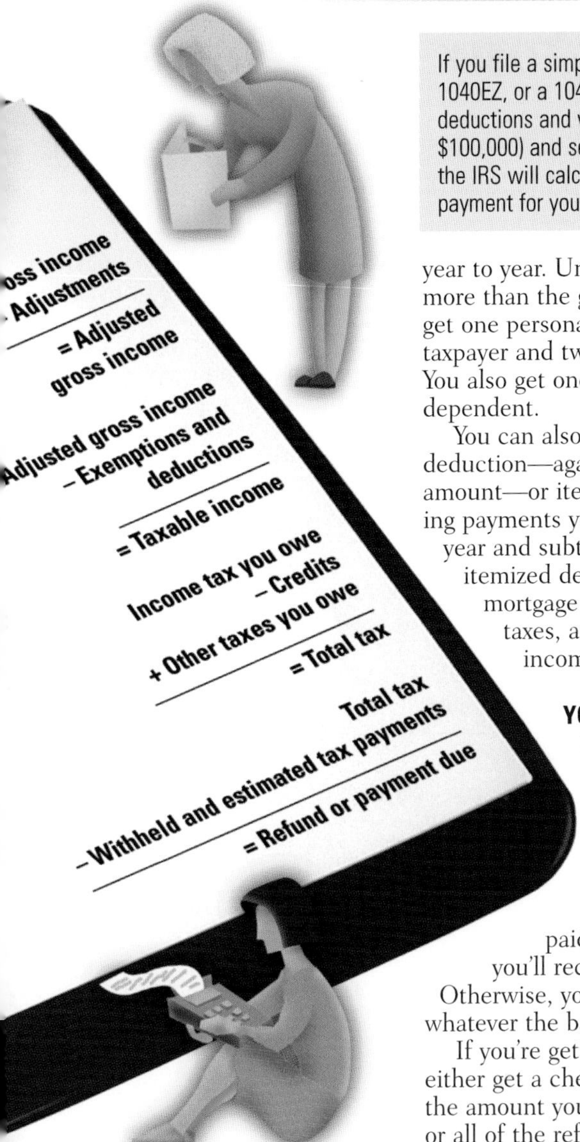

ost common adjustments include ontributions to IRAs or self-directed tirement plans (like Keoghs or EPs), half of any self-employment x you paid, qualified moving expens-, and alimony you've paid.

If your AGI is higher than the limit t by Congress, you won't be allowed deduct your IRA contribution, and our total exemptions and itemized eductions may be limited.

EMPTIONS AND DEDUCTIONS

fter you calculate your AGI, you n figure your taxable income by ıbtracting certain **exemptions** and **eductions** to which you're entitled.

Each exemption is a fixed dollar nount, and typically increases from year to year. Unless your income is more than the government limit, you get one personal exemption as a single taxpayer and two as a married couple. You also get one exemption for each dependent.

You can also subtract the standard deduction—again, a fixed dollar amount—or itemize all of the qualifying payments you've made during the year and subtract that total. Some itemized deductions include home mortgage interest, real estate taxes, and state and local income taxes.

> If you file a simple return (such as a 1040EZ, or a 1040 with no itemized deductions and with an income below $100,000) and send it in by April 15, the IRS will calculate your refund or payment for you.

YOUR REFUNDS AND PAYMENTS

Your refund or tax payment depends on what you've paid versus what you owe in income taxes. Basically, if you paid more than you owe, you'll receive a refund. Otherwise, you'll have to pay whatever the balance is.

If you're getting a refund, you can either get a check from the IRS for the amount you're owed, or apply part or all of the refund to your taxes for the coming year.

If, on the other hand, you owe a payment to the IRS, you must pay it by April 15. Otherwise, you will most likely have to pay interest and a late-payment penalty.

HELPFUL HINTS

There are things you don't need to report on your tax return:

- Welfare income
- Veteran's disability benefits
- Worker's compensation benefits
- Supplemental security income (SSI) from Social Security
- Scholarships for tuition
- Child support payments
- Life insurance payouts
- Gifts and inheritances

Filing Your Tax Return

You have three questions to answer when you file a tax return: what to file, when to file, and how to file.

You don't have a choice about whether to file a tax return, but you can decide which form to use, what payment option to choose, and how to file your return, all within a limited range of possibilities.

WHAT TO FILE

There are four forms you can choose among when you file your taxes. If you've filed before, you'll get the same form you filed in the previous year.

WHEN TO FILE

WHAT TO FILE

TYPE OF FORM	WHO YOU ARE
1040EZ	Single Married and filing jointly No dependents Under the age of 65 Taxable income lower than $50,000 No itemized deductions, credits, or adjustments
1040A	Income from several sources No capital gains, rental, or self-employment income No IRA deductions or credits for childcare No itemized deductions or adjustments (except for IRAs) Taxable income of less than $50,000
1040	Income above $50,000 Self-employed Get or pay alimony Itemize deductions Capital gains or losses
1040PC	IRS-approved tax software A computer All criteria for 1040

However, if the IRS reviews your return from last year and determines that you could use a simpler form, you'll get that form instead.

ELECTRONIC FILING

You can now file your tax return electronically. This option is becoming popular since it's faster and typically more accurate than paper filing.

Perhaps the best part of filing electronically is that you're likely to get your tax refund twice as quickly as you would if you filed by mail.

If you want to file your taxes electronically, you will need a home computer and tax software approved by the IRS. Once your return has been sent, you will receive a confirmation from the IRS.

TELEFILING

Another way to complete your tax return is to file by phone, using the IRS's **Telefile** system. The only way you can file by phone is to use the Telefile package, which the IRS sends only to those people who qualify. The qualifications are the same ones that make you eligible to file a 1040EZ.

When you call Telefile, you'll have to give your **Customer Service Number (CSN)**—you can find it in your Telefile package—that serves as ur signature. You will then be told you have a refund or balance. After ving all the necessary information, lefile will give you a ten-digit con- mation number. You'll want to keep record of that number as proof that ur call has been completed.

HEN TO FILE

ere are five payment options you n choose among when you file.

Pay by April 15. If you pay in full April 15, you'll probably save your- lf money and headaches in the long n, since there's less worry of paying penalty or interest.

Pay after April 15. If you don't pay by April 15 and you don't file for an extension, then you'll be charged penalties and interest until you pay. But you can still file for a four-month extension until August 15, which the IRS encourages you to do, rather than not filing an extension at all.

Pay after April 15 in install- ments. You could pay some or all of what you owe in monthly install- ments by sending Form 9465 with your return. The IRS will review your request, and let you know within 30 days whether you'll be allowed to pay monthly. If you don't pay on time, you'll have to pay a penalty and interest, so you might want to pay your return in full instead.

NEXT STEPS
To find out which tax software programs are IRS approved, go to the IRS website, www.irs.ustreas.gov/prod/elec_svs/partners.html.

Pay by April 15 with an exten- on. It's possible to receive a four- onth extension from the IRS if you eed more time to complete your turn. To receive an extension, you ust fill out Form 4868 by April 15. u must prepay an estimate of your x bill on time, usually at least 90% what you actually owe, on time to oid interest and penalties, which art accumulating on April 16 and ntinue until you file your return.

Pay after August 15. If you have a four-month extension and later find out that you still can't file your return, you may be able to extend your extension for two more months by filing Form 2688. You also have to explain why you need the extension, the length of time you need, and the year for which you need the exten- sion. Most advisers suggest that you apply well in advance, in case you're not approved and end up having to file by August 15.

Planning for the Future

As you get older, you'll need to figure out the pieces of your financial puzzle.

As appealing as retirement sounds to many people, coming face to face with the idea of retiring may produce a sense of uneasiness as well. While some people may be nervous about keeping busy, and others about maintaining a sense of purpose, most people's major concern is financial. Will they be able to make ends meet? Will there be enough money to do the things they've been looking forward to?

It is true that when you retire, you'll no longer receive a regular paycheck from your employer. But you may have several streams of revenue coming in, depending on the retirement plans you've made during your working years. At the same time, you may want to start sharing your wealth with the people you love.

NEXT STEPS

Once you have a sense of where your retirement income will come from, begin to think about what your spending priorities are. Here's what many people put at the top of their lists:

- Medical care
- Housing
- Food and other personal needs
- Travel or other interests
- Legacy for heirs
- Donations to charity

FROM YOUR PAYCHECK

Do you ever wonder whether the money that's withheld for Social Security or the salary you contribute to a retirement savings plan will pay dividends? When you retire, you'll se how putting money into these plans pays off.

Social Security currently accoun for between a third and a half of the average retired worker's income. You' be able to start receiving full benefit between the ages of 65 and 67, depending on the year you were bor Or you may choose to get a reduced benefit anytime after you turn 62.

Salary reduction plans let you contribute pretax dollars from your salary into retirement savings accounts. You decide how your savings are invested by choosing among the selections offered by the plan. Once you retire, you can draw on the assets to provide income.

Pensions are employer sponsored plans designed to give you a steady source of income throughout your retirement. You may have a **defined benefit plan** that pays you an annua income, usually in monthly installments, from money your employer put aside while you were working. The amount you receive depends on the number of years you worked, and how much you earned.

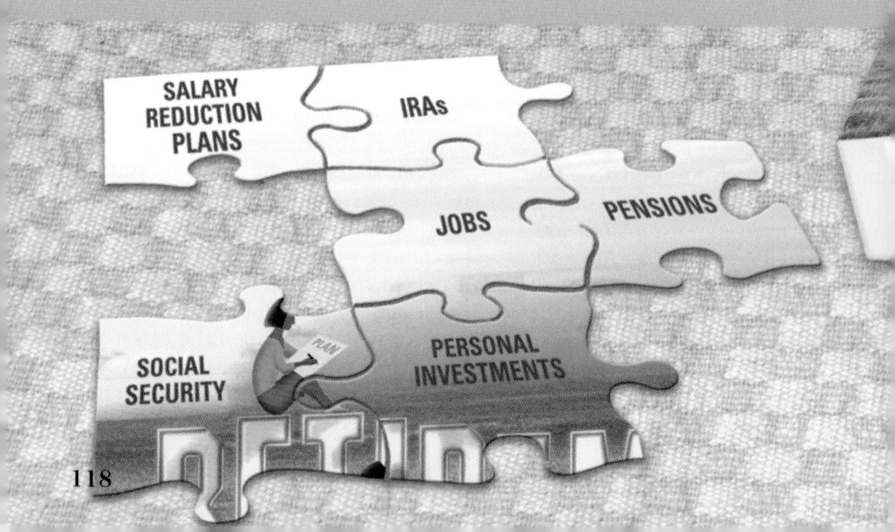

Or you might be part of an nployer-funded **defined contribu-on plan**. In that case, the income ɔu get when you retire depends on ɔw much money was invested and ɔw well the investments performed ·er time.

THER STREAMS

here are several other ·tirement savings ɔpportunities you ay take advantage during your work-g years to supple-ent your current ·tirement income.

IRAs, or Individual Retirement ccounts, are tax-deferred or tax-empt plans you set up with a finan-al services company, bank, or bro-erage firm. You can select your own vestments and begin to withdraw ithout penalty once you turn 59½.

Annuities are tax-deferred con-acts that you can use to build retire-ent savings while you're working and provide a stream of income after ɔu retire. The amount you receive om an annuity depends on the type ɔu buy, the amount you put in, and e payment option you choose.

Personal investments, such as ocks, bonds, mutual funds, real state, and certificates of deposit CDs), can be another source of ·tirement income. You may include dividends and interest from those investments in your retirement budget, gradually convert your investment assets to cash, or hold onto your assets to build your estate.

Jobs, either part-time or full-time, can also help you produce income when you need it, even after you retire.

PASSING IT ON

Once you know where your money is coming from, you can figure out where you might want it to go. The first step is to create a **will**, if you haven't already. With a will, you can ensure that your heirs will eventually receive a financial legacy.

You could set up a **trust** (or a number of trusts), which can serve different purposes depending on what your interests are. For instance, you can create a trust to save on estate taxes, one to help you distribute assets to the people you care about, or one to simply manage your property.

Another way to leave wealth to others is through **gifting**. While you are alive, you may give up to $11,000 to as many people as you choose each year without any tax consequences. Not only will you be able to see your loved ones enjoy your gifts, but you will also reduce the size of your total estate.

Defined Income

In an unpredictable world, it's nice to know that some things are guaranteed.

If you have a job, then it's likely that you're part of the 90% of the workforce that will eventually receive Social Security. And if you work for the government, a school system, or a large corporation, it's very possible that you'll receive a pension when you retire as well.

If you don't work but are married to someone who does, you may still qualify for Social Security and pension benefits.

HOW SOCIAL SECURITY WORKS

As you probably know, a specific amount of your paycheck is deducted each pay period for Social Security. Currently, it's 6.2% of your annual salary, up to an annual limit. Anothe 1.45% of your salary, with no cap, is withheld for Medicare. Your employe matches the amount you put in each pay period.

WHAT YOU GET

What you receive in Social Security depends on three factors.

Credit. To qualify for Social Security, you have to accumulate credits in the system. You get one credit for every $900 you earn in 2004 (the amount increases slightly every year), and you can earn a maximum of four credits per year. You wil need 40 credits, or 10 years of work during your lifetime, to qualify for benefits when you retire.

Age. You can start receiving partia benefits at age 62. You qualify to receive complete benefits if you wait until you're fully eligible, which depends on the year you were born (see chart).

YEAR OF BIRTH	AGE YOU CAN RECEIVE BENEFITS
1937	65
1938	65 and 2 months
1939	65 and 4 months
1940	65 and 6 months
1941	65 and 8 months
1942	65 and 10 months
1943-1954	66
1955	66 and 2 months
1956	66 and 4 months
1957	66 and 6 months
1958	66 and 8 months
1959	66 and 10 months
1960 and later	67

And if you postpone taking bene-its until you are 70, you get a credit or each year you delay, which boosts he amount you collect each month vhen you do start.

Earnings. The amount of Social Security you get is based on a lifetime of earnings—adjusted for inflation—livided by the number of months you vorked. That means you qualify for a arger benefit payment by working onger and earning more. But there's an annual cap on the benefit amount.

PENSION PAYOUTS

While you'll get a Social Security check every month once you begin to collect, the way you receive a pension depends on the payment option you choose.

A lump sum payment. If you can choose a lump sum payment, you receive all of the money from your pension at once, typically delivered by check or electronic transfer to your bank or investment account. You'll have to pay income taxes on the amount immediately.

HELPFUL HINTS

Social Security benefits are increased each year to offset inflation. This adjustment, based on increases in the Consumer Price Index (CPI), is known as a **cost of living adjustment**, or **COLA**.

An annuity. If you choose an annuity, you'll receive regular payments, typically monthly, for the remainder of your life. Most pension annuities are not adjusted for inflation, so the amount you get will buy less over time. However, annuities paid from retirement savings plans, such as 401(k)s and 403(b)s, where you can invest your money to produce growth, may have the potential to pay you increasing amounts over time.

IRA rollover. You may choose to roll over the assets from your pension into an IRA. In that case, you can preserve their tax-deferred status and invest the assets as you choose. If you don't need income from the IRA to cover living expenses, you can postpone withdrawals—and the taxes that are due—until you reach age 70½.

MORE CHOICES: ANNUITIES

If you choose to get your retirement income as an annuity, there are several more choices you'll have to make.

You can choose a **life annuity**. That means you get a set payment—based on the size of your pension account and your life expectancy—every month for the rest of your life. A life annuity typically offers the highest amount of income while you are alive.

Another option is a **joint and survivor annuity**, which covers both your lifetime and the lifetime of a designated survivor. If you're married, you may be required to name your husband as the beneficiary, unless he agrees in writing that it can be someone else. One advantage of this choice is that you and your partner can rest assured that the other will be taken care of when one of you dies. However, it's likely that your payments will be somewhat smaller with a joint and survivor annuity than they would be with a life annuity.

Finally, you can choose a **period certain annuity** to provide survivor benefits for a specified time period—often ten to twenty years. If you and your beneficiary die before the time is up, the payments continue. It's common to choose this payment schedule if you want to provide for a young survivor, such as a small child, after you die.

The Tax Issue

Balancing taxable and tax-deferred investments makes the most of your retirement income.

If you've been putting money into a tax-deferred, employer sponsored retirement plan, an IRA, or an annuity, and you've also been building a portfolio of taxable investments, you'll be on stronger ground when you're ready to create a stream of retirement income. The question is how to use taxable and tax-deferred accounts to your best advantage.

BALANCING ACT

The deal you make to get the benefit of tax deferral on money you add to a retirement savings plan is that sooner or later you have to start taking it out.

Once you reach April 1 of the year following the year you turn 70½, you must start withdrawing from your IRA and from your employer sponsored plan if you're no longer working. If you continue to work, you can usually postpone withdrawals from your employer's plan until after you actually retire. Until you reach that age, though, you can continue to let your tax-deferred investments compound, and tap your taxable investments for the income you may need.

After you begin required withdrawals from your tax-deferred accounts, you can supplement the amount you must withdraw with income from taxable investments.

TAXABLE INVESTMENTS

If you want your tax-deferred investments to continue to grow until you're obligated to take required withdrawals, that doesn't mean you have to sell all your taxable investments as soon as you retire. Instead, you might want to liquidate an investment that has reached maturity, such as a CD. Rather than reinvesting the amount from that investment, you can put the money into a savings or money market account, and use the money to cover your current expenses.

Another method you can try is to start liquidating your stocks, bonds, and mutual funds. You have several options to choose from if you decide to use this method:

- You could sell off some of your holdings and invest in an annuity or income-generating bond

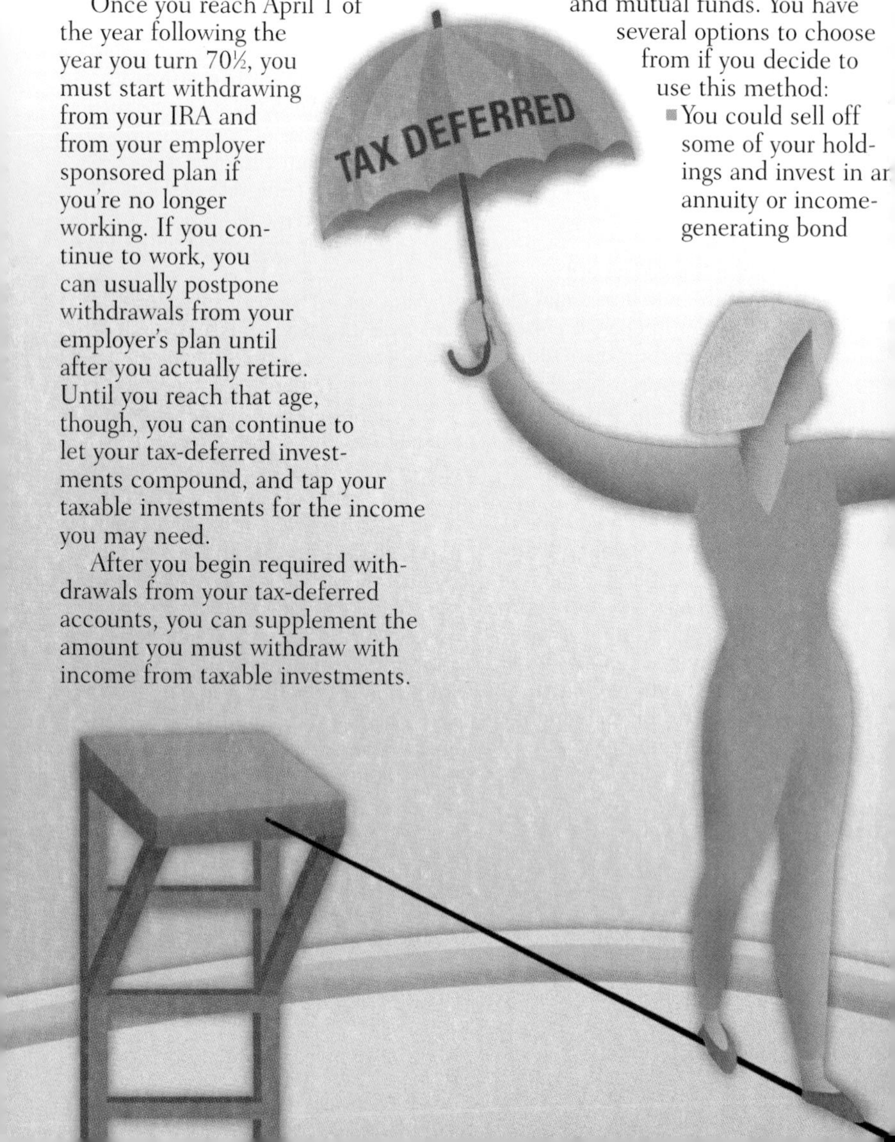

You could withdraw your investment earnings and leave your principal intact to produce earnings
You could use the earnings and a percentage of the principal each year, though with that approach you risk running out of money eventually

You'll owe ncome tax at our regular ate on interest nd dividend arnings. But you make a rofit by selling nvestments you've owned for more han a year, then you'll owe the IRS ax on your **capital gains**. That tax is gured at a lower rate than your egular income tax rate.

HE TAX-DEFERRED ADVANTAGE

f you want to preserve the tax-eferred status of your retirement avings, such as money you put into salary reduction plan, you might vant to roll your assets over into an ndividual Retirement Account (IRA). here are no limits on the amounts ou transfer, but you are only allowed o include pretax contributions and arnings in the rollover.

The most efficient way to move he money is to authorize a direct ransfer from your employer's plan to he custodian of your roll-over IRA, which can actually be the same financial institution. Another method is to take control and handle the rollover yourself.

This is not as simple because you have to follow a strict set of rules. First, you have to deposit the full amount of your retirement payout into the IRA within 60 days of receiving the check. However, 20% of that payout is automatically withheld as tax. To deposit the full amount, you'll have to make up for the lost 20% by tapping into another source, such as a savings account. You will get the 20% back after you pay your taxes for the year, provided you've met the 60-day deadline for deposits.

IRA WITHDRAWALS

When you withdraw from your traditional IRA, you owe income tax at your regular rate on the earnings. And, if you deducted your contributions, you owe tax on the entire amount you withdraw. You can withdraw without penalty when you reach age 59½, though you may wait until you're 70½. From 70½ on, you must take at least a required minimum amount each year.

You figure the amount you must withdraw starting at age 70½ by dividing the value of your IRA on December 31 of the previous year by your life expectancy. For example, if your account is worth $200,000 and your life expectancy is 27.4 years—as it is when you're 70—you must take a minimum of $7,299 ($200,000 ÷ 27.4 = $7.299.27, or $7,299).

Everyone uses the same life expectancy table, which you can find in IRS Publication 590, "Individual Retirement Arrangements (IRAs)." But if your husband is more than ten years younger than you are, you can use a different table, which produces a longer life expectancy and a smaller required withdrawal amount.

NEXT STEPS

You can access your IRA money before you turn 59½, using a process called **annuitization**. That means you create a withdrawal plan that pays you a fixed amount from your IRA each year, based on your life expectancy. Your annuitizing plan has to cover five years, or all of the years until you reach 59½, whichever is longer.

Estate Planning

There's more to your estate than you might think.

Although the word **estate** may suggest images of wealth, you don't have to be rich to have one. Whatever your financial situation, you'll leave an estate behind when you die. Your estate includes everything you own in your name and half of everything you own jointly with another person. That includes **real** items, such as land and buildings, **personal** items, such as a music collection or an heirloom necklace, and all of your other financial assets.

The reason you write a will or create one or more trusts—documents that are described on the following pages—is to be sure that the people or institutions you want to share in your estate will do so. Controlling what happens to your estate is also the reason you name certain beneficiaries on retirement savings plans, insurance policies, and other assets that are distributed directly at your death. All of those decisions come under the umbrella heading of **estate planning**.

But there's another aspect of estate planning, too, that becomes increasingly important as your net worth increases. It involves anticipating the value of your possessions to determine whether or not your net worth will be subject to federal (and state) estate taxes.

ESTATE TAXES

Under federal tax law, each person has access to a **gift and an estate tax credit**. Those credits, which apply to taxable gifts you make when you're alive and whatever is left in your estate when you die, let you transfer ownership of some or all of your real and personal property to others without owing tax on the value of those assets.

In 2004, federal law lets you give away cash or property valued at up to $1 million without owing tax. The amount you can leave your heirs in your will is $1.5 million in 2004 and 2005, gradually increasing to $3.5 million in 2009. However, the cap on lifetime gifts that are exempt from tax will remain $1 million.

If you're sure that your estate will be worth less than those amounts, you may not need to be concerned about extensive estate planning. But if you own your own home, a life insurance policy, and one or more retirement savings plans, it's risky to assume you don't have to think about estate taxes. Those assets combined could put your entire estate at a taxable level.

Similarly, if you are in line to inherit wealth from your parents, relatives, or your husband, those assets will become part of your estate.

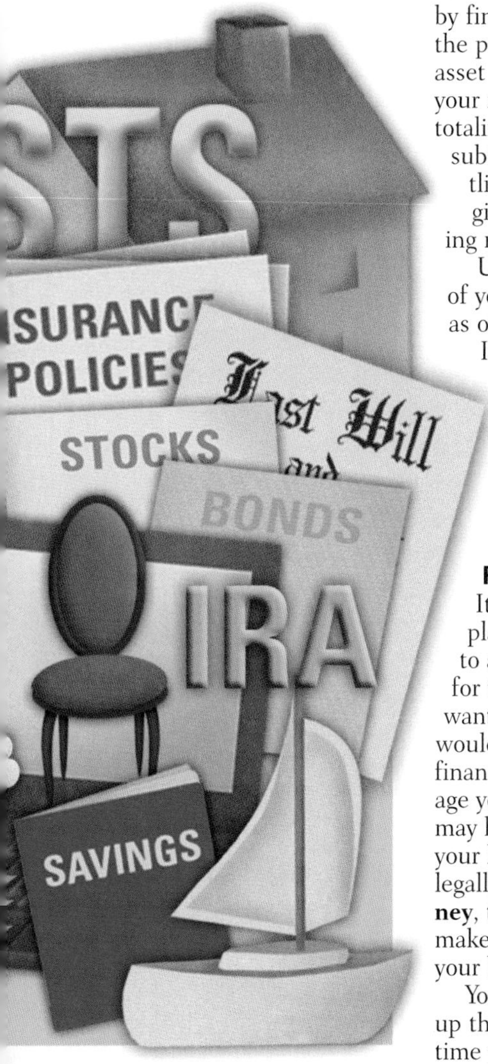

WHAT AN ESTATE IS WORTH

Estimating what your estate would be worth if something happened to you is the only way to judge whether you should be making estate plans.

To get started, consider the following major elements of your estate:

- Real estate
- Personal property (cars, furniture, electronic equipment)
- Value of any retirement plans, including IRAs
- Bank accounts
- No-fault insurance payments you are owed
- Income tax refunds due to you
- Life insurance policies you own
- Stocks, bonds, mutual funds, and annuities

DOING THE CALCULATION

You can estimate your estate's worth by finding the **fair market value** (or the price you would pay to buy an asset on the open market) of all of your real and personal property. After totaling those amounts, you have to subtract two items: the cost of settling the estate and any nontaxable gifts to your husband or a qualifying nonprofit organization.

Ultimately, the actual valuation of your estate will be calculated as of the date of your death.

In some cases, an estate is valued six months after the owner's death. That's a decision your executor may choose to make if the delay could decrease your estate's value and reduce the taxes your estate will face.

POWER OF ATTORNEY

It's important to have an estate plan in place as soon as you begin to accumulate assets. As you plan for the long term, you might also want to give some thought to who would manage your property and finances if you became too ill to manage your accounts on your own. You may have a family member, friend, or your husband in mind, but unless you legally give someone **power of attorney**, that person won't be able to make financial or legal decisions on your behalf.

You can ask your lawyer to draw up the power of attorney at the same time you make your will, or you can use a standard form and have a lawyer review it. Then be sure that the person who'll need it knows where the document is.

If you want to be sure that someone will be able to act for you if you become unable to act on your own behalf, you should use a **durable power of attorney**. If you want the person of your choice to take responsibility only in the event that you become incompetent, then **springing power of attorney** would better suit your personal needs.

Giving someone power of attorney through the signing of legal documents isn't a substitute for other types of long–term estate planning, but can be a valuable complement to your financial planning.

Will Power

A will puts your legacy in your hands.

If you've ever wondered why having a will is so important, consider this: When you die without one, your chosen family members, friends, and charities may not benefit from what you accumulated during your life. A portion of your money could even end up in the hands of your state government.

WRITING A WILL

When you're ready to make your will, you can consult a professional or write it on your own. Most financial advisers suggest that you use a lawyer who specializes in wills and estates, since you may not be aware of all the laws that apply in your state. And because the fees for a basic will are generally affordable, it's smart to look into professional help. Of course, the more complicated your estate, the greater the fee you should probably expect.

If you decide to write your own will, you can buy a guidebook to find out what you must include to make the document legal. Or you can purchase a computer program, such as the ones offered by Nolo Press, to ensure that your will meets the legal standard for your state. Once you've drafted a will, though, it's smart to have a lawyer review what you've done so that your estate won't face potential taxes or legal complications after you die.

NAMING NAMES

In your will, you have the opportunity to choose your **beneficiaries**, or the people who will inherit your estate. Whom you choose is really up to you. The only rule is that if you're married, you have to provide for your husband.

Beyond that, you can leave property to your family, friends, charities, and other organizations. When you're deciding whom to choose, it's important to be as specific as possible. Any language that isn't completely clear could result in costly court proceedings. It's also smart to designate your bequests as percentages of your whole estate rather than dollar amounts, since it's hard to tell in advance what your assets may be worth.

Another choice you'll have to make is the **executor** of your will. This person carries out the terms of the will, such as collecting your assets, paying your bills, and taking care of tax and legal issues.

Because being an executor can involve making complex decisions,

A WILL OF YOUR OWN

Many women urge their fathers or husbands to write a will. But remember if you want to choose who inherits your assets or serves as your children's guardian, you need a will of your own.

ou'll want to think carefully about vho would be best suited for the task nd get permission from the person ou're thinking about choosing. You nay want to name a back-up execu- or, in case your first hoice cannot fulfill he necessary respon- ibilities. You can also ame joint executors, vhich is a good idea f your estate is complicated, or if you vant both a relative or friend and a rofessional handling your legacy.

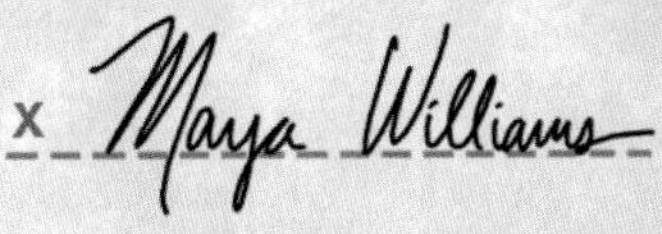

IGNING ON THE DOTTED LINE

)nce your will has been written, here's still more work to be done. 'our **execution**, commonly known s your signature, has to be witnessed y two or three people. While the vitnesses aren't required to read your vill or know what's in it, you do have o tell them that they're witnessing he execution of your will.

When you actually sign your will, ou should sign only one copy. Then, you should either ile your will at home, vith your attorney, or n another safe place. t's not a good idea o store it in a safety leposit box, though, since the box ould be sealed when you die, which neans your will would automatically ecome inaccessible.

WHY ARE WILLS IMPORTANT?

If you die without a will, or **intestate**, you run the risk that what you want to happen to your property won't actually happen. If you're married and die intestate, your property will pass to your husband and your children, if you have any. The proportion of your estate they receive depends on what state you live in—some favor the spouse, while others give a larger amount to the children. And the situation becomes more complicated if you've been married more than once or have children with different partners.

If you're not married, then the courts decide which of your relatives will receive your property. They are unlikely to name friends or charities.

PROBATE AND THE COURTS

Whatever you transfer to your heirs through your will has to go through a sometimes lengthy process called **probate**, during which the courts verify your will. The best way to move the process along quickly is to create an unambiguous will. Further, experts suggest that the more property you can transfer directly to your beneficiaries outside your will, the faster the probate process will be.

Trusts

Trusts can benefit someone you choose—and your own estate.

Creating one or more trusts can give you the opportunity to control what happens to your assets after your death. A **trust** is a legal entity, sometimes compared to a corporation, to which you can transfer property.

Different trusts serve different purposes, so you may not be able to find one trust to meet all your goals. However, you can create several trusts to serve different purposes. For example, you may be able to reduce the value of your taxable estate by putting some assets into a trust. Or you may be able to set up the schedule on which your heirs would have access to some of your assets.

THE BASICS

Most trusts work the same way: You, as the **donor**, establish the trust, and place assets in it. The trust is then run by the **trustee** whom you name, and will eventually benefit the **beneficiary** or **beneficiaries**—the person, people, or organizations that are to receive income and perhaps the principal from the trust. For example, an elderly woman may set up a trust, managed by her financial planner, to support her granddaughters while the young women are in college.

LIVING TRUSTS

If you choose to create a trust that you fund during your lifetime, the trust is called a living trust or an inter vivos trust. You must decide whether the trust is **revocable** or **irrevocable**.

A revocable trust is similar to a will. You can change what's in it and who benefits from it whenever you choose, and its value is counted in your estate at your death. But unlike a will, the assets in a trust do not go through the extensive and public process of **probate**.

An irrevocable trust is a binding arrangement. You can't change any of its terms or reclaim an item once you transfer it to the trust. Despite such restrictions, you may want to create an irrevocable trust if your goal is to reduce estate taxes.

To use an irrevocable trust to shield your estate from taxes, you ma[y] choose to keep your annual contributions under the tax-free gift limits. Or you can set up the trust using **Crummey** powers. That means the beneficiaries must be notified that they have the right to withdraw an asset within a set amount of time after you contribute it. But it gives you the opportunity, over time, to shed a lot of your estate value by passing it through the trust to the people you want to benefit.

LIFE INSURANCE TRUSTS

If you own the insurance policy on your own life, the benefit paid at your death is counted in your estate. Since that can be a sizable asset, you can reduce the risk of estate taxes by setting up a **life insurance trust** expressly designed to own the policy on your life. You might plan to have the trust liquidated upon your death to pay estate taxes.

CHARITABLE LIVING TRUSTS

If you plan a gift to charity from your estate, you might want to create a trust that makes those donations during your lifetime instead.

OTHER TRUSTS

Testamentary trusts are created by your will at the time of your death, often to minimize estate taxes. You choose the beneficiaries and terms, and the trustee or trustees oversee the distribution of your assets after your death.

Bypass trusts are used to ensure that both partners of a marriage pay minimal estate taxes. Each person creates a bypass trust. When one spouse dies, a portion of the estate equal to the amount that can be transferred, tax free, is reserved for future beneficiaries, and the rest of the estate passes, tax free, to the surviving spouse. The surviving spouse may also receive income from the first trust's assets. After the second spouse dies, the assets in the first bypass trust

If you set up a **charitable remainder trust**, you can choose to donate tax-deductible assets and collect income from the trust for your lifetime or an agreed-upon period. When you die, the trust's remaining assets go to the charity.

With a **charitable lead trust**, on the other hand, the assets in the trust pay income to the charity for a specified period of time. When the period ends, your heirs inherit the assets.

A **charitable gift annuity** is a simpler version of a charitable trust. You make a gift directly to a charity, and in turn they pay you—and a beneficiary you name—a set income for the rest of your life.

MARITAL TRUSTS

If you're married, you may create a **marital trust**. If either of you dies, this trust manages the surviving spouse's finances to help minimize financial decisions. However, you and your spouse may both feel qualified to handle your own finances and decide against a trust.

QTIP

go directly to the named beneficiaries, such as the children. So do the assets in the trust of the second spouse to die. Estate taxes apply only to any amount left in that person's estate.

A **qualified terminable interest property trust (QTIP)** is a kind of bypass trust that lets you determine who the second beneficiary will be. That might be a good way to pass extra assets on to your children from an earlier marriage, for example, without cutting your current husband's income if he survives you. However, keep in mind that if your husband creates a QTIP trust, you'll have no right to change any of its provisions.

Gift It Away

When it comes to estate planning, gifting can be as good as receiving.

One of the most common goals of estate planning is to reduce estate taxes by decreasing an estate's total value. So giving away assets before they are included in your estate can be a powerful tool.

THE BASICS

The federal government allows you to make annual contributions of $11,000 each to as many people as you like, and those gifts can be in any form. That means you can give your daughter $11,000 in cash, investments, or anything of value for her birthday each year. And the same year, you can also give $11,000 apiece to each of your nieces and nephews. If you're married, you and your husband can give $22,000 to each recipient each year.

If you know that you have more money than you'll need during your lifetime, giving some away before your death can significantly reduce the threat of ending up with an estate large enough to be taxed. It can also be a wonderful opportunity for you to witness the joy that your financial support can bring to your loved ones.

GIFTS TO MINORS

Often, parents and grandparents want to give young children monetary gifts that are too substantial to be kept in bank accounts or savings bonds. But children can't own assets until they turn 18 or 21, depending on state law. So any adult may elect to set up an account for a child under the **Uniform Gifts to Minors Act (UGMA)** or the **Uniform Transfer to Minors Act (UTMA)**.

UGMA

These are investment accounts in the child's name that a custodian maintains until the child is old enough to take control. Contributions to the account are considered gifts, and are tax exempt up to $11,000. In an UTMA, you can include assets other than cash and securities if you choose to do so.

HELPFUL HINTS
A **qualified transfer** is a unique way to fund a child's college tuition and maximize estate reduction. You make a gift to the institution—not the child—equal to the amount of tuition. The student's bill is considered paid, and you can still give him or her a $11,000 tax-free gift for the year.

If you aren't concerned about the recipients controlling the assets in the accounts when they turn 18 or 21, UGMAs and UTMAs are ways to reduce your estate while supporting a child's future financial security. You may want to focus on growth stocks and bonds, since children under 14 pay tax at their parents' tax rate on any income the UGMA or UTMA account earns in dividends and interest.

UTMA

And since any adult is eligible to be a custodian, you should consider

naming someone other than yourself. That's because if you die while you re custodian of an account that you et up, the assets return to your estate nd your potential estate tax savings lisappear.

GIFTING VS. LEAVING

Gifting, like all estate planning options, has its limits and drawbacks. Most notably, you lose complete control over the asset once you give it away. You can't access it if you suddenly need money. And you can't control what the new owner does with it.

Ironically, the other major liability of tax-free gifts is a tax consideration. Specifically, you must consider the capital gains taxes that will apply if he new owner of an asset sells it.

If you give somebody an asset and ne or she eventually sells it, that person has to figure the profit based on he original price you paid. That gain n value is what's taxed. So if the value of the asset appreciated heavily at any point between when you bought it and the new owner sold it, he new owner pays a hefty tax.

If you leave someone an asset in your will that he or she eventually sells, the taxable profit is figured from the time that your estate was valued (usually right around your death), and the price that you paid becomes irrelevant. So if the asset didn't appreciate much between the time that the new owner received it and the time that he or she sold it, the taxes could be significantly smaller.

If the new owner has to pay any inheritance taxes on the asset, though, the tax savings from selling it may be negated. And you may want to consider the emotional benefit of seeing the new owner enjoy the gift.

GIFTS AND TAXES

There are several tax advantages to giving gifts.

If you are married to a US citizen, that means you can give your husband gifts worth any amount, at any time, and will not be charged tax on those gifts.

And you won't face taxes if you give gifts to charitable organizations. However, giving large gifts could put you in the position of facing the alternative minimum tax.

Inheriting Wealth

Understanding inheritances is vital, whether you're giving or receiving.

During your lifetime, you might inherit money from a parent, relative, spouse, or friend. Or you may pass the money on at your death. That's why you need to educate yourself now about how to handle inheritances as well as help your heirs understand the implications of receiving your property from you.

THE EDUCATION PROCESS

Whether you're the person providing an inheritance or the person receiving it, it's smart to educate yourself on the emotional and financial implications of an inheritance.

When you've created a will, and have figured out whom you'd like to pass your property on to, you may want to tell those people that they will be inheriting something from you. That way, the inheritance won't come as a shock. And if there's something specific you want to happen to that inheritance, such as keeping a cherished heirloom in your family after you die, you can tell your heirs what your wishes are while you're alive.

However, if you don't feel comfortable disclosing whom you're leaving inheritances to, you might want to write out instructions—or have your lawyer document your wishes—so your heirs are informed when they receive their inheritances. The more information you can provide, the less stress your heirs may face after your death. For example, you might explain how to handle taking income from a 401(k) or 403(b) account, or which assets to liquidate to pay estate or inheritance taxes.

If you are the person receiving an inheritance, you may find that it's more stressful than you imagined. Many people feel guilty about suddenly coming into unearned wealth, while others are not prepared for the obligations that accompany an inheritance. So educating yourself on how to invest and how to manage money can help you prepare for the day when you do receive an inheritance.

GRIEVING

It's common to feel strong emotions about an inheritance, since it's often linked to the death of a loved one. Experts recommend that you postpone making major financial decisions until your initial grieving period has passed. When you start thinking of the inheritance as your money—and not as a gift or loan—you might be ready to start making thoughtful financial decisions.

CASH INHERITANCES

If you've received a cash inheritance, it's smart to list your financial priorities before you start spending the money. Be sure to weigh short-term rewards against long-term comfort. While a new car may be an affordable luxury, it may not be more important than your retirement security.

Experts recommend that you make paying off debt—like credit card balances—your first priority, especially if it's compromising your credit rating or limiting your other investments.

You might want to consider your retirement security as well. If you've fallen behind in your IRA contributions in the year you get an inheritance, consider using $3,000 to help make up the difference. While you can't put inherited cash in your salary reduction plan, such as a 401(k), you may still maximize those tax savings indirectly. If you use an inheritance in your current budget, you can contribute more of your wages to your retirement plan.

If you don't already have an emer-
ency fund that could cover three to ix months of expenses, part of your nheritance can serve as one. This und could be vital if you lose your ob or face an unexpected expense.

If you have children, you may also ecide to set aside some of your nheritance in their college fund. If ou don't have an existing education und, inherited money may be a per- ect initial investment.

ECONDARY CONSIDERATIONS

f you have already addressed your rimary concerns, you may want to onsider further options.

You might want to use part of your nheritance to treat yourself or mprove your quality of life. You could plurge on an elaborate vacation or et aside enough money to send your hild to private school. If you can fford it, there's nothing wrong with esponsible indulging.

A final option is to give a good portion of your inheritance to a charity or research organization, perhaps in memory of the person who left you the money. The emotional rewards of carrying on a legacy by contributing to a good cause can outweigh the value of spending the money on luxuries.

WIDOWHOOD

If you are widowed, your financial considerations may seem particularly hard to handle after the loss of your partner. You automatically become the full owner of all the property that you had held jointly. And you may have a large sum of life insurance money to manage. Eventually, you will have to claim your portion of payouts from Social Security, a pension, IRA, or annuity. Each of these responsibilities will be manageable with time. The advice of a trusted financial planner or lawyer can be helpful.

Getting Professional Advice

Your business can benefit from the help of experts.

Although it's tempting to believe you can run a business on your own, it's usually a good idea to get professional help. Hiring lawyers and accountants can help keep you out of legal and financial trouble, while public relations experts can get your company in the public eye.

Technology consultants can keep you abreast of recent technological innovations. And having a good relationship with a particular bank or banker is a good way to get information when you make major financial decisions, such as arranging a line of credit or securing loans.

Keep in mind that professional advice can be costly. In general, it's a good idea to figure out the areas where expert help could provide the biggest boost, and hire professionals to achieve it. As you have more money at your disposal, you can hire other specialists as you need them.

You can also get business counseling at no cost from retired executives through an organization called the Service Corp of Retired Executives (SCORE), sponsored by the Small Business Administration. To find a local chapter, you can go to their website, www.score.org.

FINANCIAL GUIDANCE

Running your own business is challenging enough without trying to handle your company's tax planning and reporting. Most business owners would agree that hiring an accountant is a good investment.

Accountants can work with you and your financial officer or controller to keep your business financially sound. Some areas that accountants can help you with include preparing

rofit and loss statements, audit eports, and earnings projections. n accountant can also troubleshoot or you and help you fine-tune our budget.

Many accountants will help you omputerize your records for more fficiency. And if you need a loan, our accountant can help you deter-nine what type might be appropriate or you.

AWYERS

s a business owner, you'll probably eed to work with an attorney. If you ave business associates who work vith an attorney, ask for their recom-nendations. You can also contact your ocal women's business association or referrals.

In the early stages of your busi-ess, your lawyer helped you decide vhat type of structure (sole owner-hip, partnership, corporation, or ranchise) would work best for you. nd as you grow, an attorney can oresee various business needs, such s zoning regulations, employment ractices, and workplace safety. It's lso important to retain a lawyer if ou are applying for trademarks or atents, because many legal issues rise during the application process. inally, it's crucial to have an employ-nent lawyer review your employee andbook to make sure you cover ll the bases, legally speaking.

It's essential to find someone who's xperienced in business law, prefer-bly someone who has worked with usinesses like yours. You may also vant to think about the size of the rm. A smaller firm may give you nore personal attention, but a larger ne usually offers a wider range f services.

Finally, you should find out how ou'll be charged for the legal services ou need. Most lawyers charge an ourly fee, and the cost of each con-ultation depends on the lawyer's illing rate. That generally depends n level of experience, the part of he country where you live, and the ype of firm it is. However, some awyers charge a flat fee for a specific ervice, regardless of the amount of ime it takes.

PECIALIZED CONSULTANTS

f you want to get your business into he public eye, you can hire **advertising** or **marketing specialists** to help you create an image and positioning scheme. A small advertising agency or independent specialist may be ideal for your small business's needs.

You can also employ a **public relations (PR) firm** or add a public relations specialist to your staff to help you gain exposure that you otherwise may not be able to attain. A PR agent can write press releases, contact the media, and generally educate the public on the latest happenings in your business.

There are **technology consultants** who can help you modernize your computer systems and office servers, as well as keep you updated with the latest software and manage the upkeep of your systems.

There are also **soft consultants**, who are trained to teach your employees how to maximize their productivity, cultivate working relationships with clients, and more.

RESOURCES

There are formal ways to establish relationships with other women business owners, who can be a source of ideas and advice.

The **National Association of Women Business Owners** (www.nawbo.org) maintains many local chapters, which host monthly meetings and programs to build business skills.

Similarly, the 93 Small Business Administration's **Women's Business Centers** (www.onlinewbc.gov) maintain and staff facilities in which these connections can form. They primarily provide training for women just starting their companies, or growing established businesses, by helping them secure venture capital, and offering programs on using technology, expanding markets, and other topics.

Another organization worth checking out is the **Women Presidents' Organization (WPO)**, which is made up of successful women business owners. The WPO organizes informal and formal meetings for women to discuss business strategies, organizational skills, and various successes and failures in their own businesses. For more information, go to the WPO website, www.womenpresidentsorg.com.

Attracting Employees

To draw new employees, it's important to have a well-rounded incentive package.

By knowing what you're looking for in an employee and providing incentives to attract skilled candidates, you can create a strong team.

YOUR ROLE

Many businesses, both big and small, have started to offer the following incentives to their employees.

First of all, most potential employees look for a company that offers a well-rounded **health plan**. Depending on how extensive your budget is, you may include dental and optical coverage, which could make your company more attractive than your competitors.

Offering a **retirement plan**, such as a 401(k), can also give you an edge when you're hiring. Some employees may want to roll over their current retirement plan into the one that you offer, while others will want to start building their nest eggs.

Finally, it's become standard to provide **paid vacation time** to your employees. One way to decide how much vacation time you want to offer is to find out what other businesses in your industry offer, since you want to remain competitive. Advisers suggest that you include your company's policy for vacation days in your employee handbook, so that your employees know when they can expect an increase in the number of days they get.

FLEXIBLE INCENTIVES

To attract employees, you may want to provide **flextime**, which lets your employees work part-time, or compress a full work week into four days.

Or you can offer **telecommuting**, which allows your employees to work from home, on the road, or even from another city.

Making these schedules work can be a challenge for you as the business

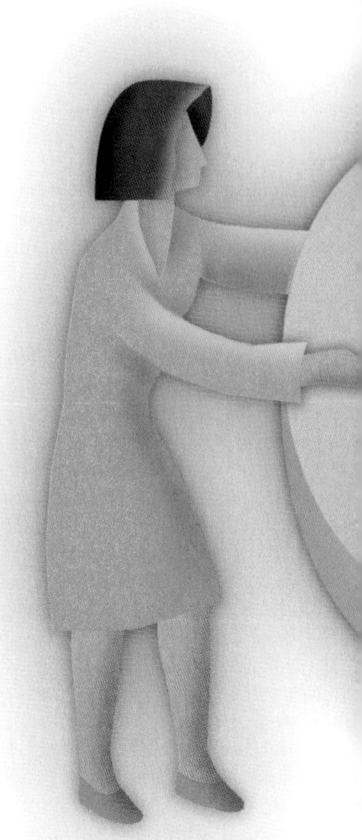

owner, since it's more difficult to create a cohesive office atmosphere if workers use flextime. But if you schedule regular phone conferences or in-office meetings, your employees will still feel connected to one another and your company in general.

INTERNSHIPS

One way to attract employees is to start young. Many companies now offer internship programs to high school and college students, either for the summer or for credit during the academic year. If you offer this type of program, not only will you have added hands in the office, but you may also find some talented future employees among the interns you hire.

SALARY DECISIONS

To come up with a reasonable salary for a potential employee, you should do some research. Find out what your competitors are offering to people in the same position you're trying to fill. Experts suggest that you read salary surveys to see what the typical salaries are in your industry.

Chambers of Commerce, the JS Bureau of Labor, and many trade ıssociations publish these surveys, ınd you can buy them from consult-ng firms or receive them through nternet subscription services. They're eported regularly in trade journals.

Another factor to consider is 'our geographical region. Salaries, specially in lower-paid jobs, and for mployees with less experience, vary rom city to city, so it's wise to get ome statistics on the salary trends n your region.

HELPFUL HINTS

While it's very important to offer your potential employees a competitive salary, you need to keep your company's financial well-being in mind as well. That doesn't mean that you should skimp on the incentives you offer, or the compensation packages that you create. But it's still crucial that your company remains profitable, so be careful not to put your bottom line at risk.

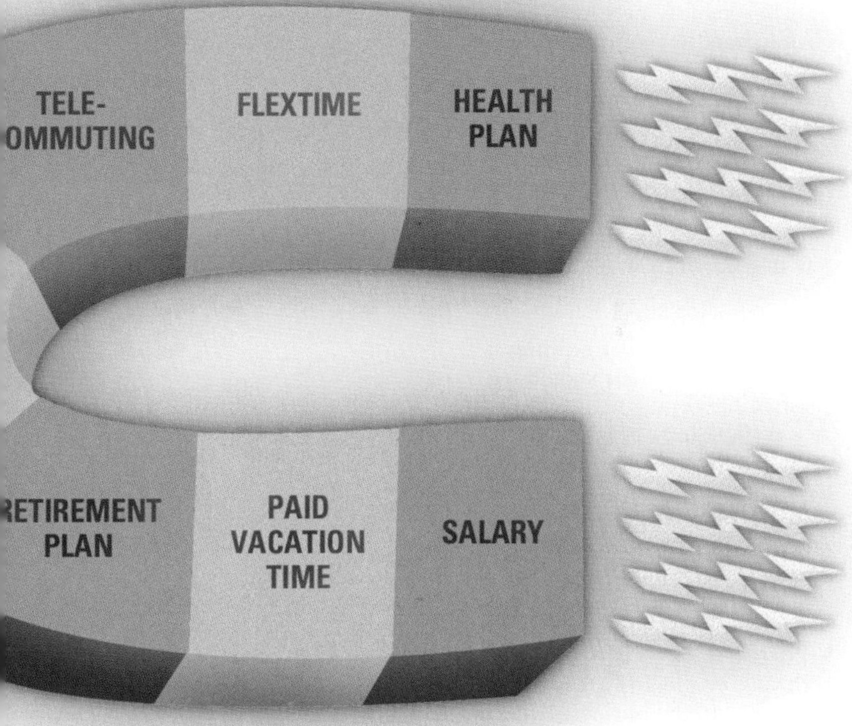

IAKING THE OFFER

'ou can either call, write, or email ɔ extend the offer to your potential mployee. But for record-keeping urposes, it may be wise to send a vritten contract, even if you call as vell. You should be specific in your ffer, making sure to include the posi-ion's title, general duties, starting alary, start date, and a general escription of vacation time and he benefits you offer.

You may also want to add a date y which you expect a response. 'hat makes it easier for you to xtend other offers if your first hoice declines the position.

THE COSTS OF YOUR OFFER

In a tight labor market, you may find that you have to offer higher salaries to attract employees. But how does that affect your current employees, who may end up making less than the new hires?

If you start offering higher salaries to your incoming employees, it's smart to adjust your current employees' salaries to reflect their skills and experience. You could also create a salary structure, in which you figure out a base salary for each job in your company. Once that structure is in place, it's also easier for you to give scheduled pay raises.

Keeping Your Employees

Creating a strong team is key to your company's growth.

You've found an ambitious, hard-working group of employees to help make your business a success. Now your challenge is to create a motivational, exciting, and productive workplace. As an employer, it's important to stay aware of your employees' feelings about their jobs, as well as provide incentives to establish a creative environment in your office.

EMPLOYEE FEEDBACK

Even if you have managers to oversee the day-to-day work of your employees, there are several ways to get employee feedback directly as well. It's an important way to hold on to an informal environment as your work force expands.

Keep communication lines open. Your employees should feel comfortable coming to you to discuss work issues. To maintain that openness as your business grows, try to arrange for regularly scheduled meetings with each employee. If you think some of them may be uncomfortable in a one-on-one meeting, try small groups.

Have staff meetings or lunches. Every two weeks or so, get together with your employees to review what's happening in the business. You can include any important updates and generate discussion about new products or ideas. These meetings are also the time to let your employees offer their feedback and creative thoughts.

REWARDS

It's very important to let your employees know when they're doing a good job, or when you feel that their work needs improvement.

Schedule salary reviews and make promotions at regular intervals. By promoting employees, you are showing that you reward hard work. When you do a salary review, it's the perfect time to go over any strengths and weaknesses an employee may have. And it's also a time to give long-term employees new responsibilities.

Give criticism behind closed doors. A working environment should be positive, so while public praise is often a good idea, criticism should remain a private matter.

INCENTIVES

If you are employing a large number of working parents, providing subsidized **daycare** or giving your workers vouchers to daycare facilities may be a wise choice. There may be other small business owners nearby who would collaborate on providing these services.

You can arrange for **on-the-job training** when an employee joins your company. Or you can offer training or workshops every six months to a year. Many employers choose to have their employees take online workshops or courses in your business or industry, such as the ones offered at www.learning.net.

NANCIAL INCENTIVES

ven if you already have retirement ıd health plans in place, or match ur employees' contributions to their tirement plans, there are additional ays that you can provide employee centives.

You can offer a **profit sharing an**. Basically, that

eans that you pay a certain percent-ge of your company's profits to your nployees. If your profits are less than ou anticipate in any year, or if you eed the money to expand, you can ways skip a year.

Many companies offer **stock ptions** or **stock appreciation rights** their employees. If the company oes public or is sold, the employees nare your financial success. You'll eed professional help to set up a plan ıch as this, but you may find it's a eat loyalty builder.

Finally, you can create an **employ-e stock ownership plan (ESOP)**. /ith an ESOP, you create a trust fund r existing shares of stock and estab-sh individual ESOP accounts for our employees who choose to participate in the plan. You contribute shares to those accounts based on a formula you set up. You can use an ESOP to give your employees bonuses and incentives or as part of a 401(k) or other retirement plan.

MORE OPTIONS

As employment rates steadily increase, there's increased competition among businesses to find and keep employees. Added incentives are often a good idea if you want to keep your essential employees.

Many companies have created mentor structures, often aimed toward women professionals, to help younger employees learn the ropes and get advice from their older, more experienced colleagues. You can implement this type of structure by matching up two people in the same division of your company, one with many years of experience and perhaps someone you've just hired. It's smart to encourage these mentor groups to meet often.

Although it may be costly, it's important to keep the technology in your office current and functioning. That means providing current computers, appropriate computer software programs, email and Internet access, fax machines, copiers, printers, and anything else that your employees will need to use on a regular basis.

NEXT STEPS

Not only do you want your business to run efficiently, but you also want to make sure that your employees truly enjoy work. So many advisers suggest that you provide added extras. These may include:

- A game room, basketball hoop, or foosball table
- Company outings to sporting events, wine tastings, or other similar activities
- Business casual attire, either one day a week, during the summer, or all the time

Health Benefits

Offering health insurance can benefit you and your employees.

It's become common practice for small businesses to include health insurance in an employee benefits package. And since group plans are generally cheaper than an individual policy, both you and your employees can be covered for less.

Remember, though, that there's a significant difference between having your company shoulder the cost of a health plan and having your employees pay the premiums themselves. One alternative you can investigate is to provide health plans for your employees, while making family coverage, which workers can pay for themselves, available.

MANAGED CARE

If you'd prefer to allow your employees to choose from a list of medical providers, then **managed care** is a

CHOOSING AN AGENT OR BROKER

Once you have a good idea of what your options are, you can choose an insurance professional to guide you through your insurance choices. If you haven't used an agent or broker before, these suggestions may help you make a choice you'll feel comfortable with.

- Get referrals from business colleagues, friends, and family
- Make sure the agent is licensed by your state's insurance department
- Look for an agent who specializes in health insurance
- Check on the agent's experience
- If the agent only represents one or two companies, you might want to keep looking for someone with a wider range of options
- Find someone you feel comfortable with and who is easily accessible, since your agent or broker should be available to answer all your insurance questions

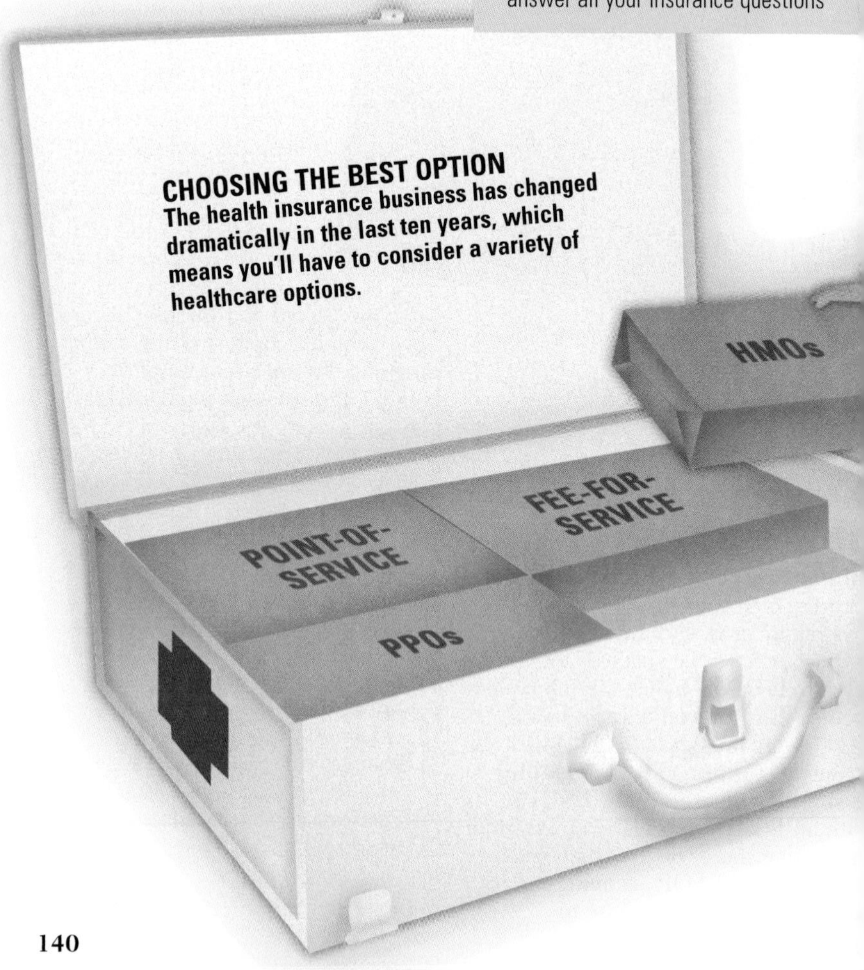

›od choice. There are three types of anaged care: **Health Maintenance rganizations (HMOs)**, **Preferred rovider Organizations (PPOs)**, ıd **point-of-service** programs.

If you choose an HMO for your ›mpany, you and your employees ın pick medical providers from the MO's exclusive provider list. The ore extensive the plan's options for edical providers, the more you'll ıd up paying to provide the plan. owever, an HMO is generally garded as one of the most cost- ficient types of plans, because if ›u or an employee goes to a doctor hospital within the plan, costs for ıre are typically modest.

A PPO is similar to an HMO ecause employees pay less if they ıoose a doctor who is considered ›referred," or included on the PPO's eferred provider list. To get the pre- rred rate, your employees may have go to their gatekeeper doctor, who ill refer them to specialists if they're need of further attention. But if you fer a point-of-service plan, they may e able to go to the specialist directly. he amount of money you, as an employer, will pay for offering a PPO or point-of-service plan depends on what your employees' **copayment**, or portion of the cost of a doctor or hospital visit, is. If your employees pay only $5 per visit, your costs will be higher because the cost to the employee is lower, but if your employees pay $15, your costs will be lower.

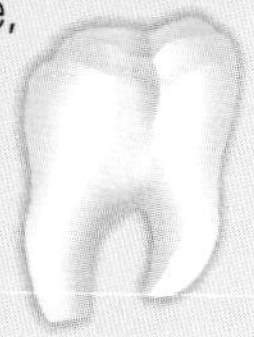

According to recent statistics, at least 70% of companies that employ 25 to 100 employees provide dental coverage. Although it's more expensive, offering this option may attract more employees, since the costs for these medical services are higher than ever.

FEE-FOR-SERVICE

If you want your employees to have the flexibility to choose any doctor, or to consult a specialist without prior approval, a **fee-for-service** plan may be right for your company. The patient pays the full cost of care up to a certain amount, or **deductible**. Once the patient hits the deductible, the insurance company starts paying a percentage of the medical costs they approve, and the patient makes a copayment, up to a set limit, after which the insurer pays.

With this type of plan, your costs will be higher if your employees have a low deductible, and the charges approved by the insurer may be much lower than the actual medical cost.

RESOURCES

When you are looking for a health plan, keep in mind that the costs change depending on how many people join the plan.

Your business is considered a **small group** if there are between 3 and 25 people (but sometimes up to 100) in the health insurance plan. Costs are generally higher for smaller plans.

If you want to save money on health insurance, you can join a small business coalition to help you get the most insurance for your money. For more information, you can contact The National Business Coalition on Health (NBCH)'s home office at 202-775-9300 or go to their website, www.nbch.org. You can also try the National Federation of Independent Business (NFIB) at 800-NFIB-NOW or on their website at www.nfib.com.

Retirement Plans

Fashion a retirement plan that suits your company's style.

When it comes to retirement plans, there is a growing number of options for small businesses. It's your job to narrow down the choices to a plan that will fit your company's needs.

EMPLOYER SPONSORED PLANS

A plan that provides a fixed income to your employees once they retire is known as a **defined benefit plan**. With this type of plan, you as employer are responsible for putting enough money into the plan to provide the income your employees are entitled to, as well as to meet the federal guidelines governing these plans. Not surprisingly, very few small business owners can afford to choose this type of plan.

On the other hand, you might choose to establish a **defined contribution plan**. The main difference between this type of plan and a defined benefit plan is that you don't guarantee a set income to your employees once they retire. Instead, the amount they receive depends on how much money is invested in the plan and how much the investments increase in value.

With some defined contribution plans, you put in all of the money that's invested. One example is a **profit sharing plan**, which lets you contribute a percentage of your company's profits each year. With other types of defined contribution plans, employees put in a portion of their pretax salaries.

BY THE NUMBERS

Any retirement plan to which your employees contribute pretax income is known as a **salary reduction plan**.

The type known as a **401(k)** is a popular choice among small business owners. With a 401(k), your employees can put a part of their pretax paycheck into a variety of investment options offered through the plan. You can match your employees' contributions if you choose, but you're not required to do so.

One drawback of conventional 401(k) plans is that your plan has to meet detailed federal guidelines. A typical solution is to find a highly regarded plan provider who specializes in serving small businesses and will handle the details and much of the paperwork for you. You might also investigate a SIMPLE 401(k), which can provide the same tax advantages for you and your employees, but is easier to administer.

BEING A SPONSOR

If your company offers a 401(k) plan, you're the plan sponsor. That means you're responsible for choosing a plan provider and deciding on the plan's options and features, including the rate at which employees can contribute, whether to match employee contributions, and whether to allow employees to borrow against their account value.

As the plan's sponsor, you have a fiduciary responsibility to make decisions in light of what's best for the people who participate. For instance, it's your responsibility to choose a menu of investments that offers your

nployees a real choice. If you follow e Department of Labor's guidelines r providing a range of options, ough, you're not responsible for how ell the investments your employees oose meet their expectations.

If you are the head of a nonprofit organization, you might want to consider a 403(b) plan, which is a salary reduction plan that works in similar ways to a 401(k). However, only employees of nonprofit organizations, schools, and hospitals are eligible to participate in a 403(b).

.PS AND SIMPLES

any smaller business owners opt r a **Simplified Employee Pension EP)**. With a SEP, you choose how uch you contribute each year for urself and your employees, and n change that amount based on w well your company does each ar. There is no vesting period with SEP, so any money you put in an count belongs to the employee the inute you deposit it.

You have to put the same percente of money into each qualifying nployee's account that you put into ur own. So if you contribute 15% your earnings into your own SEP, u have to contribute 15% of your nployees' earnings into their accounts.

Another popular alternative, known a **Savings Incentive Match Plan r Employees (SIMPLE)**, was creed in 1997. In fact, there are two rsions of a SIMPLE—a SIMPLE A and a SIMPLE 401(k). If you oose a SIMPLE, your employees can contribute up to the annual maximum a year, and you must contribute either 2% for all of your eligible workers, or match up to 3% of whatever your employees choose to contribute.

KEOGH PLAN

If you have a sole proprietorship or are a partner in a small business, you may want to create a **Keogh plan**, which provides benefits for business owners or self-employed individuals.

If you have employees, you have to provide comparable benefits to those who qualify to participate in the Keogh. That means if you put 25% of your earnings in your plan, you must contribute 25% for each employee covered by the plan. You are also required to have a plan administrator, who can be yourself or an employee. Like a 401(k), a Keogh can involve substantial recordkeeping and reporting.

Getting the Funds

Growing a business requires a steady flow of money.

Building a business costs money—usually more than you can generate from your operating revenues.

Whether you're adding a new truck to your fleet, building a new housing development, or creating software, you'll need money to turn these plans into reality. It might help to work with an accountant to calculate estimated costs for reaching the next level of development.

THE BASICS

Before you borrow, list your basic business expenses. Each time you expand your business, these costs are likely to increase:

- Employee salaries
- Rent
- Electricity, heating, air conditioning, and fuel
- Paper and other office supplies
- Purchasing or leasing operating equipment
- Decorating or remodeling costs
- Legal and professional fees
- Insurance
- Taxes
- Machinery and power tools

BANK LOANS 101

If you've made the decision to borrow money for your business, which loan is right for you?

You can get a **line of credit**, which is a type of loan that gives you short-term or seasonal funds. Basically, a line of credit is very similar to a credit card, with the notable exception tha interest on a line of credit is lower and may be tax deductible. You borrow cash, using your business assets as collateral, and pay back the princi pal and interest on any outstanding balance each month.

A **long-term credit loan** usually lasts up to five years, and is helpful i you want to have money for operatin costs until your business turns a pro it. Banks typically require that you take a mortgage or sign a promissory note on this type of loan, and pay it back in installments.

DO YOU QUALIFY?

If you're thinking about taking a loar to build your business, there are several qualifications that banks and investors normally expect from you, as the owner, and your business. Before you apply for a loan, make sure that you can provide potential lenders with the following:

- Business plan
- Balance sheet and income stateme
- Cash flow projections
- Profit and loss reports
- Personal financial statements for all business partners
- Credit report
- Personal income tax returns
- Information on business debts

GETTING THE LOAN

You may want to investigate banks that have a history of offering loans small and growing businesses, since there are banks across the country known for being friendly to small businesses. And many banks offer special lending programs specifically for women-owned businesses.

CREDIT CARDS

Visa, American Express, and Mastercard all offer credit cards aimed specifically at small businesses. These cards offer lower interest rates than normal credit cards, and often have credit limits up to $15,000.

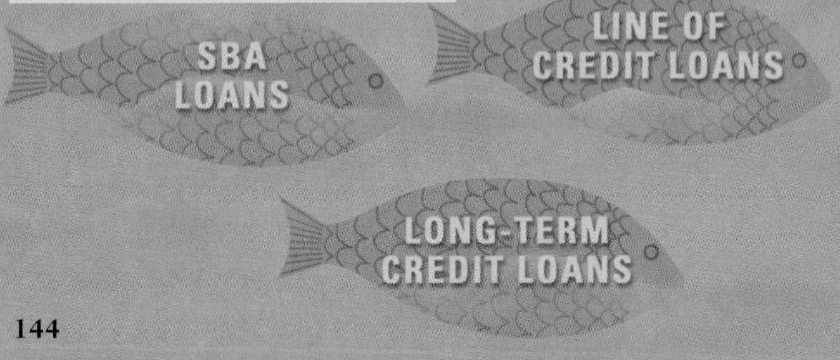

ESOURCES

ome new women usiness owners have ound it difficult to ecure bank loans, especially if they on't have significant personal assets or co-signer. One organization that pro-ides loans to women business owners s Count-Me-In for Women's Economic ndependence, which offers loans of 5,000 to $10,000. Your first loan can be 5,000, and when you pay it back in full, ou will be eligible for another loan. You an find out more about this organization t www.count-me-in.org.

ı can find out which banks are all business friendly by reading Small Business Administration's nall Business Lending study, which ublished every year.

It's good business practice to have trong relationship with a certain nk or banker, especially since she he could help you get loans when ı need them. If you don't use one ticular bank, you might want to en a business banking account or ure small lines of credit before olying for a big loan.

If you belong to a credit ion, you may be able to ure a loan through ıt organization. In ıeral, a credit ion offers lower n rates than nks or other nmercial ders.

Credit unions may also charge lower or no fees, and can provide more personal attention to help you find a loan that meets your business needs.

A LITTLE HELP

Since 1993, the Small Business Administration (SBA) has extended **Microloans** to businesses to help finance machinery, office space leases, equipment, and other basic necessities.

The most you can borrow with a Microloan is $35,000, and the average amount that borrowers use is about $10,500. Although the term of the loan depends on what you're using the funds for, and the size of the loan, the longest term for a Microloan is six years.

The SBA can also help you create a loan package and secure funds through a program called the **Prequalification Loan Program**. You can qualify for the loan if your business is at least 51% owned by a qualifying person or group, and you can receive up to $250,000. The length of the loan is anywhere from 7 to 25 years, depending on how you use the money.

For more information, you can contact the SBA at 1-800-UASK-SBA.

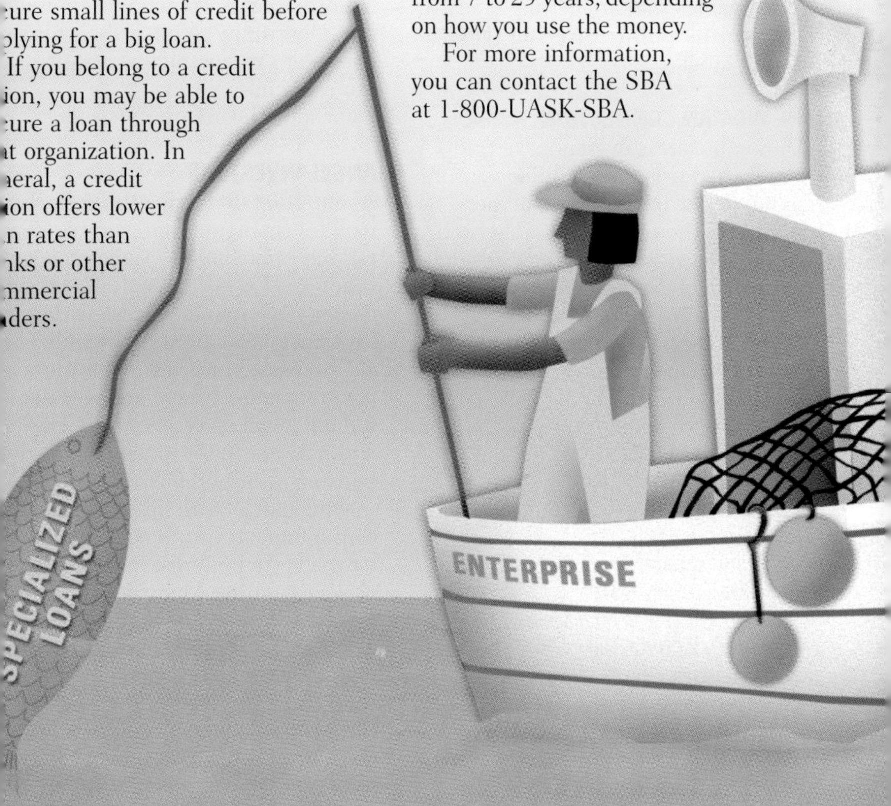

Other Funding

Bank loans are not the only option for getting money to build your business.

If you're building a business, you may be able to get funding from professional investing firms or private investors.

The money you get is known as a **private equity investment**, and the investors put their money into your business because they expect to make money. They reap the benefits of your success by getting their share of the purchase price if you sell your business, or receiving stock in your company if you take it public.

VENTURE CAPITAL

Venture capital is money an investment firm raises from institutional investors and wealthy individuals to fund business development. Some **venture capitalists (VCs)** invest in a business that's in the early stages of growth, and others specialize in companies that are getting ready to do an **initial public offering (IPO)** of their stock.

THE WOMAN CONNECTION

Women business owners have traditionally had trouble obtaining venture capital, receiving only a small percentage of the money available each year. However, there are now several organizations devoted to helping women receive money from VCs.

The National Women's Business Council organizes a series of Springboard forums throughout the country to give women entrepreneu the opportunity to pitch their business plans to potential investors. For more information, go to www.springboardenterprises.org.

BOOTSTRAPPING

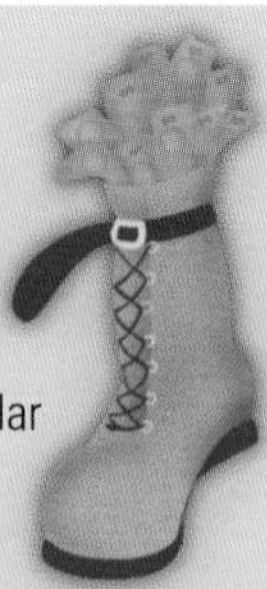

When you're growing a business, one of the buzzwords you may encounter is **bootstrapping**. That's the philosophy that every dollar counts in your business, so saving rather than spending can be worth your while. If you're on a tight budget, you can bootstrap by coordinating your accounts receivable and accounts payable so you have a continuous cash flow. Or it can mean being frugal with your inventory and expenses.

ANGEL INVESTORS

About 100,000 companies each yea look for financing from venture capi tal, but only 3,000 or so actually get funding. However, about 30,000 bu nesses have found success with **ang investors**, who are wealthy individuals interested in investing in promising companies. There are over two million angel investors in the US, and many of them specifically focus on women-owned businesses.

Since angels are investing their own money in your business, they have a vested interest in the success of your venture. Many angels becon mentors for the companies they sup port, and sit on the board of adviser One drawback is that angels often want to be involved in the way you run your business, so you may give up a bit of your management power to get the money.

There are angel investor groups located throughout the US. To find one, you might ask the local Chamb of Commerce about affiliated group

contact your local Small Business ɜvelopment Center (SBDC). And n't forget to check with your ɔfessional advisers—your banker, ɔcountant, and attorney.

ISINESS INCUBATORS

your business needs help in all ɔects of its development—from ice space to tech support and ɔre—you may benefit from a **busi-ss incubator**. Incubators nurture sinesses until they are established ough to be successful on their own. incubator can provide office ace, flexible leasing arrangements, uipment, technical assistance, and neral business advice—all in a short ne span.

In return for their help, business ɔubators often own a portion of ɜ company, and get a significant urn on their investment if the mpany succeeds.

For more information on finding a siness incubator for your company, u can check out the National siness Incubation Association BIA) (www.nbia.org or 0-593-4331).

MILY AND FRIENDS

any business owners have found ɜmselves at a dead end when it comes to attracting capital. If you fall into this category, you may have to turn to friends and family for low-cost funding for your business. About 73% of investments for women-owned businesses come from friends and family, so you're not alone if you choose this avenue.

It's good business practice to classify any money you receive from friends and family as an investment, a gift, or a loan. If the money is an investment, you're making no promise to repay, but the investor stands to profit if your company is successful. You should sign an agreement that specifies what share of ownership the investment provides. If the money is a gift and the amount from a single person is more than $11,000, the giver may have to file a gift tax return.

If you borrow the money, then you should draft a promissory note or contract that lists the terms of the loan. That should help you avoid legal complications later.

RESOURCES

There are a growing number of venture capital firms focused on helping women entrepreneurs take their businesses to the next level.

Some organizations to contact are:

Isabella Capital
513-721-7110
www.fundisabella.com

Women's Growth Capital Fund
202-342-1431
www.wgcf.com

Capital Across America
615-254-1414
www.capitalacrossamerica.org

Business Networks for Women

Being a business owner and a woman can work to your advantag

It's a well-established fact that women business owners face challenges at every turn of their professional careers. In response, a number of organizations, networks, and services have been created to help women build successful businesses.

CERTIFICATION

Some smaller and newer women-owned businesses have had trouble getting the contracts to sell their products and services that are crucial to running a business. So a number of organizations have created **certification programs** to give women business owners a better shot at securing government and corporate contracts, making deals with service providers, and creating business partnerships with other companies.

Certification by The National Women Business Owners Corporation (NWBOC), The Women's Business Enterprise National Council (WBENC), or a similar organization will give you more opportunities to work with hundreds of companies and government programs that have agreed to do business with certified woman-owned companies.

To become certified, you'll have to apply to one of the many programs located throughout the US, and meet the criteria of the program or programs you choose.

One general rule is that your business has to be at least 51% women-owned and operated. For more information on the NWBOC, go to www.nwboc.org or call 800-675-5066. To contact WBENC, check out www.wbenc.org or call their certification department at 202-872-5515.

PROCUREMENT PROGRAMS

Many companies, along with departments of federal, state, and local governments, want to do business with women-owned businesses. To do that, many organizations now support special **procurement programs**, which focus on attracting and using certified women-owned businesses t supply products and services.

As a business owner, you should contact companies to which you wou like to sell your products, and ask about special procurement programs they might have. Checking company websites may be a good way to start.

Since the US federal government is the single largest buyer of goods and services in the world, getting yo

mpany on an approved list of sup-ers can help to build your business. You can refer to the Small siness Administration (SBA), ich offers resources for women o want to secure supplier con-cts. There is a federal database led CAWBO (Contract assistance women business owners) that ks small businesses with procure-nt opportunities. For more ormation, check out www.sba.gov/ /indexprograms-cawbo.html.

One of the most extensive ources for women who want to sell oducts and services to the federal vernment is WomenBiz. It offers ights on federal procurement pro-ms and their regulations, as well as ks to specific federal departments, er women-owned businesses, d a calendar of upcoming events. eir website is www.womenbiz.gov.

For a broader perspective on opportunities for women, you may want to access the Center for Women's Business Research, established by the National Foundation for Women Business Owners (NFWBO). The Center, a source of up-to-date information and research studies about women business owners and their enterprises worldwide, offers a resource guide for small business owners. You can download a copy at www.nfwbo.org.

INFORMAL NETWORKING

Some women also create profes-sional business groups. These groups meet at regular intervals and include women from various fields, such as accountants, lawyers, and public relations specialists. The women exchange advice and ideas in their areas of expertise, as well as provide each other with places to go for fur-ther information.

There are also many organizations that encourage networking across gender lines. These include:

- Chambers of Commerce
- Trade organizations
- Political organizations
- Rotary or Lions Clubs
- Organizations centered around special interests
- College alumnae associations

RESOURCES

It's a good idea to contact organiza-tions devoted to women-based busi-nesses. Here are some suggestions:

American Business Women's Association (www.abwahq.org) stages events for career women, including speakers, workshops, and national conventions.

The Business Women's Network (BWN) (www.bwni.com) hosts a number of conferences on different "best practices" topics for various industries. BWN also produces an annual directory that features profiles of over 5,000 business and professional organizations in the US and abroad.

The Women's Network for Entrepreneurial Training (WNET) (www.sba.gov/ womeninbusiness/wnetcov.html) is a program sponsored by the SBA. The WNET matches experienced women business owners with women who are just starting out in the business world.

nual percentage rate (APR) is the t of credit expressed as a percent- of the amount you are borrowing. e APR includes interest and most s you pay to arrange the loan. It s not include late payment fees.

sets are everything you own that monetary value, plus any money t you are owed.

set allocation is a strategy for cre- ng a diversified investment portfolio putting money into different asset sses. Generally, it means you invest ercentage of your principal in cks, a percentage in bonds, and the ance in cash or cash equivalents.

neficiary is the person, people, or titution you name to receive the ets in your retirement savings plan, st, annuity, or the face value of your insurance policy. These assets are transferred by your will.

pital gain is the profit you make en you sell an investment for more n you paid to buy it. If the selling ce is lower than the price you paid, difference is called a capital loss.

sh equivalent is an investment, h as a money market fund, CD, US Treasury bill, that you can liqui- e easily with little loss of value. e cash investments, cash equiva- ts are vulnerable to inflation over long term.

rtificate of deposit (CD) is a type bank investment that pays interest a specific period of time and urns your investment plus earnings maturity.

mpounding occurs when the earn- s an investment produces are ded to your principal, creating a w, larger base on which earnings n accumulate.

fined benefit plan is a traditional nsion plan that pays a regular ome amount to retired employees. e pension amount is usually deter- ned by your final salary when you ire and the number of years you rked for your employer.

Defined contribution plan is an employer sponsored retirement plan in which each participant has an individual account. The amount of retirement income you receive depends on the amount that's invested in your account, how it is invested, and the return the investments provide. 401(k), 403(b), and profit sharing plans are examples of defined contribution plans.

Diversification means spreading your investment assets among a number of different investment categories and then among individual investments within those categories. For example, in a diversified portfolio you might own stock in six companies, each in a different sector of the economy, several bonds or bond funds, and US Treasury bills or CDs.

Dividend reinvestment plans (DRIPS) let you reinvest the dividends you earn on a stock investment directly to buy additional shares of the stock. The plan is run by the company issuing the stock.

Equity is an ownership share of property. With real estate, for example, your equity is the value of the property you own outright as opposed to the portion that is mortgaged or that belongs to a joint owner. Similarly, stocks and stock mutual funds are equity investments because you own shares in the corporation or fund.

Estate is the value of your assets, minus your liabilities, at the time of your death.

Executor is a person you name in your will to administer the transfer of your property and other details of settling your estate. Executors are also known as personal representatives.

Fair market value is the amount you would have to pay to buy a particular asset or service on the open market. The concept of fair market value assumes that both the buyer and the seller are informed about the object's value and neither is under pressure to sell.

Finance charge is the amount you pay for the use of borrowed money. With a credit card, the finance charge is the interest, figured as a percentage, that you pay on an outstanding balance on your card.

401(k) plan is a retirement savings plan sponsored by an employer and funded by employees with money that is deducted from their pretax pay. Employers may match employee contributions.

403(b) plan is a retirement savings plan sponsored by an educational institution or other not-for-profit employer and funded by employees with money that is deducted from their pretax pay. Employers may match employee contributions.

457 plan is a retirement savings plan sponsored by a state or local government and funded by employees with money that is deducted from their pretax pay.

Grace period is the time between the date a credit card bill is calculated and the date the payment is due. When there's a grace period, you owe no finance charges on purchases you made during the billing cycle if you've paid your previous month's balance in full and on time.

Gross income is the total amount you earn before any money is withheld for taxes, Social Security, or pretax contributions to retirement or other plans. When you report your gross income on a tax return, you include both earned and unearned income, such as interest or dividends.

Healthcare proxy is a document in which you give someone the right to make decisions about the medical treatment you should receive if you are unable to make those decisions for yourself. The proxy must be signed and witnessed.

Home equity loan is a loan secured by the value of your ownership share of your home. For example, if your home is valued at $200,000 and you owe $100,000 on your mortgage, you can borrow against the $100,000 that represents your share of the value.

Inflation describes the increase in t prices of goods and services over tim The rate of inflation can vary from a low as 1% or 2% a year to more than 100%. In the US, it has averaged about 3% annually since 1925.

Interest is the income—figured as a percentage of your principal—that you're paid for putting money into a savings account, CD, bond, or other fixed-income investment. Interest is also the percentage of a loan's princi pal that you pay as part or all of the finance charge.

Intestate means dying without havi written a will.

IRA is an acronym for Individual Retirement Account or Individual Retirement Annuity. Each is a tax-deferred retirement savings plan you can set up on your own, and which imposes specific contribution and withdrawal conditions.

Liabilities are debts, or money you owe. You subtract your liabilities fro your assets to find your net worth.

Life insurance is a contract that requires you, as the policyholder, to make regular payments to an insurance company to guarantee that a death benefit will be paid to your be eficiary or beneficiaries after you die

Lines of credit are revolving loans that allow you to borrow money up t a predetermined spending limit. As you repay an amount you've borrowe you can borrow it again without having to reapply.

Liquid investment is an investment that can be converted easily to cash with little or no loss of value. For example, you can usually redeem shares in a money market mutual fu for the same $1 a share it cost you t buy. However, mutual funds are not insured by the federal government a could lose value.

Living will is a legal document that you use to provide instructions for t way you want your healthcare managed if you are unable to make your own decisions.

et asset value is the dollar value of
e share of a mutual fund. It's com-
ıted each trading day by dividing the
tal value of the fund's investments
the number of existing shares in
e fund.

et income is the amount of your
rnings after withheld amounts,
ıch as taxes and Social Security,
e taken out.

et worth is the value of your assets
inus all of your liabilities.

ar is the face value of a bond, or the
nount you pay if you buy at issue
ıd receive if you redeem the bond at
e end of its term when it matures.

ortfolio is the collection of invest-
ents you own. A diversified portfolio
cludes investments from different
set classes and a variety of invest-
ents within each class.

rincipal is a sum of money that can
fer to an amount you invest, an
nount you borrow, or the face value
a bond.

robate is the legal process of prov-
g, or verifying, your will. The court
which this process occurs is known
probate court, surrogate's court, or
phan's court.

rospectus is a formal written docu-
ent that outlines the background,
ɔjectives, and performance of a
utual fund. It must be issued to
ch investor who purchases a new
sue of a registered security.

eturn is what you get back on an
nount you invest, including interest
dividend payments, plus capital
ins or losses. A positive return
eans you end up with more money
an you started with, and a negative
turn means you end up with less.

evolving credit is a form of credit
at allows you recurring access to a
xed amount of money. When you
pay an amount, it's available for you
use again.

ollover means you move an invest-
ent from one custodian or trustee to
ıother. For example, a lump sum
ıyment from a 401(k) plan can be
lled over into an IRA. Or, one IRA
ın be rolled over into another IRA.

Securities are another name for stocks, bonds, and certain other investments. Originally a security was a piece of paper, such as a stock certificate, that proved your ownership.

Tax deferred describes investment amounts and investment earnings that are not taxed until you withdraw them from an account.

Tax exempt means that no tax is due on earnings an investment produces.

Trust is a legal entity that owns property, which you transfer to it. A trust is administered by a trustee, and can provide tax savings, financial management, or other advantages if it is set up correctly.

Underlying investments are the investments a mutual fund makes. The performance of the underlying investments determines the performance of the fund.

Venture capital is business financing provided by institutional investors—such as pension funds and endowments, wealthy individuals or families, and investment divisions of corporations—to new or growing companies that they expect will provide a strong return. Venture capital is also known as risk capital.

Vested interest is an employee's right to receive benefits from a pension, profit sharing, or other employer sponsored plan at retirement. Department of Labor and Internal Revenue Service (IRS) rules establish the amount of time an employee must work to be vested.

Will is a legal document you use to transfer ownership of your property to your heirs. You can also use a will to set up trusts and to name guardians for your minor children.

Yield refers to the amount of income, expressed as a percentage, that an investment produces during a certain time period. There are several different ways to calculate yield, depending on the type of investment. For example, the yield might be calculated based on your investment's original value or its market value.

A

B

C

F

G

H

I

K

L

M